The Early Correspondence of
Hans von Bülow

Nach einem Aquarell von Frau v. Lüttichau.

Gravure Meisenbach Riffarth & Co.

The
Early Correspondence
of
Hans von Bülow

Edited
by
His Widow

Selected and Translated into English
By Constance Bache

With Two Portraits

VIENNA HOUSE
New York

Originally published by D. Appleton and Company
New York, 1896

First VIENNA HOUSE edition published 1972

International Standard Book Number:
0-8443-0009-8

Library of Congress Catalogue Card Number: 71-163788

Manufactured in the United States of America

PREFACE TO THE GERMAN EDITION.

WE seem to have known but little, until now, of the first five-and-twenty years of Hans von Bülow's life, beyond a few general dates. Whether and how far the process of development of the artist and of the character may arouse the sympathy of the world, it is impossible for a single individual to decide. But there is no doubt that the picture of the transformation period of his life, in conjunction with all he became, when fully developed, both to Art and to his own day, is an important and even indispensable contribution towards a correct estimate of him. An intimate knowledge of the soil which produced him, of the atmosphere which surrounded him, of the impressions which he received, will help us to understand him better, to follow the often apparently complicated lines of what he felt and said, and will also help us to apprehend him, where a hasty and fragmentary impression seemed likely to confuse, rather than to satisfy, one's judgment. And therefore I feel it to be my duty not to hesitate in bringing out these letters of my husband, in order that those who were in direct touch with Bülow's personality both in Art and life, and who felt a degree of sympathy with him which must of necessity be wanting to a later generation, should have this help.

The chief importance of this work lies in the biographical details which the letters contain, and these are of all the more value because Bülow, with his ever-restless and onward-striving mind, was always averse to retrospective contemplation, and therefore left behind him but few indications as to his life, with the exception of transient notes in later years. ' Life is too short for reflection; il ne faut pas remuer le passé; it is better to utilise the time for fresh work'; these were the things he was in the habit of saying when people approached him on the subject of 'Memoirs,' ' Recollections,' etc.

There is no trace to be found of the diaries which, at his mother's express wish, though to him very much against the grain, he was in the habit of keeping in his early youth. Nor are there any rough copies of letters or rough drafts—such as there are, for instance, of Schumann or Liszt, which could be of use in bringing out the letters of those masters. There is every ground for thinking that Bülow's letters were written straight off, spontaneously, according to the feelings and mood of the moment. Moreover it would have been an impossibility to do otherwise; it would be inconceivable that he could write down twice over such a voluminous and ample correspondence, whilst at the same time he was doing so very much, not only in the domain of Music, but also in that of Art and of learning. It was only in the last ten years of his life that he occasionally had copies of his letters made for some special reason.

He wrote a small, clear, regular hand, which changed but little with the course of years, and but rarely made a mistake or an erasion. Thus a letter of Bülow's, even outwardly, bears witness to his inborn sense for the beautiful and aristocratic in form, satisfying the *eye* as well as the *mind*, without puzzling the former by riddles such as now and then perplex the latter. Whoever will pass in review Bülow's life in the light of his writings will meet such riddles, and will more than once feel the most elevated frame of mind suddenly interrupted by them. But it would be misconstruing the right to truth, it would be incompletely estimating the historical personality of Hans von Bülow, if one perhaps timidly avoided them. This personality can lose nothing of its beacon-power by a flashing word here, or a contradiction there; the few dark touches do but make it gain in corporeality, and thus bring it nearer to the heart, for they just go hand-in-hand with all that was most worthy of honour in him.

A passionate desire, emanating from a profound sense of truth and justice, to help on any true artist-nature—and this long before the tide of fashion had turned in its favour; the manner in which he combated whatsoever stood in his way; the personal courage which overlooked all difficulties, or even the disadvantage which might accrue to himself from the position he had taken up—these are some of Bülow's most striking characteristics. They can be traced through his whole life, and are the basis of all those words and actions which have been set down as 'inconsistencies' by those who held aloof from him. They are the guides that enable us to read his life aright, and fully explain those sides of his character which need any explanation.

> Lives of great men all remind us
>   We can make our lives sublime,
> And, departing, leave behind us
>   Footprints on the sands of time ;—
>
> Footprints, that perhaps another,
>   Sailing o'er life's solemn main,
> A forlorn and shipwrecked brother,
>   Seeing, shall take heart again.

MARIE VON BÜLOW.

HAMBURG, *Autumn* 1895.

PREFACE TO THE ENGLISH EDITION.

THE contents of the present volume are a selection from two volumes of Letters brought out in Germany by Marie von Bülow. To make a selection from the 240 original letters has been deemed advisable, as there are many of them which, whilst interesting to Bülow's fellow-countrymen, would hardly appeal to the general English reader. At the same time nothing has been omitted that is of vital interest or importance in enabling us to understand the sequence of events which moulded Bülow's youthful life and decided his career. I may add that Frau Marie von Bülow has authorised and approved such condensation as I have thought it necessary to make.

Hans von Bülow has been, with one exception, the "best abused" musician of our day. He has been more misunderstood, more laughed at, and even sneered at, than any other except Wagner. The reasons for this judgment are superficial, and are not far to seek. Bülow had a hasty tongue, and he was apt to say *exactly what he meant*, without softening down the edges. Wagner did just the same; and think of the "Schimpfwörterbücher" that his enemies published about him! These are the things that stick fast in the public mind until—the tide of fashion turns the other way, and then—well, then they are forgotten. Twenty years have cleared away many of the mists and clouds that hung over Baireuth, and have shown us the man as he was, both good and bad. I believe that these Letters will do more than anything else to clear away the atmosphere of mist and cloud that has hung around Bülow's name, for they let us see *behind the veil,* and the real man is revealed to us. It must be borne in mind that very many of these letters are to his parents, and in these he gives the rein to his aspirations, disappointments, and confidences, with a naïveté and absolute truthfulness rare even between parent and child.

The turning-point of his life, when he undertakes that journey to Wagner on foot, "to see if he has the necessary strength of endurance"; the heart-broken letters that follow his father's sudden death; the exciting and characteristic extremes of the letters that describe his first experiences in concert-giving—these are among the gems of the collection.

A good many French words appear in the course of the Letters. They are, almost without exception, Bülow's own expressions interpolated into German letters; these I have therefore retained. A few of his letters, notably those to Franz Liszt who wrote in French by preference, are written in that language, and in those I have merely retained such expressions as seemed to be more "telling" in French than in a translation.

It will be seen from the Letters how Bülow suffered from ill-health, more or less, all his life; and this, added to an intensely nervous, highly-strung temperament, at length broke him down. In 1894 he was taken, ill as he then was, to Cairo, to see what the change might do for him. But this forlorn hope of restoring his shattered health was, alas, not realised, and he expired there, a few days after his arrival, on the 12th of February 1894. His remains were brought to Hamburg, the city of his adoption and of his preference, to be cremated, according to the great Master's own desire.

CONSTANCE BACHE.

LONDON, *Autumn,* 1896.

CONTENTS.

ILLUSTRATIONS.

INTRODUCTION

HANS VON BÜLOW.

INTRODUCTION.

FROM the family book of the von Bülows we learn that Ernst Heinrich Adolph, the grandfather of the subject of the present volume, was born on the 21st July 1766, and brought up for the army. Wounded in the battle of Smolensk, he received the Royal Saxon Order of Henry and the Imperial French Order of the Legion of Honour, was pensioned off after peace was proclaimed, and resided in Dresden until his death in 1842.

Of his three sons, one only grew to manhood—Carl Eduard, who was born in the year 1803. He was destined for the mercantile line, and with this view was put to work for some time in various banking houses. But his tastes lay in other directions, and he went for some years to the University of Leipzig, where he made a special study of the dead languages. In the year 1828 he returned to Dresden, and devoted himself thenceforth exclusively to the career of letters.

In the year 1828 Eduard married Franziska Elisabeth Stoll, who was born at Leipzig in the year 1800; and there she had lived for many years in the house of her celebrated elder sister and the latter's husband, Herr Kammerrath Frege, helping them in the education of their son Woldemar. Her immense talents, lively disposition, and good musical education enabled her to exercise a powerful influence over the young Woldemar, who preserved throughout his life a faithful and grateful feeling towards his aunt. Franziska left this home for Dresden, on her marriage with Eduard von Bülow.

Here the young couple lived in the midst of a pleasant literary and artistic circle, which included such names as Herr von Lüttichau, the Intendant of the Dresden Theatre, and his accomplished wife, Countess Hahn-Hahn, the widowed Countess Bülow-Dennewitz with her daughter Louise, besides Eduard's faithful friend Tieck. In the Bülow family music played always a conspicuous part, Franziska having regular prac-

4 HANS VON BÜLOW.

tising *réunions* with the violoncellist Henselt, who afterwards became
the first piano teacher of her son Hans.

On the 8th January 1830 Hans Guido von Bülow was born at 19
Kohlmarkt, Dresden-Altstadt, now known as 12 Körnerstrasse, at the
corner diagonally opposite to the house where Theodor Körner was born.
A weakling from his very birth, Hans (as we shall see from his later
letters) never enjoyed robust health. Five times, as his mother related
in after years, he suffered from brain fever, although some doctors maintained that, had that been so, it would have been impossible for him to
cultivate that marvellous memory, and to attain to such a degree of
mental development as he actually did.

Be that as it may, Hans and his sister Isidora, three years younger
than himself, did not, either of them, enjoy a happy childhood. For,
apart from physical weakness—which however did not prevent the boy
from keeping pace with his schoolfellows in the examinations, and even
surpassing most of them—the sharp eyes of the children were not long
in discerning the differences and want of harmony in the characters of
their parents. This point cannot remain unmentioned, because it
exercised a deep influence on the future man's destiny, and it forms too
important a factor in Hans von Bülow's life and experience to be passed
over in silence.

Franziska's passionate character, to which from her childhood up she
had given way, unrestrained by education and position; her religious-
ness, which to her appeared inseparable from prescribed forms; her ever-
increasing preference for Catholicism, to which she finally went over at
the ripe age of eighty-four; her sympathy for the Conservative side in
politics; the absence, as it seems, of a certain cheerful element in her
nature,—all this stands out in glaring contrast to Eduard's amiable,
fantastic nature, his enthusiasm for the ideas of freedom with which at
that time all the rising generation was filled, his antipathy to the
clerical party and to the condition of things in the Germany of that day,
which betrayed itself, amongst other things, by his disinclination to
acknowledge himself as the subject of any individual German State.

Something of an almost effeminate gentleness and nervousness, com-
bined with a hot, hasty temperament and a want of strength of will,—
these seem to have constituted the shady side of what was otherwise such
an attractive personality, and it was these which must have made the
daily intercourse with him somewhat difficult.

The children were not at all systematically educated by their parents,
except as regards the French language, for which Franziska had such a
great liking that she made them learn it thoroughly at a very early age.

When he was nine years old, Hans received his first pianoforte lessons from Herr Henselt (already mentioned). Louise von Bülow, who became afterwards Eduard's second wife, often visited at their house in those days, and remembers hearing that when the boy was confined to the house or to bed by illness, as was frequently the case, his favourite occupation was music-reading. She also relates that he often went to the Catholic Church to hear the fine music there, and when he came home he would play from memory any melodies that particularly pleased him. Herr Henselt soon declared that he could teach the boy nothing more, and he was then placed under Fräulein Schmiedel for piano lessons, and Herr Eberwein for theory.

"All these indications of a special gift for music," wrote Louise von Bülow, "delighted his parents, but it never occurred to them to bring up their son as an artist, especially as he was distinguishing himself at the Dresden Gymnasium, and learned with the utmost rapidity what to other boys cost great labour and pains. His parents, especially his mother, thought that great musical talent would beautify his life, would keep him away from many useless, foolish things, and would always ensure him an agreeable position in society."

It must have been between the years 1842 and 1844 that Franziska made Liszt's acquaintance, as it was about that time that he was playing in Dresden, arousing enormous enthusiasm. He also went much into society, and the Bülow family also enjoyed visits from him. It was probably at that time that Liszt, at an evening party at a house close by, declared that he would only play if they fetched the little Bülow, which was of course immediately done, although the little fellow had already gone to bed.

It was in the lessons with Fräulein Schmiedel that a friendship was begun, which accompanied Hans von Bülow faithfully throughout his whole life : this was with Miss Taylor, afterwards Madame Laussot, and now the widow of the eminent writer Karl Hillebrand, a widely-known and highly-esteemed woman, whose great talents, especially in music, and whose enthusiasm for art, and noble nature, procured her the friendship and respect of all the greatest musicians of the last forty years. And yet another important friendship of Bülow's must be mentioned here, namely, that with the brothers Karl and Alexander Ritter. This friendship exercised an immense influence, musically, on Bülow's youth. The mother of the two Ritters—a well-to-do widow from Narwa, who had settled down in Dresden—lived a very retired life, and there was no intercourse between her and the Bülow family. But from a mother who, firmly believing in the genius of Richard Wagner, had helped him over his hardest years of exile, her sons had inherited a glowing enthusiasm for art, and this knit together the youthful hearts of the three school friends, Hans and the two Ritters. In common with them, he received the first great musical impression of his life, when ' Rienzi ' was performed for the first time in Dresden in the year 1842. What was then written in letters of flame on his youthful fancy was extinguished only with his last breath.

During his schooldays in Dresden, from 1840-45, Hans frequently visited his relations, the Freges, in Leipzig. Woldemar, now grown to man's estate, had become Professor of Law at the Leipzig University, and had married Livia Gerhardt on her eighteenth birthday. In spite of her extreme youth, she had already attained notice as a talented singer; she was also on terms of friendship with Mendelssohn, who dedicated many of his works to her. The young couple occupied half of the old family house of the Freges, Woldemar's parents living in the other portion.

Further mention will be made of this later on, at the time when Hans came to spend the University period of his life with them.

DRESDEN—LEIPZIG

CHAPTER I.

DRESDEN—LEIPZIG.

1830—1846.

TO HIS MOTHER.

LEIPZIG, 23rd May 1841.

DEAR MAMMA,

So at last you have decided to go to Baden-Baden, to get yourself well and strong again. I am always so glad of a letter from you, as I am longing to know how you are, etc. Papa was here on Monday and Tuesday, and wanted to take me with him, but has after all left me here at the general request. I am now quite settled; I have two lessons a week from Herr Hesse, who corrects my work, and gives me fresh work to do; I also have French lessons every day from Fräulein Hackstädt. I have lots of amusement at the riders' booth and in a panorama, and I have been to a Bellini opera! The best first—'i Capuleti et i Montechi!' O, when I heard that this heavenly opera was going to be given, I was quite beside myself for joy, for I could already flatter myself with hope, as Aunt had promised to send me to a Bellini opera. Demoiselle Kreutzer (daughter of the Kapellmeister) was starring it here from the Cologne Theatre, and played Julia, and she will also play in ' Robert le Diable,' and in her father's ' Nachtlager' (so she says). She pleased me very much; her voice and appearance are beautiful, only she makes such faces when she sings. Romeo, Madame Schmitdgen, I did not like. The three men I liked. But the choruses were very badly sung; I had expected them to be much better. At the riding booth they did some beautiful and extraordinarily difficult athletic exercises (Glohia is mere child's play in comparison), but these would not interest you, so I shall only say that Demoiselle Louise Zischek is a wonderfully charming and graceful rider; there are Bedouins, and the training of the horses is very good, and the decorations are very pretty. I have been to a panorama by Enslen, ' A Journey to Germany and Italy.' One quite imagines oneself in the town and neighbourhood. It interested me very much, although I don't care particularly about pictures, especially of Italy. The lovely cities of Naples, Venice, Florence, Rome, and the glorious monuments of Pompeii, and Berlin amongst the German cities, pleased me most of all. Aunt sends you her best love, and is going to write to you soon. Goodbye, dear Mamma, and continue to love—

Your obedient Son,
HANS VON BÜLOW.

I forgot to tell you that I have got to know the celebrated actress, Madame Crelinger and her daughter, and have heard Clara Schumann, who unfortunately only accompanied Livia.

From that early period there are but two letters extant. We have contented ourselves with taking the second of these, as being the more interesting. We now pass on to the year 1844, when, still in Leipzig, he writes to his mother as follows, on the 24th July :—

I must tell you plainly that I don't at all want to go to Tetschen even for a couple of days, as I can enjoy fresh air here also, and it is extremely necessary for me to stay *as long as possible* in Leipzig, both on account of the Rakoczy-cure and the drilling lessons, and also on account of the *music*, as it is of the utmost use to me to hear Madame Schumann, and this more than anything else will urge me on to more practice. I am also reading French, and Aunt borrows Racine, Molière, Florian, and Voltaire for me, all of which I find rather tedious.

I am keeping my diary, but I don't know in the least how to 'meditate a little and then write it down,' as you recommend. How is the theatre going on now the Lipinskis are gone?

I am playing Bach Fugues, 'Poème d'amour,' Mayer's Studies, Beethoven's D minor and C sharp minor Sonatas, and keeping up other pieces, such as Hummel's A minor Concerto and Septet.

And on the 9th May 1845 he makes the following remarks about his music in a letter to his mother, also from Leipzig :—

I practise *steadily* two hours a day, and have got up again what I had lost by a few days' stoppage. I am playing Chopin, Henselt, Bach and Hummel, and have begun to study the Fantasia 'Oberon's Magic Horn.'

I have already had two lessons from Herr Hauptmann.* I like

---

* Moritz Hauptmann (1792-1868), composer, Master of Theory, Cantor of the Thomasschule, and teacher at the Leipzig Conservatoire.

him very much; he is very friendly, and it gives me almost more pleasure to learn from him than from Herr Eberwein. Yesterday he was pleased with the exercises I had done for him.

Yesterday I went *twice* to see Herr Plaidy;* he was not at home. I begged for an appointment with him, and he has sent me word today to go to him at six o'clock.

P.S.—I have begged Aunt to tell you whether I have grown more sensible.

TO HIS MOTHER.

THURSDAY, † 4.30 *in the morning,*
30*th May,* '45.

DEAR MAMMA,

I woke today exactly at four o'clock, dressed, have had already half an hour in the garden, and now come back to finish this letter to you, of which I wrote a rough copy yesterday. I can't write to you at any other time, for today is Aunt's birthday, and we want, if the weather keeps fine, to make a party and go to Halle and the Giebichenstein, for which we must start by rail at a quarter to eleven. I will write to Isa about it very soon.

With regard to my piano-playing you may set your mind at ease. ' *Je travaille comme un nègre,* ' I can truly say. Every morning I play shake exercises, scales, simple and chromatic of all kinds, exercises for throwing the hands (for these I use a Study of Moscheles, one of Steibelt, and a two-part Fugue of Bach's, which I play with octaves in both hands ; it was Goldschmidt ‡ who recommended me to do this), Toccatas of Czerny, which Herr Plaidy gave me, and Moscheles' and Chopin's Studies ; so that I don't find any others of Bertini, Cramer, or Clementi necessary ; I have enough to do with the Chopin Studies, which fully take the place of all these others, and I hope you will think I am doing right. I finished Field's A major Concerto yesterday ; I have only studied the first movement—Herr Plaidy thinks the others are not worth much—and at my next lesson I shall begin Mendelssohn's D minor Concerto. Besides these, I am studying by myself Bach's Fugues, Klengel's Canons, Oberon's Zauberhorn, Hummel's Fantasia, a Beethoven Sonata (the 'Pastorale,' in D major), and am keeping up my old pieces, such as Chopin's Tarantella and Nocturnes, Henselt's Variations and

---

* Louis Plaidy (1810-74), pianoforte teacher at the Leipzig Conservatoire.

† Probably 5.30.

‡ Otto Goldschmidt (1829), pianist, pupil of Mendelssohn, later on married Jenny Lind.

Frühlingslied, and Hummel's B minor Concerto pp. I played Beethoven's C major Sonata to Herr Hauptmann, whose lessons are a great interest and pleasure to me. He praised my conception of it, and gave me a few hints and some advice now and then, which it would take too long to tell you about. Then I played him a Fugue of Bach's, in which he found fault with the Czerny edition, which gives it *staccato*, as I played it, but Herr Hauptmann thinks it would suit the character of this Fugue (C minor) better to play it *legato*.

Plaidy is in every respect a *good* teacher, and I am convinced that I shall be able to learn much more under his and Hauptmann's tuition, with the *great* encouragement which I get here from the musical boys of my own age, than in Dresden.

I have often played duets with Goldschmidt; he has also dined with us, and is invited again for next Sunday with Joachim.

The piano from Klemm has been tuned again, but it is in such a condition that one can only play finger exercises on it, and even that is scarcely endurable. For the rest, I have gained in tone and strength in my playing. Sometimes I borrow a Beethoven Symphony in score from Klemm, which I then study.

Count Reuss, who is in every way extremely kind and friendly to me, has given me leave to practise on his grand piano, as he is away from home nearly the whole day. It is rather a stiff touch (it is an Irmler), and has a magnificent tone. It is too stiff for the Count, and I am therefore, as it were, to break it in for him. The Count also played duets with me once when I went to see him.

Chancellor Müller * from Weimar came to call on Livia yesterday, who had to occupy herself with him the whole day. He sends you his very best remembrances. He has grown rather deaf. He told us a lot of interesting things about his life, and his meeting with Napoleon, which also entertained me very much. Aunt gave him a little dinner, to which Dr. Auerbach was also invited, and I liked him very much. Champagne and *Maitrank* were drunk. I am extremely fond of them both, and hope that you will also have some of the latter to enjoy.

Livia often sings; I accompany her, and composed two songs for her lately when I lost a *Vielliebchen*.† I read lately in the Vienna paper, in the news from Prague: "(*Delayed*). Herr Litolff ‡ has given

---

* Friedrich v. Müller (1779-1849), Chancellor of Weimar, a friend of Goethe's.

† 'Vielliebchen,' commonly known in English as 'Fillipine,' doubtless a corruption of the original.

‡ Henry Charles Litolff, composer and celebrated pianist, was born in London in 1818; died in Paris in 1891. Was for a long time an intimate friend of the von Bülows.

five concerts with enormous success ; at the last of them he was assisted by Prume. He interested people both by his playing and compositions, as well as by his adventurous life. He possesses uncommon delicacy, and with it great energy, and might in many respects be compared with Liszt, though in the latter one recognises always the Hungarian, in Litolff always the Englishman ! "

Hiller's opera has been given again in Dresden a few times, but does not seem to have been well attended.

Madame Birch-Pfeiffer is starring here. She has had ' Thomas Tyrnau ' given, which has not taken at all here. I have been again twice to the theatre—to the ' Freischütz ' and to ' Alessandro Stradella,'— a romantic opera by Flotow, which contains some pretty, lively melodies in the style of Auber.

STUTTGART

CHAPTER II.

STUTTGART.

AUTUMN 1846—SPRING 1848.

IN the year 1846 Eduard von Bülow, with his family, removed from Dresden to Stuttgart. It was about this time that, during a summer holiday at Bingen, Hans made the acquaintance of Joachim Raff, the celebrated musician and composer, an acquaintance which ripened into a lifelong friendship. Raff was eight years older than Hans, so that the latter, while on a par with him as a friend, was able to look up to him as a *mentor* in music. In Stuttgart also about this time Hans got to know Molique, then just approaching the zenith of his fame as a violinist, and in his house Bülow spent many happy hours, and played much with the Virtuoso. One of Molique's daughters, writing of those days, says : "There was nothing angular or helpless about Bülow. When he was at the piano, one soon saw that it was a young *Master* who was in command of the instrument."

The Bülows left Stuttgart in 1848 and returned to Dresden.

The following letter, giving Hans' first impressions of Stuttgart life, is the only one obtainable of the year 1846 :—

* TO FRIEDRICH WIECK † (DRESDEN).

STUTTGART, 29*th September* 1846.

DEAR SIR AND MASTER,

You wished me to write to you from Stuttgart, and I avail myself of this permission in order to thank you for your kind letter of introduction to Herr Concertmeister Molique. I went to see him shortly after my arrival ; my playing seemed to please him ; at any rate he spoke in terms of praise of it, and said he would write to you himself. He gave me two Sonatas of his own composition to take away with me, and says he will play them with me. I am now busy

---

* Taken from Kohnt's 'Friedrich Wieck,' Pierson, Dresden.

† Friedrich Wieck (1785-1873), pianoforte teacher, father of Clara Schumann.

studying them; they are certainly difficult, but quite suitable to the piano, and extremely beautiful, so much so that one can truly say that no such grand duets for piano and violin have appeared since *Beethoven.* I am surprised that they are not yet better known, and I much wish that you could get to know them. He has begged me to go and see him often, and I have to play a good deal before his daughter, who loves music, and who plays with much facility and spirit, although she complains that she has had no opportunity here of a good training in piano-playing. The pianist Krüger * is away. Concertmeister Bohrer's † wife and son are considered the best pianists here; I have not yet heard them, but Molique thinks the wife is only a drawing-room player, and that the son (who plays in a blurred and unclear manner) is unworthy of mention. There is also Madame Heinrich here, who gives lessons, and who studied in Paris with Chopin.

Just lately I saw Kapellmeister Benedict ‡ from London, whose father is a banker here. He came to Molique's to hear the latter's new Trio, a really grand, original, and well worked-out composition, far surpassing the Sonatas in wealth and beauty of ideas. The piano part is very difficult, and was played by his daughter in a very finished manner. Benedict stays here some weeks longer, and I hope to see him often. Later on he intends to make a tour in Germany. A new pianist of the name of Kuhn is here, and intends to give a concert. But, from what I hear, he is no good.

There is even less classical taste here then in Dresden. Mozart, Beethoven, Weber—these can only be played in the king's absence. . . . But it seems that at the winter concerts, which take place twice a month, one does hear some better music.

I have plenty of time for piano-playing just now, as the Gymnasium does not open till the 15th October, so I am working pretty hard at it. I am learning to understand the excellence of your teaching more and more, and am trying to follow your directions.

I have not yet myself tried the Stuttgart pianos of Schiedmayer, but, judging from hearing them played, they seem to have a powerful, beautiful, and singing tone; but they have a stiff touch. The mechanism is English, and the prices low—500 gulden (or about 300 thalers).

Lindpaintner's new opera ' Lichtenstein ' has met with no success.

---

* Wilhelm Krüger (1820-83), composer and teacher at the Stuttgart Conservatoire.

† Max Bohrer (1785-1852), first violoncellist at the Stuttgart Theatre.

‡ Julius Benedict (1804-85), operatic composer; lived in Vienna, Liverpool, and London.

I hoped to be able to write to you about it, but it has not been given again.   As there is no more musical news to tell which would be of any interest to you, I conclude by signing myself,

Yours very obediently,

HANS VON BÜLOW.

TO HIS MOTHER.

STUTTGART, *Monday,* 30*th August* 1847.

. . . . I am now quite well again.   I have not yet begun to take riding lessons again, but I must begin soon, as it is maintained here among my comrades that, in consequence of an accident, I have given the whole thing up, and, of course, I must now give a brilliant contradiction to such reports. . . . One Sunday lately I was in the Schloss Church, where Grüneisen was preaching again for the first time. There are a great many holidays just now, and this week there is again an examination, which gives me some free days.

In the autumn—in the middle of September—there is to be, as usual, a prize recitation for every class.   Seven in my class, including myself, are going in for it.   I think I shall recite Schiller's ' Verschleiertes Bild zu Sais,' and hope I shall win the prize ; but, if I should not, I shall not be in despair.   I have now been studying Mendelssohn's Rondo, which I like immensely, and then Liszt's magnificent arrangement of the Oberon Overture ; I am also playing Mayer's Studies, a Toccata, a new number of Czerny's ' Schule der Fingerfertigkeit,' some of Bach's Fugues, and a Scherzo of Mendelssohn's.   Now I am taking up again Hummel's Fantasia, which I like much ; it is difficult, and only here and there a little unpleasantly old-fashioned ; I am also studying the new edition of Liszt's ' Sonnambula,' and Litolff's charming ' Invitation à la Polka.'   I am keeping up Beethoven's D minor Sonata, and think of studying one of Weber's, which are really beautiful. I have had the piano tuned lately, but as it has had some new strings it is again awfully out of tune.

I was with Molique on the two last Sundays, and played two Beethoven Sonatas with him.   He was very friendly, and will lend me with pleasure some of his scores of ancient operas by Piccini, Lully, Paësiello, which will interest me immensely.   I played Mendelssohn's Rondo to him lately, and he was much pleased.

As soon as I have drummed the Hummel Fantasia into my fingers,

I shall let him hear it. He does not know it at all. Fräulein Molique has been ill, and is not going to give any more lessons henceforth.

. . . .

Things are going on somewhat better than formerly with my little pupil;* certainly I still get very cross, but as far as possible only inside myself—one must postpone its effects, I think.

. . . .

Writing to his mother on the 7th September, he says :—

Yesterday Ritter sent me a letter, and a parcel containing compositions, some Songs, a Sonata dedicated to me, and half of a string Quartet. There are some pretty original ideas in them, but the form is of course still rather awkward and abnormal.

With them was a letter from Kapellmeister Wagner to me ! ! ! —" Your works, dear Herr von Bülow, have given me much pleasure ; I did not wish to give them back to your friend Ritter without accompanying them with a cheering word to you. I do not add a criticism to them, for you will have enough of criticism without me ; and I feel all the less disposed to pick out weaknesses and other things which did not please me, as I see from all that remains that you will soon be completely able to criticise your earlier attempts for yourself.

" Go on trying, and let me soon see something more."

I think that it is superfluous for me to try to add a single word to this. When Ritter came to the Kapellmeister, who just at that time had visitors, he said quietly to Ritter, pointing to my work, "an undeniable talent."

TO JOACHIM RAFF.

STUTTGART, 30th December 1847.

MOST HONOURED FRIEND,

This rather bad weather prevents me from coming to you myself, to thank you once more for your note to Lindpaintner. He desires his kind regards to you, would much like to get to know you better, and says he has " never yet heard your name mentioned in general." So it is now settled and decided that I shall play your masterly ' Prätendenten' Fantasia on Saturday, the 1st January, at the close of the first part.

Besides that, there will also be Méhul's ' Jagd' Overture, Mendels-

---

* Fräulein Scheuten.

sohn's 'Meerestille'; Molique will play, and Jäger, Lehr, and Demoiselle Basse will sing. So I am delighted that your splendid Fantasia, which I will take the utmost pains to play as little badly as ever I can, will appear in pretty good company. Tomorrow I shall have a practice at Schiedmayer's . . . I shall omit my class . . . I can choose what instrument I like best, and shall, if possible, get the one on which Madame Heinrich played at her matinée. I should be extremely indebted to you if you could come there at any hour that suited you, and that you liked to fix, to help me with your advice, which I trust absolutely.

Yours ever,

* Guido v. Bülow.

Apropos, Lindpaintner prefers to call me Hans ! !

---

* Bülow's second Christian name, for which he sometimes showed a preference.

LEIPZIG UNIVERSITY

CHAPTER III.

LEIPZIG UNIVERSITY.

SPRING 1848—AUTUMN 1849.

IT was already intimated in the Introduction that the position young Bülow held towards the Frege family would need further explanation. Much that there is of what is rough, passionate, and therefore one-sided in the following account can neither be omitted from the picture nor left to stand by itself *alone.*

A greater contrast in tradition, nature, education, and politics than existed between Hans' father and the Frege family, it would be impossible to imagine. The well-to-do patrician house in Leipzig, with its conservative religious and political principles, and the poet, enthusiastic for "freedom and regeneration" —who, moreover, had not succeeded in providing an assured position for himself and his—these differing elements could never become mutually sympathetic, and it was impossible entirely to abnegate the opposition to Hans' father in intercourse with the son, which the latter felt bitterly, and fell into prejudices on his side also.

But, quite apart from this point, there were such *utter* contrasts between Hans and the Freges. On the one side, the two married couples : Kammer-rath Frege and his wife—he the head of a great banking house, a man of high position both privately and publicly, and famous for his love of botany and his magnificent hothouses ; she, a very tender mother who, having lost several children in childhood, was absorbed with the health of those who remained to her, including her nephew while he lived under her care ; the younger couple, Woldemar and his wife—he twenty years older than his young cousin Hans, Professor of Law, religious, conservative, patrician ; she the lively and talented musician—both much taken up with the education of their son Arnold, with the claims of society, and of a large circle of friends. On the other side, the young relation entrusted to their care, endowed with a strongly independent spirit, only kept under by a deep sense of duty, and a tenderness and goodness of heart which made him, all his life long, feel any dissonance or disagreement absolutely unendurable.

And then the years 1848-9 ! Could any period have been more trying for men of such opposite feelings and temperament to have to come daily and hourly into contact with one another, dwelling under the same roof, and meeting at the same table ?

Such was the position of things when young Bülow was an inmate of the Freges' house. Yet it was no lack of goodwill or kindly feeling on their part, but solely the force of circumstances of that excited time, and the radical differences of character above described, that finally caused so much pain to both sides.

TO HIS MOTHER.

LEIPZIG, 24*th June* 1848.

DEAR MAMMA,

Please forgive me for not having written to you for so long, but for some time I was unwell, and then I had a good deal to do ; but the chief reason is that I did not want to bother you with complaints until I had got somewhat accustomed to the life here. For, if I may speak openly, I don't feel happy here. I daresay I had got a wrong idea of the freedom which, as a student, I should enjoy ; no doubt that is it. I don't mean to say that they are unfriendly to me, or treat me like a child—it is not that. But I can't do anything right, they find so much fault with me. If a friend comes to see me, he does sometimes get a cup of tea, certainly, but he is not allowed to smoke in my room. I myself am not allowed to go out late in the evening, say half-past eight, to see anything such as there is to see in a pretty lively town like this. Please don't think that I am not trying to be agreeable to them all. I go in to Aunt every morning, and am as friendly as I can be, but I don't know what to talk about ; they don't have any sympathy with me. At table politics are talked, but in a way which makes me turn dumb and give all my attention to my plate, although I have very little appetite. Visits, which are pretty seldom made, don't interest me in the very least ; nor do I care much more for the singers who come to Livia from time to time. I have been twice to the theatre. Except for that I don't go out, so I live very quietly and receive very few callers, because I can't do as I like in my own room. Late in the evening, that is to say, after ten o'clock, I must not play the piano any more, which I should often much like to do. I seldom make a joke ; I rather acquiesce in that, and have become reserved from experience. I may never say how I like this or that—nothing to do with anyone in the house, for I might be venturing on an opinion different from the authorities—that is the hardest of all. I am in a sort of middle position. They don't say " You must not behave like that here," which I should be only too glad if they would, for I want to give as little offence as possible. But I am not on an equality with anybody. I am supposed to consider everyone else as high above me, which—forgive me for such unpardonable arrogance—I can't always do. But I would even do that if they would leave me just a little bit of independence. This, alas, only consists in my being able—with due regard to the hours— to play the piano, read and write when I like, in my own room, where I am fearfully plagued with flies, and where, even in the great heat, I must open the windows, in order not to catch cold at night. But do not misunderstand me, dear Mamma ; I think it is a good thing to go through a sort of schooling like that, only I can't understand how Woldemar can call this year the happiest of my life, by praising up my academical freedom, which consists in being able to miss any lectures I like, if I am a careless fellow. I hope, before God, it is not to be my happiest ! I will, I must, try to make myself more independent. I will not do anything that can be blamed, but I must emancipate myself in order to be happier. Otherwise I shall grow too bitter ; I am so already, and suffer often from headache, which I don't let them know.

Of the household I get along best with Friedrich, who is *good* towards me, and little Arnold. My six songs, which I dedicated to Livia, and which were really not bad, she has once hummed through ; she found some pretty ideas in them, then she called me a crack-brained fellow, then she found they were a wonderful mixture of Schumann, Chopin, Döhler, and so on. She apparently does not want to spoil me by praise ; but she might, for instance, have shown them once to Kapellmeister Rietz, for he might have given me some hints about them. Woldemar did not like the songs at all, except one bit, which reminded him of Weber—that was very flattering to me ; but Livia could have sung the songs beautifully if she would have done.

Under these circumstances, a letter from Ritter to me is very refreshing—he loves me truly as a kindred spirit. Thode is also a really good fellow. He gets my compositions and then plays them to me, and I am delighted when, after he has studied them for some time, he finds out what is tolerably good in them—he shows me, by this interest, that he feels a friendship for me ; I know how to discriminate between this and flattery or depreciation. I occasionally read French and German books with him. His pronunciation of the former is not at all bad.

Pray forgive me that I have destroyed, by these foolish outpourings, your expectations of a sensible letter, but you wished me to be quite open, and that I have been. But please don't mention a word of it to my Aunt. I have everything I require—am even much better fed than is necessary—so there is every reason to be satisfied. And my indiscretion was probably that, owing to the heat, I have had my hair cut *à la mécontent*. For the rest I am free according to my title of Student—

a good step above the Gymnasiast (schoolboy), and I have, at any rate, a certain independence, and can think what I like.

I will make myself as freely happy as I can : if that is not possible, then I must drag along as well as I can; Woldemar found things *much* worse in his student days.

Now I will continue in a more reasonable strain.

I shall not want so much money in future; this time I had to get several necessary books, student's portfolio, inkstand, etc., in which Woldemar, and especially Friedrich, helped me much. With my washing I am not extravagant, and I always write out two bills in an orderly manner; in fact I keep everything in order. I go to bed at ten to half-past, and get up at half-past five. The lectures I am attending are— Psychology and Logic from Weisse, every day from seven to eight, (very clever lectures, sometimes rather obscure, but he dictates a great deal, so that one can think it over afterwards at home). And it is very nice that he gives his lecture so early, because then one is obliged to get up early. Four times a week Wachsmuth reads Universal History from eight to nine, which is rather interesting and useful. W. is no very great man, but he knows how to make his lectures very interesting, especially by quoting the sources of his information. Twice a week Haupt reads, from ten to eleven, Tacitus' 'Germania,' which is of much interest both grammatically and historically. He is also, in my opinion, the best speaker, as he always speaks in an equal tone and never interrupts himself.

Hermann I hear four times, from eleven to twelve. His lectures are intended specially for philologists, but they are also useful to me, and it is interesting to see again this celebrated old man, who comes into the room every time rattling his spurs with such an energetic step. Fechner lectures on Wednesdays and Saturdays, from three to four, on the Last Judgment. His audience diminishes every time—first there were fifteen, then eight, now five. He is a profound thinker, and I enjoy listening to him very much. He tells us how many of the teachings of Christianity are not fulfilled, and the extent to which one may use one's own reason in judging of them. (Original sin, freedom of will, God's everlasting decrees, etc.) First of all he occupied himself with philosophical premonitions about Idealism and Materialism, and began by placing before us an interposed doctrine of these two extremes.

Flathe's lectures on Shakespeare's Tragedies, twice a week, from four to five, are very popular. At the first two lectures there were 120 students (the doors were left open); many of them had to stand, as they could not get into the room. As yet he has been speaking in general terms about ideas of art, and making æsthetic preambles; his delivery is too declamatory to be a standard one, but he often makes very witty, striking points. Papa repudiates him, but I listen to him nevertheless. That makes twenty lessons in the week. I wanted to go twice a week to hear Rathgeber's lectures on the Rudiments of the Italian Language, but Papa won't have it, and so I have left that. The attending of the lectures fits in very well with the rest of my time. I always do my piano practice from nine to eleven or from eight to ten, and sometimes go then to Härtel, and I also have the afternoons to myself for composing and other work.

I am very much pleased with the piano I have hired. It has quite a fair tone, and keeps in very good tune; I also often play on Livia's— she wishes me to do so very much, as her piano has not yet been half enough played upon, and is very unequal; for otherwise, as you may well imagine, I would not do so. The Chopin Fantasia did *not* please Livia. I play Studies and Nocturnes of Chopin, some new 'bad' pieces by Kullak, Heller, a new Fantasia of Thalberg, Sonatas of Beethoven. Raff's things I cannot play to anybody; firstly, I never do play to anybody, for which I am very sorry, as I might again inure myself to my nervousness, and, secondly, Livia thinks some of them very bad.

I have not seen Ascher for five weeks. I play Moscheles' 'Capriccios'; firstly because they are such good practice, secondly because they are so suitable for playing to anybody, and thirdly because through Ascher's playing I have learnt somewhat how Moscheles wants them played, and because they are more attractive to me, as being something new, than the somewhat trite Studies.

He has now been a week in Dresden, so it is only now that I can go to him.

Hauptmann has been ill the whole time with cold and fever, and has given no lessons at all, but *hopes* to be able to begin next week. I have really often inquired after him, but Papa seems to lay the fault of my not having yet begun my lessons with him onto my negligence. I must confess that I should be very glad if I had a little more encouragement in my piano playing. It is not that I am lazy; but, after all, one does not play merely for one's piano. It need be merely a hint of encouragement, but another kind than what I can give to myself. Today I am not very well again, with some giddiness and headache.

The theatre affair is very unpleasant to me, because it is to you. But I did, truly, not behave in the very least improperly in the pit. Besides, I was always with the Ritters, and they must surely know something. In the 'Prinz Eugen' I hissed, like the Ritters, as people applauded, and that everybody does; that is no 'stupid prank.' The people who sit in the best places do that; of course not the ladies.

Otherwise I am not conscious of having done anything out of the way, beyond having clapped the Valentine very loudly ! For the rest, as you are vexed I beg to be forgiven.

I saw here a most wretched performance of ' Robert,' especially by the orchestra. The *tempi* too were much too fast; except Wagner, I don't know any conductor who does not commit this fault. (Berlioz relates that Mendelssohn did it too.) . . . I beg you earnestly, dear Mamma, to write me word fully what Wagner lately inserted in the *Anzeiger;* Ritter gave me only very short, clever hints of it. He sent me an article for the musical *Signale,* which was very well written. It was a refutation of the thesis that ' the present time is unfavourable to art.' But it is sure not to be accepted. A performance of Hamlet enchanted me. It was the greatest pleasure I have had yet, except the Ninth Symphony, at a concert of which I have not yet told you. I got a relapse of my headache and fever at it.

The concert was very full. 824 tickets were sold, and 632 thalers taken. Many people had paid a louis d'or for one or two tickets. Uncle had defrayed the expenses, 175 thalers, out of his own pocket. It was very good of him, and it gave universal satis- faction. The concert opened with an Overture of Gade's, ' Im Hochland,' which was really very charming, fresh, and original (with occasional reminiscences of Mendelssohn), and was very well played. An Aria from Figaro was well sung by Frl. Schwarzbach. David played some bad variations of his own very cleverly. The sextet from Don Juan was beautifully played. Livia had a reception on making her appearance. Moscheles played a very beautiful Rondo of Mendels- sohn's with orchestra very delicately, but I think I have played it much more in the spirit of the composer. This commonplace really astounded me; I exclaimed, ' Extraordinary ! also a Jew and a musician, and yet so little kinship ! ' Livia sang two songs by Rietz, which are very pretty and made a perfect *furore.* They encored the second ; she did not understand, and thought the applause was for Rietz. A little song of Mendelssohn, with which she concluded, was not at all suited to the concert, and made but little effect. If she had only followed my advice ! —for my choice was in every way better—but at last, from diffidence, I said nothing more. The Ninth Symphony went very well—I was absolutely and entirely in heaven. Rietz conducted in a praiseworthy manner, as well as he could. The ladies' parts were much better done than in Dresden, the rest not so good. I will write again to you very soon.

This morning, Midsummer Day, I heard Howard, who otherwise always preached at the same time as Harless. He is not so popular, not so strikingly powerful as Harless; but he has profound and beautiful thoughts, only he speaks excessively slowly. . . .

P.S.—I am feeling somewhat more softened again, for Livia sang my songs again yesterday, and said many kind things about them.

Writing to his mother on the 4th December 1848, he says :—

I heard Cherubini's 'Requiem' lately in the Church (at B.'s funeral). It is a magnificent, grand, and yet clear, sacred composition, and wonderfully beautiful. And what I did not venture at first, out of diffidence, to assert—namely that, as a whole, it is much grander than Mozart's — I now don't hesitate to affirm, seeing that Franz and Hauptmann say the same—two such diverse musical characters, and yet both of them authorities.

The civil disturbances in Germany during those stormy times were not without their influence on young Bülow's life in Leipzig. And then came those terrible May-days in Dresden, which affected him powerfully, both on their own account and on account of his parents and friends there. The members of the Frege family naturally felt annoyed at what they considered Bülow's want of sympathy in their anxieties and views, and even expressed a suspicion that he was following these events with joy, and that he was connected with the democrats. But, whatever inconsiderate and hasty words may have been spoken on both sides, nothing more keenly touched Bülow's consciousness of his own loyalty than to perceive that it was called in question. The following letter betrays in every word the painful state of overwrought excitement under which he was labouring :—

TO HIS MOTHER (*Fragment*).

[LEIPZIG, 7*th May* 1849.]

There are things I wanted to keep silence about, but it is impossible —I must come out with it : I cannot stand being in this house any longer, for I am a man, and not a machine. Every hour here is torture to me. The plainly-outspoken contempt, and even suspicion, latterly, is perfectly unendurable. Day and night there is the greatest excitement here, and noise everywhere ; and yesterday it was carried to such an excess that there were eight killed and several wounded. Now that they know my opinions they dare to implicate me in it all. I must know everything. If I can't appear sufficiently gloomy and serious, then they mistrust me in the most marked manner, *and they beg Uncle to take care what he says before me, because I should pass it on to the democrats !* Could anything be worse? . . . I implore you, write to Aunt, or, better still, send me somewhere else ; dry bread would be preferable. I mean it! I don't know whether, in this fearful state of things, this letter will ever reach you, but I write to you all the same; perhaps also there might be a possibility of things soon taking a turn, or coming to an end of some sort. . . . Studying and practising are just now absolutely impossible to me. I wish I were not a man, but a poor, unreasoning brute, that I might not feel the sensations I do. How happy among our comrades is he who was yesterday struck down by a cannon-ball in Dresden! . . . If only you in Dresden are not suffering! I am so anxious about you, although you are pretty far away from the scene of action. If only I could come to you, to hear a few *friendly, tolerant* words! If only Wagner does not get shot!

Beautiful Dresden! To think that so lately I was glorying in the many art-works in her picture-galleries, and that only a few weeks ago I was hearing the grandest of all music in her opera-house! And now the one is given up to the flames, and the other is the scene of the most horrible murder! Heaven grant that the seed sown in blood may blossom into something beautiful, everlasting, and divine. . . .

To this letter, written under the strain of unnatural excitement, he added another very shortly afterwards, in a calmer frame of mind, in which it appeared that the proclamation of martial law having quieted down the overwrought feelings on both sides, he would be glad to remain on until Michaelmas under his Uncle's roof :—

TO HIS MOTHER.

WEIMAR, *2nd June* 1849.

DEAR MAMMA,

Thank you for your last letter and the two letters of introduction. Please give my thanks to the lady who gave them for me, as they have been a pleasure to me. I am writing to you in a great hurry, for reasons which I will explain to you presently. I shall send you, later on, a sort of diary of my doings here, by which you will be able to see more particularly how very useful this stay is to me in many ways, and how I am right in begging you to give me the means to prolong it still a little more. Liszt answered very kindly last Monday that he would do everything he could to make my stay here interesting to me. I forthwith went on Monday at mid-day to Halle, and stayed there till Tuesday.

After some futile attempts, I met Liszt at one o'clock (Wednesday). He had to go to the Grand-Ducal dinner, but we had an hour's talk together on various subjects—Raff, Wagner, who, Liszt hopes, is in

Paris. In the afternoon he appointed me to meet him at half-past four at the Altenburg, the abode of the Princess Wittgenstein, where Liszt is also accustomed to spend the whole day. There I met a pupil of his (sixteen years old), young Winterberger,* a very talented fellow. Liszt was with us both till nine o'clock. I played the Schumann song to him, and he was pleased with my manner of playing, although I had not got his conception of the piece. It was also very interesting to me to see how he let his pupil play Beethoven's E flat Concerto; and his splendid hints with regard to the conception of it, even in the apparently most trifling matters, are of great use to me. He played some things for four hands with me, then some new compositions, amongst others the paraphrase of Wolfram's song; finally, he took a long walk with us in the castle garden. It would take too long to tell you all the details here. On the same afternoon he received also a most sensible, excellent letter of apology from Raff. On Thursday he dined with me at the Russischer Hof, where I am stopping. He came with the most notable artists and singers, who all adore him, and whom he treats with unspeakable kindness. He is a quite perfect man. Today I was at Stör's,† the leading violinist, who has also done something as a composer —there was no end to his praise. Liszt's playing, and his whole personality, have completely enchanted and inspired me; all the brilliant gifts of former days he still possesses in the fullest measure, but a more manly repose, an all-round solidity, complete his truly exalted character.

Early yesterday I was with him at the rehearsal of ' Fidelio.' I was perfectly carried away by his conducting—admirable, astounding! In the evening he played Trios at the Altenburg. We were again with him from seven to eleven. Tomorrow he is going to have my Quartet played. He has placed his room, piano, and musical library at my disposal every morning; naturally I have frequently availed myself of the permission.

In short, I myself know best of what use it is to me to see, to talk with, and to hear Liszt. I—who before the Whitsuntide days was bitterness personified, and thought of nothing but revolutionary terror-ism *in spe*—cannot now even read a paper, think no longer of politics, but am able again to enjoy life; and the intercourse with some first-rate and *real* artists, the chief representatives of their art—an inter-course which I have had to do without for so long—does me indescribable good.

---

* Alexander Winterberger (1834), organist and pianist, a pupil first of the Leipzig Conservatoire, and then of Liszt.

† Karl Stör (1814-89), later on conductor at Weimar.

So I beg you most earnestly to let me stay on till Wednesday, and for this to send me as soon as possible three reichsthaler more—I can spend it out of my own money-box—for I cannot use the money in a better way than this. I have pretty confident hopes that you will fulfil this wish, because I shall wait for your answer, and thus I must overstep the proposed time of my stay here. I am really not wasting my money, as you will perhaps see from the accompanying paper of accounts.

Yesterday I dined at Herr v. Schwendler's,* today I go to Frau v. Pogwisch,† in the evening is ' Fidelio,' and after the opera Liszt will come to the hotel. As I heard today from Liszt's own particular *famulus* (Stör, the first violinist), I may also be of some little use to him; but of this more anon.

" I also brought some of my songs with me, and it is quite easy for me to get them sung by artists here, as, owing to Liszt's extreme kindness to me, I have already got quite a good position among them.

In a long letter to his mother from Leipzig on the 21st June 1849, he writes as follows :—

Thank you again a thousand times for having allowed me to stay a few days longer in Weimar; I think the visit has done me good both musically and in other respects.

Liszt sent me a short time ago, through Kistner, his newest work, three great Studies; I wrote to him lately, after I had executed his commissions, and I hope I may perhaps get an answer from him soon, giving me R. W.'s address.

I believe I have already told you that he had my Quartet played twice at his house. The first time it was done he was prevented from hearing it, by a sudden, long call from the theatre Intendant; I was, however, very glad of this, as it was played in an excruciating manner, whereas the second time it went quite nicely, including the Scherzo (some of the musicians having looked over their parts at home). Liszt said several times, ' Very nice,' ' Very pretty,' but also ' Very difficult.' I begged him to allow me to send him later on my Overture, at which I am now working steadily, a permission which he very kindly granted. Liszt gave us an immense pleasure that same day (Tuesday) by his performance of the ' Tannhäuser ' Overture, which he has paraphrased in a most wonderful manner and with the greatest assiduity (he made three

---

* Herr v. Schwendler, a State official of high standing in the Weimar and Coburg service.

† Henriette von Pogwisch, one of the ladies of honour to the Grand Duchess Luise of Saxe-Weimar, and mother of Ottilie von Goethe.

different arrangements of it); he has managed to give the effects in such a wonderful manner on the piano, as no other pianist, I am sure, will ever be able to do. In all probability he will publish this arrangement, as well as the transcription of Wolfram's song. The latter is not particularly difficult; and the former does not look so very awful on paper, yet the playing of it was such a strain upon him that he was obliged to stop for a moment once near the end, and he very seldom plays it because it exhausts him too much, so that he said to me afterwards, ' You can write down today in your diary that I have played the " Tannhäuser " Overture to you.'

I had read the *Journal des débats* of the 16th (?) May a month ago, but thank you for telling me about it. I strongly advise you to get Liszt's article in the *feuilleton*, not necessarily to get a ' sympathy ' for ' Tannhäuser,' but simply because the article is written in a perfectly masterly, superb manner. Liszt reproduces the contents of the opera almost in Wagner's own words, in a way that one would have hardly thought it possible to render German poetry into French, and I hope it will have done Wagner much good, although, as Liszt himself avows, it is impossible to give ' Tannhäuser ' with any success on a French stage. . . .

After frequently hearing Liszt, I have now made a special study of what was particularly defective in my piano-playing, namely, a certain amateurish uncertainty, a certain angular want of freedom in conception, of which I must completely cure myself; in modern pieces especially I must cultivate more *abandon*, and, when I have conquered the technical difficulties of a piece, I must *let myself go* more, according to how I feel at the moment; and, if one is not devoid of talent, of course anything absurd or unsuitable does not come into one's mind. Please give me your opinion fully on this point, and tell me what struck you formerly as faulty or ugly in my playing, for I want to perfect myself as far as ever I can ; and with the idea that I shall sometime give lessons I have always tried to become more confident, and it is not at all improbable that it may yet come to that.

According to what Liszt tells me, there is really a foundation for the report that he has begun some big works, and that several piano Concertos with orchestral accompaniment are lying completed in his desk, with which he means to ' pay off some of his debts,' and an Italian opera, ' Sardanapalus ' (after Byron's) is far on towards completion. These are secrets at present, which he does not want all the world to know.

He usually worked at the Altenburg in the mornings, so that I seldom saw him at that time, but in the afternoons and evenings I was almost always with him. His talk was always intensely interesting, and he hardly ever said an insignificant thing. He spoke French by preference, and even when he talked in German he constantly interpolated not merely words, but whole phrases in French. . . .

Writing from Leipzig again on the 2nd August 1849, he says to his mother :—

Quite by chance I met Litolff. I was feeling very hungry one day between two of my lectures, and went into a baker's in Peters-strasse. Suddenly, as I was turning a corner, I saw a well-known figure standing before a picture-shop; I fixed my eyes on him, hesitated a moment, and then was so struck with the resemblance that I went up to him; it was really Litolff, and he knew me directly too. Litolff looked so very much better that this explained my doubts as to his identity ; except for the unavoidable nervous twitching of his face, which affects strangers so unpleasantly, he is much quieter, and has become much stronger and healthier ; but unfortunately, as I found from his conversation, as he has got stronger bodily he has grown weaker as regards the productiveness of his brain. In order to excite his brain sufficiently seems, or seemed, to require such an excited life, such a deranged health : now he has already settled down into the Philistine repose of a good humdrum citizen ; may the Fates preserve him from sinking into this and nothing more !

A German genius—I cannot include Mozart in the category of *German* geniuses—can perfectly well fulfil his calling apart from the outer world, in the quiet peace of his own family, and among the homely concerns of everyday life—indeed he is even at his best thus ; but a non-German, a Frenchman, or a Pole, or indeed any foreigner of talent or genius, such as Litolff, cannot do this. He requires the perpetual alternation of joy and grief, he requires 'great passions,'—in a word, the great outside world. Such a man as Litolff will occasionally be inert, perhaps sink into the mud for a moment, but will then arise and create anew, with superhuman, demoniacal power and perseverance, something very great, although to a certain extent imperfect, if looked into very closely. Such a life as this is, in my opinion, the most natural for Litolff.

BERLIN UNIVERSITY

CHAPTER IV.

BERLIN UNIVERSITY.

IN the autumn of 1849 the divorce of Hans' parents took place. In the same year Eduard married Louise von Bülow, daughter of Count von Bülow-Dennewitz, the Prussian Field-Marshal, who attained celebrity in the war for freedom. She was a charming creature, highly cultivated and witty, enthusiastic, and full of goodness and kindness of heart, which was always shown in an equal measure towards Eduard's two children by his first marriage.

The pair went to Switzerland, and bought the beautiful castle of Ötlishausen in Canton Thurgau, intending to make that their permanent home.

In the late autumn Franziska went to Berlin with Hans and Isa, for the sake of the former, who was there to continue his University studies. Eduard's cousins, Ernst and Paul von Bülow, the former of whom was in the Prussian State service, and the latter in the army, together with a few acquaintances of Franziska's among the literary people of the Berlin of those days, formed the pleasant circle into which the new-comers stepped. Fräulein Henriette Solmar, a well-known personality in the Varnhagen circle, wrote to Eduard in the most friendly terms about Hans, and Varnhagen himself took a deep interest in the young man, an interest which he maintained in later years.

It was in this winter (1849) that *Hans' journalistic-literary work began.* In the autumn he obtained the post of musical reporter to the *Abendpost,* a democratic paper of the day.* He was also occasional correspondent to other papers, not in Berlin. He was studying music at this time without any practical or theoretical help, but with the greatest zeal.

In the spring of 1850 Franziska and her daughter Isa left Berlin and returned to Dresden, Hans going with them for the Easter holidays, after which he returned to Berlin to continue his studies, accompanied this time only by his faithful companion of many years—his dog Wach.

From Berlin, writing to his mother on the 6th July 1850, he says :—

I am giving lessons in harmony to another student—I don't have

---

* Some of these writings, partly critical, partly polemical, will appear in a separate volume.

anything to do with swaggerers and ranters and scandal-mongers—and he gives me lessons in English in return ; I am reading the ' Vicar of Wakefield,' which I can understand quite well without any help except from the dictionary.

And on the 4th August he writes as follows (also to his mother) :—

For Griepenkerl's * poor tragedy 'Robespierre' Litolff has written an Overture, which has met with the most universal, undivided praise. I ordered it for myself, and, if not exactly a classical Beethoven Overture *à la Egmont*, it is nevertheless a very talented piece of music, with undeniable flashes of genius, and, so far as I can gather from the instrumentation, full of interesting effects ; and moreover there is a unity about the whole, which is all the more surprising to me as he is otherwise rather split up and piece-meal in his writing. The principal subjects are the very ones which he had formerly fixed upon for Catherine Howard in the Overture. When I went to see Geyer lately he gave me a new Trio by Litolff to take home with me (the second Trio, just out), and I confess I have truly rejoiced over Litolff's progress and the quickness of his power of production. There is a wealth of genius and ideas in it, and some things are of an excellence which is rare nowadays. It is rhythmically and melodically original without oddity ; almost everything sounds well ; there is freshness and life throughout ; a specially beautiful Andante, and a Finale overflowing with humour. Geyer had begged me to review it for him, which I have done, and, though I praised it most tremendously (and the Leipzig *Signale* wrote in even far more favourable terms of it), that dry old fellow did not agree with what was said, because Litolff had violated what he considers the inflexible, sacred, unimpeachable old Trio-form. But Litolff has kept as strictly as possible to the old forms, only not pedantically ; the last movement especially he has carried out further, and in a very happy manner. For it is a very bad habit, and in the highest sense a want of form, that composers always lay out their Finale on as large a scale as the first movement, and if possible spin it out even longer. The hearer cannot stand it, as this repetition grows wearisome ; and on the other hand there seems very little justification in a fourth movement at all, if the form of it is not new, but just a reproduction of the introduction, and only individual owing to its being of a lighter character, in place of the more heavy earnestness. The Rondo-form, in such a manner, is old-fashioned and insupportable. L. has taken the

---

* Wolfgang Robert Griepenkerl (1810-68), Professor of the History of Art at the ' Carolinum ' in Brunswick ; in his writings a partisan of musical progress.

right road; he has 'hit the nail on the head,' as papa would say, whether by instinct or in conscious imitation of the Finale of many a Beethoven Symphony. In the first movement and the Andante the composer must give himself over to the purest subjectivity; the last movement, and perhaps also the Scherzo, must be treated as objective, so that the hearer may be satisfied in recognising the necessity for a conclusion; in order that the objectivity may not be insipid—for musicians and music-lovers do not require an insipid objectivity, like Hofrath Carus, & Co.—the composer has *carte blanche* to introduce here a piquant, a *capriccioso* element. And this is what Litolff has done. And then a Flodoard Geyer puffs himself up and cries, 'The critic must be the guardian of the sacredness of form,' etc. All the same, I hope my criticism will be printed in the musical paper here, and, if it is, I shall write to Litolff so as to bring myself into connection with him again if possible. I must say I long to see the dear man again, and if it were not for Weimar I should like to go to Brunswick.

Forgive my tremendous garrulity; '*l'objet m'a emporté malgré moi.*'

I have been living rather a dull life here lately, but now I mean to go in for a little amusement, especially by going to the theatre. When the opera reopens after the holidays they are going to give 'Cosi fan tutte,' which I am very anxious to see. And then Rachel is here, and was lately playing Camilla in ' Horace,' and also playing in ' Andromache.' Everybody is in raptures, or pretends to be, as that is the correct thing. There is no doubt that she is something very extraordinary and specially gifted, and, according to her portrait, she looks very interesting. I intend to see her in her next part, Phædra, which is said to be one of her best. I don't think one ought to put off a thing like that, for it is not probable that she will revisit Germany very soon, and who knows when I may get to Paris, apart from all other eventualities ?

I lately made a call on the Court preacher Strauss, to whom Herr v. Gall had as good as introduced me (though not in person), and about a week afterwards I was invited to an evening party there. The family, in addition to his kind and courteous wife, consists of two sons, who are also clergymen, and the younger of whom is musical (church music). The company was not particularly interesting or attractive, but there were a good many young people there, and, apart from a very nice supper in pretty rooms, I was most kindly treated, and, after I had played, I received tremendous attention. For I really had played pretty well and with great ease, as I had had a little wine at supper, and then one plays one's best and surest. I had played the Prophète Fantaisie (No. 1), and had petrified everybody. A clergyman—I don't know who it was—compared me with the ' Edel von Hornau,' with this difference, that he could only boast of *one* thing, whereas I knew much more and was more daring. Then some of the ladies begged for something ' soft,' and I played them, *con molto sentimento,* a transcription of Kullak's on an air from ' Norma,' which is very pretty and effectively arranged, and which gained me the reputation of ' many-sidedness.' . . .

Bülow persuaded his mother to accompany him to the Herder Festival at Weimar at the latter end of August. After a short stay there, which she appears thoroughly to have enjoyed, Franziska wrote to her daughter :— ' After the Festival came Liszt ; he pressed my hand, and thanked me that we had both come, adding, as he kissed Hans in farewell, " Je suis très attaché à ce garçon." '

SWITZERLAND

CHAPTER V.

SWITZERLAND.

AUTUMN 1850—SUMMER 1851.

THE turning-point in Hans von Bülow's career was now at hand. On the 10th September (1850) he arrived at Ötlishausen on a visit to his father, and to see his sister Isa, who was also there on a short visit.

In spite of the inward agitation through which he was passing, he appears to have shown a calm exterior, and to have evinced a self-command which, on all the really *great* occasions of his life, never failed him.

His step-mother, speaking of those days, says : " Hans appeared in good spirits, and was constantly talking ; we often went walks in the beautiful neighbourhood. . . . But the pleasant time in Ötlishausen did not last long. One morning Hans had vanished. He was absent from breakfast, dinner, and supper. All inquiries were unsuccessful. Bülow soon said, ' Hans is gone to Wagner at Zurich.' I could not but think the same thing. Bülow took the post at the next station, Rorschach, for the railway in that part was not yet finished, and went to Zurich. The next day he came back, very much upset and excited. Hans had fallen at his father's feet, and implored him to let him become a musician. His father had then yielded, on condition that his mother agreed to it. I did my best to calm Bülow, and my endeavours were not without result. By degrees he became more composed about his son's bold and hasty resolve—but Hans would have to come to an understanding with his mother himself."

Before taking the decisive step Hans had made the attempt with his mother in the following letter :—

TO HIS MOTHER.

ÖTLISHAUSEN, 16*th September* 1850.

. . . Now as to *my affairs.* And, please, hear me patiently to the end. I might have gone to work a roundabout way, and prepared you little by little, but I prefer to go direct to the point.

Kapellmeister Wagner proposed to me some days ago that I should make practical studies under his direction in Zurich next winter, and conduct the opera there in turns with Ritter, for which I should then draw half of the salary. In the larger concerts, in which Wagner would himself conduct the Beethoven Symphonies, I might come forward as a pianist, and thus become known, and be enabled, by giving lessons, to keep myself. This is at least a proposal worth consideration; an opportunity which, for anyone who wants to embrace a musical career, would be joyfully seized upon by any young artist; an opportunity which will not soon offer again, and certainly not in a better or more attractive guise. It is a great question whether Wagner will still be in Zurich during the winter of 1851-2.

Now, I implore you most earnestly, listen to the result of my reflections, made after the first excitement was overcome, and thought out in wakeful nights. The question of my future career presses for a speedy and definite solution. I have passed my twentieth year, and have had no clear, definite aim before my eyes—as yet. The last half-year in Berlin found me more than ever occupied with thoughts of my future, and, from some remarks in conversation which we had when we were last together, you will remember that the wishes were not newly formed by the sudden event (falling, as it were, from the clouds) of Wagner's proposal, but that they were simply formed into clearer and more distinct expression.

In all the conversations which we have had together over my career since that time you have said most distinctly that you would not place any obstacle in the way of my free choice, but only your advice; that you would never employ compulsion; that I might have complete confidence in you; and that you would let me be happy in my own way. We then agreed that I should study Jurisprudence (as one of the most general branches of the profession) as far as was necessary to pass an examination, so as to keep all roads open to me. I yielded the question, seeing the good sense of your advice, and that you wished to protect yourself against all responsibility, and to have done all that lay in your power to give me the previous preparation, by the help of which I should be enabled to choose, among a number of similar careers, the branch which I should prefer to pursue. I promised you that I would study Jurisprudence, and still intend to keep my promise, and do not ask you in the least to release me from it. But I can no longer conceal from you that I am too much wanting both in talent and inclination, and love of such a profession, ever to be a good lawyer or an erudite man. It is absolutely impossible for me to devote myself to the Government service; I am too little adapted to this—to me—indescribably hateful profession, especially under present circumstances. My views—and they are not of a superficial nature—I cannot sacrifice for the love of you. I cannot stifle or tear myself away from the principles which are a part of myself, nor can I strip off my ideas of honour to accommodate circumstances. I would rather not live at all than have to serve in a German State—in Prussia. All I can do is to sacrifice and renounce myself in so far that I will take no active part in the work of demolition of the old order of things, and that I will keep my opinions to myself. The more I should have to occupy myself with political matters—an integral part of Jurisprudence—the stronger would be every temptation, the harder every conquest of self. What is there left ? To be an advocate in the old sense—and that is something extremely disagreeable—I am neither sharp nor shrewd enough ; to be one in the modern sense—to become a barrister—I am wanting in oratorical talent, the outward means which insure success. I have only this alternative : either I must embrace a juridical-political career, which could then be only that of a Revolutionary ; or a musical career, where the danger is rather that of becoming an aristocrat, and in which I can so steep myself that I should cry ' apage ' to political strife and discussion.

I feel the inclination to both these careers within me, but the weight of the scales turns in favour of the latter. It is nobler, more beautiful, purer, and appeals to me incomparably more, apart from any confidence in my own powers.

Unfortunately music was for a long time placed by me in the background. That time is now past. The movements of the Revolution years, the contagion of the excitement—these outward causes, which I truly cannot help, brought out all the violent fanaticism, the feverish madness, before which all my youthful enthusiasm for freedom and the like had vanished. That time is, thank God, now over. The reading of the papers has lost its charm for me ; I can do without knowing about things, and if I am left in peace I can keep myself quiet. Just in an equal degree has my love for music again obtained the ascendancy. The musical life in Zurich next winter would foster this love in the best and richest manner. To be able to write for orchestra, to have the opportunity of having what I write at once performed, and of thus studying instrumentation—I cannot imagine anything more delightful and more attractive. To play Beethoven's Pianoforte Concerti in concerts with orchestral accompaniment, to make my first essays in conducting under Wagner's direction—what could there be that would more spur a man on to activity and industry ? And I need not on that account give up the law studies, and, should it come to pass, I firmly intend not to give them up ; I could thoroughly go over all that I have hitherto learnt, and fix it more clearly and firmly in my head; if necessary I could also attend some courses at the University there, which is not at all a bad one, and at which, for example, Keller and Bluntschli have taught for a long time. In the summer I could then go either to Bonn or to Berlin, and carry on my juridical studies to their completion, that is to say, till they were brought to an end by the first examination. The winter half-year in Zurich might be considered as a test—the best for me; I would make music the principal subject, and see to what results I could bring it.

Weimar would be preferable to me, on account of the piano-playing under Liszt; but he has so much to do with others that he could not devote much time to me, and I should not have there the enormous and immeasurable advantage of the orchestra. The useless rushing about and trifling away one's time, together with the innumerable temptations to waste one's money, which are always occurring in Berlin, would not occur at all in Zurich.

Please think this over carefully, and wait at least two to three days before you refuse your consent irrevocably. I too have thought the matter fully over before arriving at this result. If you refuse me per- mission—as I almost fear you will—well, in that case I shall of course obey you, and go to Berlin for the winter, but how long I shall be able to stand it is a great question.

If you should suspect that it is Ritter who has influenced me in this wish you are entirely mistaken. I could not imagine where you could have got such a poor idea of my firmness of purpose and indepen- dence. Papa says little; he lets his permission, *i.e.* his willingness to wait and see, which he has granted, not without great fear and mistrust, depend on yours.

I beg you once more not to follow *your* antipathies, but to think it over; make me some concessions, I pray. It is, after all, no such great and formidable matter—one trial-half-year.

.   .   .   .

Our life here is very simple and monotonous. I hope we shall have a piano as soon as possible, for I want one dreadfully. In order not to let my fingers get quite stiff I practise a good deal on the dumb keyboard of Charles Mayer—*ápropos*, have you seen him again?—which now makes up to me for the inconvenience of having had to drag it about on the journey. A further occupation of mine is the working out of some musical ideas I got on the journey, and the copying of Liszt's manuscript, a work demanding great care and pains. By the help of the

clever valet, Karl, I have learnt to handle the music-pen; and as I want
to do the thing well, and to keep the pages perfectly neat—and I don't
know a more perfect pattern than the neatness of Raff—it gets along
slowly. The weather is continuously fine, and, though autumnal and
very cool in the mornings and evenings, yet one may still call it warm.
The view we have is magnificent, and has been very much improved by
Papa's order to cut down a lot of box and underwood which was in the
way of it. I work with him now and then in the garden, although I am
rejoicing in a quite imposing cold. In the rooms, especially the dining-
room, it is cold, and when we sit there I generally put on my overcoat.

I am very anxious that my letter should be posted today, so as to
reach you as soon as possible, and therefore I cannot write about the
journey now. I will therefore tell you only the most important things
about my visit to Stuttgart.

.   .   .   .

I hope you are well, and will not take my letter very much amiss.
Write soon and kindly.

How the two great artists, who exercised the most decisive influence on
Hans von Bülow's life and work, and who, together with him, constitute a
powerful epoch in the history of German music—how these two spoke up for
their young *protégé* at this crisis, will be seen by the two following letters to
Hans' mother.

RICHARD WAGNER TO FRANZISKA VON BÜLOW.

ZURICH, 19*th September* 1850.

MY DEAR MADAM,

My young friend Karl Ritter, who was desirous of increasing and strengthening his musical knowledge by practice in conducting, has, upon my recommendation, obtained the post of musical conductor
at the theatre here for the coming winter season. As it was only
by binding myself to superintend the practical work of my young friend,
and to a certain extent to direct it anew, that I could make the necessary
guarantee to the Director, Ritter has hereby a good opportunity of learning in a practical school, such as he might not easily find again under
such favourable conditions, as circumstances might not allow of this
everywhere. Now in this practice two can just as well take part as one,

D

and I told Ritter, as he is in the neighbourhood, to tell your son this, together with the offer, on my side, to help him in the same measure as I am about to help Ritter. Well, yesterday I received a letter from your son, in which he thanks me with the utmost warmth for this offer, in the accepting of which he sees the chance of quickly qualifying himself for the practical post of a musical conductor, by which he would soon be enabled to obtain a position suited to his powers and his most ardent inclinations. With all the deeper sorrow he confesses to me that he almost despairs of obtaining the sanction of his dear mother to accept my offer, as she has all along cherished the desire that he should embrace the career of a lawyer, and that therefore he must first at least finish his studies for that object.

Will you now permit a man who has attained to riper years, and who has been accustomed, as far as in his power lay, to think and act not by halves, but fully,—will you permit him to give his opinion on this point? I have followed the youthful, developing period of your son's life with cognizance and sympathy, without exercising any other influence upon him than that of my example as an artist, and of my most cautious advice. I have observed that his love of Art, and especially of music, is based upon no mere transient excitement, but upon great, indeed uncommon, powers. It was with my special concurrence, and indeed at my suggestion, that he went on with his law studies with undiminished zeal, as there is nothing so repugnant to me as a musician who is that alone, without any higher general culture. At the wish of his family he applied himself also to the study of Jurisprudence; full of devotion to his mother he tried hard to take an interest in this study, which in reality went dreadfully against the grain. And now what is the perfectly clear and evident result of all his pains and experience? Simply the outspoken and absolute conviction that the more he sets the one thing against the other the more he feels that it is Art alone—in other words, Music— that he can love unceasingly. This one thing, my dear lady, stands first and foremost as an undeniable fact, and I cannot doubt that, when once you yourself are convinced of this wish of your son to devote himself entirely to music, you will make it your own wish also. I should probably be doing you the greatest injustice did I in the least doubt this; but anxiety about your son's future might suggest *one* wish to you, namely to secure him from the possibility of repenting his decision, and from the consequences which might arise to his so-called position in life. You would wish your son at least to finish his studies for the law, so that, in the possible event of his not succeeding in his artistic career, the other might remain open to him. Whilst acknowledging therein the warmest motherly love and solicitude, I must nevertheless be permitted to reply that I consider the carrying out of such a wish would be ruinous ; ruinous for the further development of the character and powers of your son, ruinous for the continuation of a healthy, loving relation betwixt son and mother. After the unusually rapid development of the powers and the character of your son, you would be guilty of an open injustice if you did not recognise this, and mistrusted it owing to your own doubt ; but by holding fast to that second wish on your side this mistrust would be distinctly expressed. The germ of all radically ruinous evil is mistrust, and I feel sure that is your experience also : should you now—just at this time— show it to your son, by using your mother's influence to constrain him to return to a study which in his innermost soul he loathes, without the wish, without the bent, and therefore without the prospect of reaping any advantage from it, you destroy his zeal for work in general, shatter and weaken his power, and lay the foundations of a broken-down and only half-developed character, which will remain so for the rest of his days, and you will reap for certain that most unwished-for reward—the reward of an equally broken and shattered love. I cannot recall without great pain a number of years of my life in which I, for similar reasons, had entirely separated myself from my good (but on this point mistaken) mother ; and yet I cannot say otherwise than that I wish your son an energy similar to what mine was when I had strength to resist even the noblest tie of nature which would have hindered me in the exercise of my free choice !

If you will further permit me, on the ground of my own experience, to give advice which I trust you will not consider intrusive, but tendered from the purest human sympathy, it is this : give willingly and speedily your consent to this, so that your son may not go on living a moment longer in coercion against his well-founded and well-tested inclination ; grant him permission to spend the coming winter season with me here in Zurich, so that, with his friend Ritter, he may learn under my direction the practical work of a musical conductor ; wait with patience and see what further turn his life as a practical artist takes ; have full confidence in whatsoever depends on my small powers of help, but especially in what our friend Liszt may be able to do to help him on ; and in every case where trials await him, where trouble threatens him, where he needs help, do all that lies in your special power to sustain him with your self-sacrificing support ! You will thus have the satisfaction of calling a worthy, perhaps great, artist your son, of presenting to the world a contented and self-dependent man, and of having won and preserved the unspeakable happiness of his truest and deepest love as a son and a human being !

Pardon the candour and plain-speaking of my letter ! I address myself to no one to whom I may not venture to speak plainly and candidly, but I do so tq you in a special and sacred cause, in which I am convinced that the happiness of a human being—or rather, considering your deep love to him, of two human beings—is at stake, whom I would fain see happy.—With deep respect and devotion,

I am

Yours,

RICHARD WAGNER.

LISZT TO FRANZISKA VON BÜLOW.

WEYMAR, 28th September 1850.

MADAME LA BARONNE,

Several friends of your son's have spoken to me (unknown to him, as I believe), to beg me respectfully to submit a request to you. Little as I am calculated to serve as a negotiator with you for wishes and hopes—a noble and legitimate ambition,—yet I confess that the knowledge of the duty, as well as the sincere affection I bear to your son, will not permit me to put entirely aside the pressing requests which, I feel sure, are in accordance with your son's vocation. Whatever decision you may come to with regard to the future of his career, pray excuse, Madame, the liberty I am taking in meddling thus with questions of a nature at once so serious and so delicate, and do not impute to this letter any motive contrary to my habits and convictions.

Hans is evidently gifted with a musical organisation of the rarest kind. His executive talent will easily place him in the front rank of the greatest pianists, and his essays at composition denote quite exceptional qualities of imagination, of individuality, and of conception. Besides, Hans has taken an antipathy to every career which would sever him from Art. Permit me, then, to confide to your motherly love the happy solution of the noble struggle between his natural vocation and that destined for him, however bright and alluring it might be; and, in view of the sentiments which dictate this letter, pray pardon the intercession I have ventured to make to you today.

I have the honour to be, Madame la Baronne, with deep respect,

Your devoted Servant,

F. LISZT.

TO HIS SISTER.

ZURICH, 26th October 1850.

DEAR ISIDORE,

It really made me very unhappy to have to leave Ötlishausen so abruptly, without seeing you again, without saying good-bye to you. But I could not help it; I was forced to act as I did, and I do not repent it, and trust I never shall do so. I had almost let myself be over-persuaded by Papa, and had resolved to travel back to Berlin without even seeing Wagner, when Ritter brought me a letter from Wagner, which made me instantly resolve to go to Zurich, there to fill the post of musical conductor under W.'s direction. We did the trip on foot in two days: firstly in order to escape any possible pursuit on Papa's side, and also because I wanted to test whether I had the energy to do that piece on foot in the most awful weather, amid ceaseless rain and storm. Wonderful to relate, it did not hurt me. I arrived dead-beat, but the next morning I was pretty well refreshed and jolly, a sign that hard bodily fatigue does not do any harm. In fact, in spite of the unhealthy climate and the cold weather, I feel myself pretty well (low be it spoken), and I look well, and have nothing to complain of beyond some little pain in head and stomach, whereas I had more than twenty most beautiful opportunities of catching a downright good cold. That I have not done so is chiefly thanks to my habit of always pouring perfectly cold water over myself every morning, without regard to the temperature, and now I have got so accustomed to this that I do it almost with pleasure. I am now tremendously busy with rehearsals, early in the morning and in the afternoon regularly, from three to four hours each time. I have already conducted four times in public; twice it was the farce, 'Einmal hunderttausend Thaler,' and of operas, 'The Daughter of the Regiment' and 'Czaar und Zimmermann.' It is not such an easy task as it appears; it requires a thorough, extensive study, almost to the point of learning the operas by heart, and that is a great strain, and also takes a great deal out of one. The reason I have so much to do now is that Ritter (somewhat unpractically) is at present not conducting at all until I have had a thorough drilling in it, which will take till New Year. Ritter is now composing an Opera; in January and February I shall probably do the same.

The singers, who for a wonder are all extremely good, at first intrigued with the orchestra against me, because I am so young and inexperienced, and had not yet commanded sufficient respect. However Wagner, who is perfectly satisfied with me, held them in check, threatening that he should resign—i.e. that he should withdraw his interest, his

superintendence, and his conducting-in-chief—if they did not behave
properly to me. People here have a tremendous respect and esteem for
him, and a small portion of these will now be transmitted to his pupils.
I have already made some friends among the artists, and soon I hope to
have them all under my thumb.

The *Federal Times,* which is the first paper here, said of my conducting in ' The Daughter of the Regiment : ' " Herr von Bülow, a pupil of
Wagner's, has already shown himself in this performance to be a very
talented conductor ; and the one or two slips that occurred were merely
the result of the orchestra not showing enough confidence in the young
man." In order that you may not doubt the truth of this, I send you the
next critique in print.

With a monthly salary of fifty gulden, Ritter and I must both get
along till the New Year. The morning coffee is suspended, and we
enjoy a water-soup, which we make ourselves, and to which I have grown
quite accustomed. We dine with Wagner, where the cooking is capital.
His wife thoroughly understands it, and she is most kind and obliging ;
for instance, the other day she mended my (I was going to say *thy,* for I
have got so mixed over the *mine* and *thine,* owing to the Zurich Com-
munism) umbrella—which I should really have been ashamed to take out
with me—without saying a word. Forgive me for writing so hurriedly
and carelessly, but in a moment I must go to rehearsal. So only a word
more.

Write me word very soon how you are, how the journey went off,
how you like Dresden, also how Mamma seems disposed towards me. I
don't know whether she would allow me to write to her about myself
and my life. You say you truly love me, and Mamma has often said so
too ; well now, for love of me, do be very good and gentle in your behaviour towards Mamma ; try to make her forget me in you, that thus
she may not continue to feel so aggrieved and angry with me. Then
perhaps gradually, later on, you may become the mediator between us.
My address for the present is : Oethenbacher Gasse in der Akazie, 4th
floor. Love to Wach.*

TO HIS MOTHER.

ZURICH, 26*th October* 1850.

DEAR, HONOURED MOTHER,

I have long hesitated and delayed writing to you, for I
have an uneasy conscience with regard to you ; I have violated all the

* The dog.

duties of a child towards you, and am fully conscious of it, for it was no levity that carried me away, no upset that has taken place, or else repentance would have followed, and I should not have remained here, and our relation to one another would never have been broken or disturbed. I do not, however, repent the act which, from the standpoint of my sacred duties towards you, is to be condemned, and I only fear that your just anger has won the day over your motherly love : I fear, and tears come into my eyes at this most terrible of all fears, that you might want to know nothing more about your son, who separated himself of his own accord from his mother ; that you would not recognise him as such any more ; that you would perhaps destroy his letters unread. I have not made myself any pleasing illusions ; I made it clear to myself that this would all be quite natural, that I alone am guilty and have not deserved anything different. And yet I could not abandon myself to it, I could not believe it, and the dread of the unhappy, terrible certainty that it was so has kept me from writing. Although I still feel the same dread in all its intensity, it leaves me no peace, and impels me to try to ask you if it is really true that I have irrevocably broken the tie that bound us together, that I have for ever forfeited my mother's love by my act of rebellious disobedience. I cannot believe that it is really possible that your unconquerable antipathy to the man whom I so highly esteem, and who, by his warm and hearty sympathy, by his fatherly solicitude for me, has the greatest claims on my love and gratitude, can be so powerful as to tear your son from your heart. And even if it were possible that at this moment your dislike of the noblest, the most loveable and honourable man could be so deep-rooted as to have the upper hand—yet I hope that the future will make you feel kinder, more forgiving, more tolerant towards opposing views and ideas, and that you may even feel a little esteem and interest in the man to whom, in a sense, I gave over the decision as to my life's calling, even before I went to Switzerland to see my father. That it is only Music that I love, and for which I have a true inclination ; that it is only in this career that I can find happiness and inner peace, in spite of outward troubles and bothers; of this I have long been convinced ; and that I should be of use in the life of an artist, and should be able to make the most of my talents for my own and others' benefit, this has been perfectly clear to me for a long time past. The career of a lawyer, the service of the State, in which I foresaw that I should only vegetate, without aim or influence, without being of any use to my fellow-men, but rather the contrary—these long ago appeared absolutely impossible to me ; and it became only a question whether I could postpone the decision until I had finished my studies—that is to say, till I was a half-fledged lawyer, with my head crammed full of a lot of useless, prosaic stuff, which might have supplanted everything better and nobler in me by the weight of its bread-earning possibilities, and perhaps stifling more worthy germs, so that my life after a year and a half would have been spoilt, dead, and broken ! I kept thinking I should be able to hold out, but in Leipzig and Berlin I was often on the point of making a great resolution to come to a decision, which I have now done. Wagner's letters to me at Ötlishausen brought my resolve to a speedy crisis. To be with Wagner, to live near him, to study in a practical way under his direction, so as to become an artist—this is tautology, since my ambition is to be an artist, not a mere musician, for which latter there was ample opportunity in Berlin, Leipzig, etc. It is my determination, based upon the tendency of my powers and talents, to strive to follow Wagner without slavish, childish imitation. I say now—better even a medium musician than a good, so-called able lawyer. Wagner thinks I shall become a good musician and an artist of importance ; it is for me to justify his confidence in me in the course of time. This winter I hope to finish my bread-earning studies, and to become a good all-round conductor, for which Wagner says I possess the most decided talent, by the keenness of my ear, my quick perception, rapid survey, and finished playing. As a conductor I can then earn my bread anywhere, and should be in a position to compose, without any anxiety on that score. When you wrote to me that you consented to my devoting myself now to music, my father made out that you had granted the main thing, and that it was only a secondary matter that you were refusing, and that I was wrong to confound the one with the other. Papa acted wrongly towards you, and later on he must have regretted his over-haste, and must have felt that it was his duty not to thwart your plans and wishes, for he never left off working upon me, till he had almost over-persuaded me, and I had resigned myself. Then suddenly Wagner sent Ritter to me with a letter which he had written me : this one letter threw all my resignation to the winds ; it was this letter that made everything clear to me ; it was this letter that made me undertake the journey to Zurich on foot ; it was this letter, and still more my own personal talk with Wagner, that made me firmly resolve to spend this winter with him in Zurich, and no one in the world can talk me out of it. I felt I must act so as to leave no possible road of return open, no possible way of regret. Now the die is cast. I am going to be a musician ; I am doing that from which I cannot separate myself, and I hope thus to become a happy and contented man.

If you still condemn me, I hope that, by my own talent, and by my musical powers, which Liszt and Wagner affirm to be unusual, I shall bring you round to a different point of view. Let this be my care ; do not let every spark of love for me die in you ; at least allow me to write to you from here how I am living, what I am doing, and how I am.

Would it really be the same thing to you if I died?

Now farewell, and be happy. May Isidore bring you happiness, for I cannot in the way you wish. Perhaps you will write me a line sometime, when your indignation has abated. I shall go on writing to you until you forbid it.

TO HIS FATHER.

ZURICH, *9th November* 1850.

DEAREST FATHER,

You have no idea how terrifically I am working here. Rehearsal upon rehearsal, looking through and correcting the orchestral parts, in which the most flagrant disorder, the crassest carelessness, reigns, composing couplets and that sort of thing for farces, so that I have hardly a moment to myself, and have had to neglect my piano-playing more than I could wish.

At this very moment too I have not time to write a decent letter, so I must beg you for today to be satisfied with the mention of the most important facts.

Next Tuesday I play at the first subscription concert, and shall play two brilliant and startling pieces (which at a *début* here is a necessity *per se*) by Kullak and Liszt, upon 'Norma' and 'Lucia.' At the second or third concert I am sure to play again, and should then certainly choose a Beethoven Sonata and the 'Tannhäuser' Overture in the Liszt arrangement. So I must make use of every free moment for practising, so as to avoid the danger of a terrific fiasco. I hope and believe also that it will go well, and that I shall have a success.

With regard to conducting, I have directed three operas since you were here: 'Czaar und Zimmermann' was regularly murdered; I had only received the score overnight; it was a mere makeshift of a performance, and Wagner was ill, so could not appear instead of me. I had some scenes with the singers and orchestra, who, enticed by Director Kramer with the bait of the Wagner conducting, thought they could push matters so far as to insist on Wagner always conducting, and not allowing me to do so until I had gone through the necessary routine— (without the practice in conducting!). Wagner issued a kind of manifesto to the rebels, which brought them in some measure to reason.

The second opera was the 'Barber of Seville.' The singers and

orchestra took great pains; the public was more well-disposed than it
had ever been, and showed unusual interest and appreciation. I myself
had the score in my head, was thoroughly sure and master of it, and
everything went capitally. I had shown that my conducting could
make a success; the public had at last comprehended that not merely
the person of the conductor, but also the musical forces in general, ought
to awaken sympathy; so that by this performance, about which I have
received friendly congratulations from many sides, I feel that I am fixed
rather more firmly in my seat. Next Monday the 'Barber' will be
repeated.

The third opera I conducted came to grief through the apathy of
the public, and the consequent disinclination and reluctance of the singers;
that is to say, it did not actually fail, but on the stage they intended
to make it do so, in order perhaps to throw the blame on me afterwards.
It was Auber's 'Fra Diavolo;' pretty music, but cold, written by the
composer twenty years ago for *one* season, but raised by the Germans to
the rank of an immortal work, whereas even in France no one thinks
of it now. The dialogue is weak, and the opera is based upon a story
uninteresting when once one knows it, and can only maintain any zest
by the help of the actors, and by adding any humour that is possible to
it; and even this was wanting. Thus it came about that the public,
which happened not to be in such a good humour that night, remained
cold, whereas in the 'Barber' people had been carried away by the excessively comic situations and personages. Then began the old story
over again. The matter is even less ideal than we all thought at first,
and the fault lies both in the false perception of things on the side of
the public, who will hardly allow themselves to be attracted except by
Wagner's personal conducting, and also on the side of the singers.
However the chief thing is that I should learn conducting; and this I
shall do, and, I hope, much more besides, which at any rate is not improbable, as we have only one month behind us and six still to come.
Under these circumstances Ritter cannot yet take part in the conducting, but has to wait till I am thoroughly broken in and all prejudices
are overcome. By New Year, I hope, the work will be divided between
Ritter and me, and that I shall then have time for other things. Last
Monday I conducted a concert which an Italianised Swiss singer, Stigelli,
gave in the theatre, and at this I had also to play the piano accompaniments, so that I had to keep running backwards and forwards from the
stage to the orchestra. Next Friday 'Masaniello' is to be given, and
probably I shall conduct it, as well as the 'Water-Carrier' and Méhul's
'Joseph,' which are to follow next.

Yesterday was 'Don Juan,' under Wagner's conducting, with an overflowing house, and yet a most dull, stupid, and thankless public. Wagner had taken exceptional trouble, and we had all three been several days and nights correcting errors in the orchestral parts, replacing instruments which were wanting, such as trombones, by others; deep trumpets, etc. Wagner had had the Italian recitatives translated into good German dialogue, some even admitted in their original form; he had also simplified the scenery, and had cleverly reduced the ever-lasting scene-changing to a single one in the middle of the first act; and further he had arranged that the last aria of Donna Anna, which is usually sung in a room, should be given in the churchyard, to which she goes with Octavio, for whom a little recitative, composed by Wagner, precedes the aria as a sort of introduction to it. Thus a sensible con-sistency was given to the entire dramatic action, which, alas! is almost always wanting to a performance. It has driven me nearly wild when I remember how Wagner used to be accused in Dresden of conducting Mozart's operas badly on purpose, and how he could not bear this music in his own self-conceit. The warm and living artistic feeling of reverence for Mozart, shown by this disinterested act, will not be brought to light by any of these would-be adorers. It is clear that 'Don Juan,' as given everywhere up to now, does not give the pleasure or make the effect which it can and ought to do; and there is need of ample reform in this matter.

Not a line from Mamma yet. I did not know her new address, so have gone on sending to the old one.

At the end of this month we are leaving Oethenbacher Gasse, and removing to a better lodging with some very respectable people, silk manu-facturers. We shall have two nice rooms, separated by a passage; and for lodging, fire, attendance, breakfast, and dinner, we shall each pay four Zurich gulden a week. One could not well have anything cheaper.

Thank you for the news about yourself and your life. I am delighted that Willi * is well, and is gradually growing out of babyhood.

I will write to you after the concert. Next time I play in public you will come over, won't you?

TO HIS FATHER.

ZURICH, 2nd December 1850.

DEAREST FATHER,

Yesterday we removed, and then, to finish up, I hear from my landlord that the servant lost a letter which I had given about

---

* Hans' half-brother, by his father's second marriage.

three weeks ago to be posted to you, because I was so busy with rehearsals that I could not find time to post it myself. I need not say how vexed I have been about this, and all the more so because by this carelessness I have lost my passport, which, together with Wagner's article on 'Judaism in Art,' I had put into the letter, in order to beg you to send the passport to Leipzig to get it extended for me. In the same letter I also begged you for ten gulden, which however I do not now require, as Mayer-Wordmüller, the financial director of the concerts, has meanwhile sent forty francs (French) for my performance, which has succeeded well, as far as success here goes. He has also asked me to play again at the fourth concert, which will take place early in the new year.

I came home today after the rehearsal, and then something happened which peremptorily demands our (Wagner's and my) retirement from the theatre. Today I conduct for the last time in 'Masaniello.' Wagner will look after my immediate future. Possibly the termination of my engagement with the theatre may be a gain for me as regards my mother. Enough that it is simply impossible to continue the affair as hitherto. The people and the circumstances are so odious, and there is perpetual friction. At any rate the two months have not been wasted; but I have learnt some things which will be of great use to me. I cannot tell you all the details; I only know that the principal reason why we must give notice today—an eventuality that we have long been anticipating, and have well thought over—lies in a quarrel with the husband of the first singer, who has herself given notice, because she will not continue to sing under my conductorship. She is such a favourite that Kramer would be ruined if she went away, so I must make up my mind to be the sacrifice. No sort of adjustment is possible; and even if things could be made straight again—which would only be possible by the humiliation of Wagner and myself—they could not last; on the first opportunity there would be a fresh scandal, and things would come to the same end. Therefore better today, when we can retreat honourably, than tomorrow.

You will readily understand how excited I feel about the matter at this moment. I hope on that account you will excuse, first, this letter, and secondly, my long silence, which has been so long owing to the loss of my letter without any fault of mine.

The gods alone know what is to be done about the passport.

TO HIS FATHER.

ZURICH, *9th December* 1850.

DEAR FATHER,

Your letter has pained me dreadfully, and I can only console myself by thinking that you have misunderstood my last letter in several points, possibly owing to my haste and want of detail. Perhaps we shall see each other soon, and a personal talk may scatter the dark cloud which hangs over my love for you, owing to your threat of having nothing more to do with me if I remain in Zurich without having any active practical work to do with Wagner. I have become a man by my own energetic act. I have a conscience and a conviction, upon which I consistently act, and I think these ought to be respected by everyone. I am a musician, and intend to remain one. I am a follower—now a pupil—of Wagner's, and shall prove this by my actions. That is irrevocably decided. Why then your doubt, which almost becomes a serious prohibition? Why not say : "Go on as you have begun, my best wishes shall go with you ; you have not yet proved yourself unworthy of my confidence"? Why cannot we be on terms of affection, so that, when I recognise your handwriting on a letter, I may break the seal joyfully, and say, "It is from my good father!" Save yourself reproaches till I have done something really wrong, I do implore you. If you withdraw your love from me because I place Wagner, whom I love and honour more every hour, above everything, then with tears I must say to you, "Well, do it then, and give it all to your Willi, to whom I on my side will give all a brother's love in place of my filial love." But believe me that I am so steadfast that I am not afraid of anything, and take the consequences of my actions upon myself with my eyes open.

To return to my mother is impossible. I have wept bitter tears in thinking of her, but I see that her fanatical feeling is stronger than her mother's love, which makes my heart easier.

As regards my immediate future, chance has interposed so favourably that I might almost be superstitious. Yesterday I received an offer of an engagement as musical conductor of the theatre at St. Gall, from Herbort, the director, who had heard that I had broken with Zurich.

The conditions are acceptable, the principal one being that I should go there speedily. Wagner was at first against my taking it, but after thinking it over he advised me to accept it, which I have already done. I leave here on Tuesday evening; Ritter goes with me, and will begin by being chorus-master at the opera under me as conductor.

The position will be more agreeable than here, as I shall come out quite independently, without any teacher at my back ; and I shall have to deal with smaller powers, it is true, but also less arrogant. I shall also have no rivals, as I had here, wanting to step into the position of musical director. So for the present I am away from Wagner, and in your neighbourhood ; when the winter is over I shall probably return to Wagner, in order to write an opera under his guidance and help. I want immensely to write a Christus, but W. thinks I should do something more practical for the moment. It is just possible that through Wagner I might get something to do with Liszt in Weimar. Perhaps— but this is only an idea of my own—I shall make the suggestion to my mother that I might spend the summer in Paris, where, with a little help, I could soon earn my own living.

So perhaps we shall see each other soon.

Give my love to Louise, and thank her for the woollen socks. I don't require them, as even in this pretty cold weather I am not freezing in my cotton ones. Besides, I am systematically hardening myself.

Your loving,

HANS V. BÜLOW.

TO HIS FATHER.

ST. GALL, 17th December 1850.

DEAREST FATHER,

For today only a couple of lines, to go with the packet of books I am sending you. I have put in the *Kladderadatsch* almanack, which I bought at a moment when I felt obliged to lighten my purse, and which I now send for your amusement.

Many thanks for your letter, which has calmed me down, and given me great pleasure. Do not take my last one too much amiss ; I replied *stante pede* to yours, and was somewhat excited : it is not much to be wondered at if I sometimes see things as black as at other times they appear rosy to me.

I have as yet not found rooms. I am not a quiet man, as I make music—that was one stumbling-block ; the other was the high prices. After New Year it will not be so hard to find something. For the present we are staying at the Gasthaus zum Schwan ; it is very bad, and for this sort of commercial-traveller inn also very dear ; but the food is passable, and I was tempted by the fact that the innkeeper also lets out pianos, so that I was able to get one at once, on which I am practising industriously at Liszt's paraphrase of the 'Tannhäuser' Overture, which I am to play in Zurich after the New Year.

On Sunday I conducted my first opera, 'Der Waffenschmied von Worms,' by Lortzing. The house was well filled, and the public very responsive. I was much congratulated, not publicly, but by all those who knew the circumstances, on the way in which I discharged the duties of conductor to an orchestra out of practice, composed almost entirely of amateurs, and never up to its full numbers. After the first rehearsal I had almost come to the conclusion that there was nothing to be done with these people, for it did not even go infamously—it simply did not go at all ; so that I quite began to admire myself that after three rehearsals I had got them so well in hand that it went off without a disastrous fiasco. Wagner is right in saying that I have a great talent for conducting.

The orchestra was composed partly of merchants, lawyers, some officials, and a couple of musicians by profession. Herbort, the theatre manager, a thoroughly honest, friendly man, begged me most particularly to treat these gentlemen with tact. To the most rigid strictness, and energy often amounting to the greatest excitement, I yet united so much amiable courtesy, that the gentlemen—the best of the amateurs—assured me that I was already much liked by them, that it was a great pleasure to them to play under my bâton, and that they would, as far as their professions allowed, gladly attend all the rehearsals which I might think it necessary to call. I have the greatest hopes from this, and I know that I possess the capability of creating a very passable opera out of almost nothing.

With regard to the *personnel*, all the members are more obliging and more friendly towards me than in Zurich. The *spectacle* is as proportionately good as it was wretched there. The opera is certainly more insignificant, but something may be done with the singers here if one does not aspire to too difficult tasks. Perhaps also there will be a possibility of arranging some Symphony concerts, Trio soirées and the like, though not until New Year. Until then the theatre is closed ; but there is so much to be studied that I don't even know whether I shall be able to come to Ötlishausen for Christmas.

Bülow was not able to get to Ötlishausen for the Christmas Eve, but he paid a flying visit there before the end of December, on the last day of which he writes to his father :—

I am still firmly resolved to stick here till Easter; I shall have to try to compensate myself for the miseries of a conductorship here in some other way. What sort of animals I have to deal with in my orchestra it would pass the powers of natural history to imagine. If one could only get at them somehow, but they understand absolutely nothing; I would gladly learn how to grunt and to low in order to accomplish something, but it would not help matters. In the end there is nothing else for it but to laugh (that is, in derision).

Thirty-five years later—in 1886—on the occasion of a Pianoforte Recital, Bülow again saw the scene of his first musical winter campaign, and, after the end of the concert, when he was enjoying himself with the musical people of the place, he drew a lively sketch of the state of the orchestra as it was when he first had to do with it. As so many important instruments were taken, not by paid and engaged musicians, but by amateurs, who gladly gave their time from love of the art, and who on that account had to be carefully dealt with, the young conductor had to go through many an anxious moment when he mounted his desk. To quote Bülow's own account : " There were also two bassoonists in the orchestra—imagine, amateurs !—they were my dread, and kept me constantly on tenterhooks. If they had nothing to play, then I was in a state of terror that they might come in, and I was constantly warning them ('not yet !'); but if they really had to come in, then I had not the courage to give them the sign—and I warned them as before."

An amateur kettledrum-player, on the contrary, who received honourable mention, must have been a perfect marvel of a timekeeper, for when he had very long pauses he counted them inwardly, and used to pay little visits to an adjoining café without endangering the *ensemble*, as he always got back punctually to his post in time for his next entry.

Bülow also did not omit a visit to the same café, where he found the self-same landlady, who, it is true, could not any longer remember him. The old woman begged him not to let so long a time pass before his *next* visit to St. Gall, as he would not find her there if he did. And he promised to come again soon. " But the honoured Master came not again." So ends the account of Bülow's visit to St. Gall on the 25th and 26th February 1886.

TO HIS FATHER.

St. Gall, *5th January* 1851.

Your advice to me to freeze in the cold, I am following, with a peculiar expansion in the frosty feeling. Thus I never have any fire, as the iron stove makes it so unbearably hot for an hour that I am obliged to throw open the windows, and then that brings back the original temperature. Besides, it would be a luxury, as I only get up at seven, and from nine, and occasionally ten o'clock, I have rehearsals—

chorus rehearsals—which would drive one to distraction, if the ladies were not so amiable and the gentlemen so good-humoured. For we have no separate chorus singers, but all the *personnel* of the play and of the opera is obliged to take part in the choruses. In this noble occupation we go on until mid-day, when we dine; then we go to the 'Löwe,' drink our coffee, have a look at the *Augsburger* and the *Siècle*, regale ourselves with *Charivari*, which just now has some capital caricatures about German affairs, and meet our friends; or else I pay a call, etc. In the afternoon I am again schoolmaster, and have my ears martyred from half-past two to half-past four. In the evening there is either orchestral rehearsal or theatre, and the day is ended before one is aware of it. If it is then very cold, I get into bed and study scores, which have the advantage over books that one does not go to sleep over them. I have now thoroughly studied the 'Freischütz,' *i.e.* the score, so that I am learning it by heart. I think it is only when one has gone so far as to know every note, every *nuance*, the exact place and significance of every instrument (that is, in a good opera), that one is fit to get it by heart and to conduct it, which one can only do when one does not have to look at the score any more. It is really a good thing that you cannot come now, as you ought to come in six days' time.

For next Friday, with the help of God Almighty, the 'Freischütz' will be given. I hope it will go pretty well; I shall certainly have three orchestral rehearsals. At length we have got a leader, a young and very good violinist and musician (though a somewhat coarse and arrogant man) from Erlangen. His assistance will make the thing go with more spirit.

With regard to my critique, old Greith is delighted with it, and sent it at once to his son in Winterthur. Although he did not agree with the chief points, yet he was much pleased with a good deal that spoke to him from my soul; moreover he is free from prejudice; his eyes sparkled when the name of Proudhon was mentioned. What you say about extravagantly long phrases is true, and I must get out of the habit of them; yet I think they were not awkward and incomprehensible; it is difficult to write in short, concise phrases when one has to be circumspect, and to weigh one's words.

I am going to live on at the 'Gasthaus zum Schwanen.' The landlord, a Saxon from the neighbourhood of 'Dräsen,'* is an honest, reasonable fellow. At New Year we paid a bill which, apart from lodging, which moreover is no cheaper in private houses here, we found very reasonable in every point, without any 'sticking it on.'

---

* Colloquial or local for 'Dresden.'

E

P.S.—The reason I have written so large on the first page and so small on the second is owing to the cold.

Franz Liszt writes as follows to Eduard von Bülow, in reply to the request from the latter for Liszt's advice as to the most important steps for his son's future :—

LISZT TO EDUARD VON BÜLOW.

EILSEN, *4th January* 1851.

MONSIEUR LE BARON,

I am too deeply sensible of the honourable confidence you place in me not to endeavour seriously to justify it to the utmost of my ability, both now and at any future time.

In the career which your son has embraced, a career for which he is evidently remarkably gifted, there are four points to be considered. (Pardon me for putting it in this apparently pedantic manner, but it is much the most clear and convenient) :—

1. The years of apprenticeship and preparation ; the opportunities to be sought or avoided; the places to be accepted or refused, etc.

2. What direction should he follow, and what sort of work should he undertake ?   Ought your son at once to set about writing a grand opera, or would it be more profitable to him to work, either preliminarily or simultaneously, at some less ambitious compositions—symphonies, quartets, solos, morceaux d'ensemble, etc. ?

3. Up to what point might he leave in the background his great talent as a pianist ?   Would it not be better for him to cultivate that (after the example of Mozart, Beethoven, Weber, Meyerbeer, and Mendelssohn in their youth), and to attain a high position as a virtuoso, which—with his execution and the *verve* he possesses—he could easily do ?

4. What pecuniary results does he expect from the exercise of his musical faculties ?   Would he do without money gains, and work solely for the love of art ?   What sum will he have at his disposal per annum, and for how many years, before he is in a position to earn an honourable existence by his art ?

With regard to the first point, allow me, Monsieur le Baron, to observe that the harvest your son will reap from a conductor's position similar to that which he now occupies might be rather problematic *in the long run ;* and that, unless he found a solid and somewhat lucrative position, whether materially or morally, there would be every reason to advise him to give up at once this business of little-enviable luxury. Perhaps also a visit to Paris and London might be desirable. Paris in particular is especially adapted for developing, in an individuality of so good a stamp as his, what I may call a *European sense* in matters of Art ; and Wagner himself, thoroughly Teuton as he made himself out to be (doubtless with good reason), will agree, if he speaks in good faith, that his stay in Paris has been eminently useful to him.

Hans must only be careful to choose a favourable time for going there—the time of the concerts and dramatic performances—that is, the six months of winter and spring ; and before he goes he must give you his word of honour that he will refrain from taking any part in politics during that time.

It is very difficult to give reliable advice as to the particular direction a young artist ought to give to his fancy, and as to the mould into which it is best for him to adapt his ideas. I could not venture any decision in this respect, for it would go too near to overweening conceit and pedantry ; but, all the same, if Hans has enough confidence in my experience and in my friendship for him, I will gladly talk it over fully with him the next time he comes to see me at Weimar, which I hope he will do in the course of the next few months. I may say, in passing, that I entirely agree with your opinion in regard to his project of an opera of Jesus Christ ! What theatre would produce it ? What actors would play it ? And what public would accept it ?

The career of a German composer is full of hindrances and difficulties ; Wagner, and some others of far less talent, furnish a proof of this every day. The very real interest I take in your son makes me hope that circumstances will allow of my being serviceable to him. Unfortunately at the moment I am unable to offer him any post near me, as you do me the honour to wish ; and besides, I should have to be clearer about his ideas, projects, and the limits of his ambition, to come to any decision of that kind ; but as soon as ever an occasion arises, be assured that I shall neglect nothing which can prove to you the sincerity of my attachment to your son. Pray accept this assurance, Monsieur le Baron, together with that of the esteem and consideration of

Yours most sincerely,

F. Liszt.

I shall be back at Weymar about the 20th January.

After this statement Eduard appears to have been considerably easier in his mind, and to have seen things in a brighter light. On the 19th January he writes as follows :—

EDUARD TO ERNST VON BÜLOW.

Hans is now, as you know, at St. Gall. There he has formed an opera out of almost nothing. I was with him a week ago, when he conducted the 'Freischütz,' which he had studied by himself. The house was full to overflowing, the applause tremendous, and the performance excellent. Hans conducted in every respect like a *Master, and without looking at the score.* The orchestra, some sixty in number, followed implicitly and with pleasure their twenty-years-old conductor. The most notable men of the place—wealthy merchants, professors, doctors—play in the orchestra, partly for Hans' sake, and in order that the affair may succeed. Hans is working almost day and night. . . . I heard things privately about him from many sides; the whole town is well disposed towards him and respects him, both on account of his modesty, lively disposition, talent, and quiet behaviour. He is invited to the first houses, and my banker had already invited him three times before he knew that it was my son. In a concert for the poor that Hans gave, both his playing and his compositions met with enormous success.

. . . . Let me disabuse your mind of one other error: you, as a good Prussian, will naturally have been anxious, like myself, lest Hans should be through and through republicanised by Wagner, and brought up an arch-traitor. Therefore I give you my word of honour that Hans was only bitten by the political mania whilst he was wavering between two professions, as he was in Berlin. Once fixed in his true calling, as he is now, and he thinks and dreams of nothing else but music. . . . .

Hans has chosen his career, *not* lightly, but after severe struggles with himself, and therefore has not acted wrong towards anybody. I, as his father, with whom he also broke off, say this. Hans will do all in his power to obtain a reconciliation with his mother, and I assure you of his deep grief over his present misunderstanding with her.

TO HIS SISTER.

St. Gall, 26*th January* 1851.

My Dear Good Sister,

You may be sure your loving wishes for my unhappy birthday were not necessary to make me think of you. I am not estranged from you, and shall as little alienate myself from you as from my mother, in spite of her having discarded me and ceased to be a mother to me. I shall hail with joy, with a thousand joys, the day when I can be allowed to give both a sign of my love and my gratitude, but the impossible must not be expected of me. I shall not have a long life, and therefore I wish so to live that life shall appear worth living. I will not be bound down to circumstances which seem to me more hostile and detestable than the most bitter death, which I should greet as a friend in comparison. A drawing-room musician I cannot and may not be without doing violence to myself; the vocation to which Heaven, and my own desire, lead me is that of a dramatic composer; and, as one must also have the means of earning one's livelihood, I think it is wisest to educate myself for a theatre conductor, because, with my capability for it, I shall be able to get a sure and solid position as such. That is why I could never dream of repenting the step I have taken.

Now look here! Today I will indulge my inclinations by telling you everything, by pouring out my heart to you, and I think you need not think less of yourself because I do so.

You, too, know the respect and love which I have long felt for Wagner. I do not know if you can understand it, but it is through this respect, which necessitates also an understanding of his works, that I really came to my right self. I have become more and more conscious that this esteem, this understanding, is the best germ in me, the one by means of which, if properly fostered by me, I shall become a man who fills a distinct place in the world, and in humanity. For among thousands who exercise the same activity—to my thinking, not merely useless but even injurious—running about as a lawyer or a drawing-room musician, *I* could never be inspired by such an idea, which would give me no pleasure—no interest in my profession. For this I was and am too aristocratic—too exclusive. According to my ideas, every man ought to deserve his existence, and to show his fellow-men that he has a right to exist, and that he does not risk stealing away from more worthy ones the enjoyment of the earth.

Now you cannot blame me if, with all respect for the domestic virtues of W., E., and P., for example, I consider it highly unnecessary and quite a luxury for them to exist. The fact that I have recognised, as perhaps few others have yet done, the greatest artist who has appeared in our age, and who will perhaps have a still higher historical importance, has awaked in me ambition, self-confidence, and the spring of life. It became clear to me that I was able to *share the spirit* of this man, that I was able to become his pupil, his apostle; and with such an endeavour, such an aim as this before me, life appeared to me worthy of living. For him I felt an enthusiasm such as I had never felt before; and the

musical talent, the fineness as well as weakness of which (for I am under
no illusions) I perhaps owe to my mother, had fitted me to love and
to honour him. I had always wanted to be a musician, but a
morbid want of self-confidence had kept me from seriously opposing the
doubts and contrary wishes of my mother. I thought my life was
spoilt; I was full of deep dissatisfaction with myself and vegetated *au
jour le jour.* Then began those unlucky politics; as a man of feeling
and intelligence I could not get away from my inward revolt, and that
day on which I did not go with them to Dresden still seems to me
the most ignominious of my life. I often think how much better it
would have been if I had followed the insignificant, but at that time
noble and effective, calling of loading the cannon !

The career on which I have fixed by the judgment of Wagner,
whom I had indeed long regarded as a competent judge in the matter,
this career I earnestly wished to carry out under the guidance of his
hand, until I had attained my mental majority. I could not follow
after him at a distance; I have so much to learn from him; he stands
so high, I comparatively so low—it seemed to me absolutely indispensable for the attainment of my life's aim. He has been so fine, so
noble, so fatherly towards me that I owe him eternal gratitude for it all.
All the more am I grieved at the behaviour of my mother towards him,
especially as I was intending to sacrifice myself to her wishes—for I
cannot bear this disunion any longer (believe me, it has cost me many
tearful hours)—by leaving Wagner at Easter, and either going to
Weimar to study with Liszt, or else to Paris, though I recollect that
Liszt most particularly recommended the winter season for Paris.

My father has to some extent supported me in this project—I
fancy from various motives. In any case the separation from Wagner
can never be more than a temporary one. I cannot do otherwise.

If mother will allow me to write to her, I shall do so.

Papa came here lately for the 'Freischütz,' and was excessively
pleased. I was not with him for Christmas Eve. I had one sole
pleasure on that evening; the previous Sunday I had played in the
theatre; a charity concert had been arranged under my management; I
had had works studied, such as the sextet from 'Don Juan,' also a
portion of Wagner's 'Rienzi,' which they had at first said were impossibilities. It was a very good concert. My piano-playing had an
immense success, and I was called forwards over and over again. The
following Wednesday I received a laurel wreath tied with satin ribbons,
on which were embroidered my name and a verse from Schiller. I can't
yet learn from whom it came. . . .

But now I must close. Do all you can to make things right again between mother and me. Today I have not asked you a word about yourself and your doings.

On the 19th February he writes to his father :—

Herbort is always courteous to me, although to others he is sometimes a Brutus in the accusative ; certainly that redounds to his credit, or rather the *contrary* to his prejudice. His interest requires him to keep me for his establishment, as I am of use to him, and to a certain extent help to bring credit on it. Last month I was very unwell, with a very bad cough and pain in my chest, and complete hoarseness. Dr. Diethelm met me again for the first time at the ' Löwe ' after a long interval. I often see Fräulein Dardenne, and when my cold was at its worst she knitted me a first-rate shawl, which has been tremendously useful to me ever since. Next Tuesday week I play the ' Tannhäuser ' Overture at the subscription concert in Zurich ; Wagner conducts the ' Sinfonia Eroica.' . . .

TO HIS FATHER.

ST. GALL, *2nd April* 1851.

DEAR FATHER,

For the last ten days I have had to work like a dozen niggers. *Ten hours'* rehearsal daily ; I am perfectly ruined, and going to the dogs. The first thing I shall do when I have a free afternoon will be to take an emetic to get rid of all the gall and vexation which have accumulated within me. I used to behave in a courteous manner, and have now to become classically rude—a new lesson in the school of life ! For my benefit Herbort has, after many inquiries, given me the second performance of ' Czaar und Zimmermann.' That will bring in poor receipts—a couple of wretched gulden perhaps ! Nevertheless, if I have to fag so, I will at least have something for it. My benefit will take place *next Tuesday, i.e.,* the *8th April.*

After we have been having holiday for ever so long it suddenly occurs to the Director to give operas offhand, and to have such a heap of rehearsals that today everyone is pretty hoarse for the performance. Friday we are to have opera again, ditto Sunday, Tuesday, Wednesday, and Friday in next week. You can just imagine how things are going when everything is pressed on so, almost without the proper means, and now, in addition to that, operas which it is a perfect folly to give here such as Flotow's ' Martha.'

Next Tuesday, then, I shall expect you for certain ; am delighted to think of seeing you.

My March salary of 40 gulden Herbort still owes me. Tomorrow I shall send my landlord for it. The fellow will have to pay in any case, for he stays the summer here and keeps a hotel, and no one who is known to be insolvent dare do that.

Tomorrow evening Wagner is coming to see us for a couple of days. I shall hardly have time to see him. On Saturday Ritter leaves, and goes to Freiburg (University), where Feuerbach this summer is to read about Classical Art ; Ritter intends also to compose his 'Frithjof,' the poem of which is ready.

As the last drop in the cup, this morning comes an artist with an introduction to me, a clever violinist and very agreeable man, Gulomy (a Russian), a friend of Lipinski. The Munich pianist Speidel,* an old acquaintance of Stuttgart days (perhaps you may remember him), introduced him to me. How ever does he know that I am living here ? Now I shall have to give myself up to the man, which however I would do with pleasure if there were plenty of time.

My head is all in a buzz. Today is ' Czaar und Zimmermann.' It *must* go well. If Gulomy gives a concert on Monday, then you'll come that day, as I should probably play ; but I will write about it before then. Isa's letter herewith. The letter from the Berlin friend has pleased me greatly. Tell me, how did you get it ? Where had he found out that I am vegetating here ?

Farewell ! my head is buzzing, my head is buzzing—bz, bz, bz, bz !

The above-mentioned concert took place, and he writes to his father on the 16th April :—

What pleases me is that I am universally respected by the public, with whom, however, I have otherwise nothing to do ; they have never blamed me for any ill-luck in performances.

Just lately (on Monday) I played Beethoven's great A minor Sonata with Gulomy the violinist, a very clever artist, and made a *furore* with it. On Palm Sunday he gives a second concert, in which I shall also take part. On that Monday I could scarcely find time to dress myself and get to the place, and directly I had finished I had to rush from the piano to the orchestral rehearsal.

---

* Wilhelm Speidel (1826), a pianoforte teacher, virtuoso, and composer ; a friend of Liszt, Thalberg, and Schumann.

TO HIS MOTHER.

ÖTLISHAUSEN, 30*th April* 1851.

DEAREST MOTHER,

The deep need my heart feels that the sad and unnatural relation should be removed which, through my wrong, has been subsisting for half a year between mother and son, led me to ask my sister whether, after your indignation at the bitter mortification I had caused you, you would allow me to write to you again. Isidore's answer was favourable : she said I *might*, and I *was to* write to you again. The hard work which took up all my time in St. Gall, to enable me to earn my livelihood, and the bodily and mental fatigue induced by it, and, let me also confess, an unchildlike defiance, now vanished, which refused to acknowledge any wrong towards you, and which was strengthened by the certainty that I could make my way as a musician in Switzerland (even if with difficulty), without thinking that it was you I had to thank for my talent, my education in music ;—all this kept me from fulfilling my sister's wish sooner, as I had really in my innermost self wished to do.

But none the less strong was the longing which I felt, after the relaxing of the unhappy state of tension between us, which, besides the misery it brought me, seems also like a bad augury for my future in the career which I chose with such an inconsiderate disregard of all duties towards you, and in which I closed every road of return. Of melancholy hours, in which I was conscious of my loneliness and my almost orphaned condition, there were many : my birthday, Christmas,—seasons which we had always spent together for twenty years, and which I this time spent as far apart from you in spirit as we were separated in distance—these anniversaries made me doubly feel the need of a reconciliation. What kept me from taking any steps on my side was the uncertainty whether your anger against your disobedient son, whom you had driven out of your heart, would allow you to read my letter. Later on, it was the reasons I have already given you which prevented me from seeking this reconciliation. I am doing this now from Ötlishausen, where I have come to recruit after having finished my duties as conductor at the St. Gall theatre, to restore my health, to practise—which I have had rather to neglect during the winter—and to devote myself to some big compositions. You know my old dislike of great show and demonstration—therefore let me just say in simple words, *I am deeply sorry to have grieved you in the way I have done.* I cannot yet tell, as the future alone can answer this, whether I have done wrong towards myself by the way

I have acted, but I readily acknowledge to you that I have acted wrongly towards you, ungratefully, and contrary to my duty. The grief I have caused you I heartily repent, and implore you to forgive me.

With this hope within me, I think it is now my duty to give you at least an idea of what my life has been, and to tell you of my practical education in the career of a musical conductor. Whatever may be the final judgment as to the step which I took in flying to Zurich, thus much I can truly affirm, that the half-year from October 1850 to April 1851 was not only not useless in the way it was spent, but that it has been a gain for me in every respect, in knowledge and experience. On the whole, the thought of being now devoted to *one* object, the reconciling of freedom and necessity in the choice of a career, the ending of the vacillation between the profession to which I was pledged and that which I desired, has matured me ; and one result of this is that I have stripped off all dilettanteism, the consciousness of which often formerly embittered the pleasure of my talent—a talent which I know I possess. This is also evident in my piano-playing, although this has been pushed rather more into the background ; I have gained in certainty and in precision of *tempo*, and have lost, or at any rate begun to lose, that restless, inartistic haste, for which I have so often been found fault with. The frequent piano rehearsals for solos and chorus (for they had no special chorus director at St. Gall) have been of great use to me in this — in knowledge of the parts, vocal parts especially : I have learnt to express myself, to make myself intelligible, if my musical feeling told me that such and such a thing was wanting in taste, and how it should be rendered. I have become very keen and sure in regard to sounds, for, as I had to teach difficult choruses to people, some of whom, though otherwise educated, could hardly read their notes, I was also obliged to sing with them and to them, which cultivated my ear still more, and which also enabled me to sing correctly at sight, even the middle parts, a thing one can't do without practice. The conducting of the orchestra has been of still greater use to me, especially in such a poor-conditioned one as that at St. Gall, which consists mainly of amateurs ; the routine in the mechanism of time-beating, circumspection in reading the score—to say nothing of playing it and understanding it at sight—the art of getting the orchestra in time again when it has got out, the knowledge of the instruments and the instrumentation, quality of sound, etc. I am now in a position to teach quite a strange orchestra my own compositions, for instance ; even very important composers (Meyerbeer, Schumann, and others) cannot do this unless they have learnt the mechanical part early. Of operas I have studied, since I have been in St. Gall, ' Freischütz,' ' Martha,' ' Stradella,' ' Nachtlager,' ' Czaar,' ' Waffenschmied,' and the ' Daughter of the Regiment ' (to say nothing of operettas), and have frequently made possible the impossible, a fact which has met with acknowledgment.

There I was far away from Wagner, whom you look upon as my ruin. Our correspondence was unimportant, and when he came on a visit to St. Gall I was so busy that I hardly had a couple of hours with him. I had at that time to work on an average ten hours a day. Since the beginning of December, when I left Zurich, I have only been once at Wagner's, and that was on the 24th and 25th February, for a subscription concert, at which I played the Liszt paraphrase of the ' Tannhäuser ' Overture successfully.

Think what you will of Wagner, but at any rate do not disregard the distinction between the artist and the man. No one can now say a word against his merits as an artist ; otherwise would Liszt, one of the most gifted and remarkable of artists, have relinquished, in his riper years, everything which tended to his own ambition and the success of which was certain, because he thought it more noble to make propaganda for Wagner and his works, and entirely to subordinate himself to this aim ? If I am mistaken in W., a later insight will reveal it to me. But musically I am greatly indebted to him, from Zurich onwards. You cannot deny that, as I *have* become a musician, this practical work has given me experience and knowledge, has taken me considerably onwards in my career, and has at any rate the material advantage of providing me with a livelihood, as the profession of a conductor will ensure me this for the future—good conductors not being innumerable, and I having a special aptitude for it. Circumstances could not have been more favourable for learning this— that is to say, more *adapted* than in Zurich and St. Gall ; for one learns more from a bad orchestra than from a good one.

As regards my plans for the future—first of all, I shall stay here some three weeks longer, and then go to Weimar, where Liszt, as he lately wrote to Wagner, will take me as his pupil, and where I shall try to perfect myself in composition and piano playing. No doubt Liszt's influence will be able to recommend me later to some town or other.

I should so like to hear from you again—how you are living, whether you are well, and how you feel towards me. Please let Isidore write to me about this. Once more—I beg pardon from my whole heart for the wrong I did towards you.

Your loving, grateful son.

TO HIS MOTHER.

ÖTLISHAUSEN, 14*th May* 1851.

DEAREST MOTHER,

It has given me the greatest joy that you have answered my letter yourself, and have thus shown me that you did not give me up on account of my disobedience, and that you have not taken your love from me ; and I thank you from my heart for this. You give me this assurance at the end of your letter, because you foresee that I should miss the old warmth of your letters. It is true I do miss it sorely, but I also understand that you can only be reconciled to me by degrees, for somewhat of " forgetting " must also go with "forgiving." If I only have the hope that the old relation between mother and son may be restored in the course of time, and that you won't shut your heart against me on purpose—that you won't thrust away the feeling of reconciliation ! How much the wrong I did you by my mode of action, which so deeply shattered our feelings for one another, and in a way I had never imagined— how this has troubled me I told you in my first letter : here I can only repeat it, and you need not doubt the sincerity with which I beg your pardon. Be assured of this, that, wherever it is possible, I shall be guided by your wishes in the carrying on of my career. I shall in any case not stay beyond the end of this month in Ötlishausen, and I should like then to know whether you approve of my going to Weimar, and asking Liszt if he can help me by his recommendations to a post as conductor, or anything else. I should be glad to hear from you soon about this, and beg that you will write to me, as I am almost afraid you won't like the idea of a conductorship, which would certainly be the surest way of earning a livelihood.

This brings me to the mention of Ernst's letter. " You placed before me," wrote Ernst to me, " as a special condition of your reconciliation, the following of a solid musical career." I only beg you to tell me more exactly what sort of a career you have in your mind, and what you consider most advantageous for my further education. For I cannot believe that I have grown to be such a stranger and so indifferent to you that you just coldly wish me success, and that my decision to become a musician, with which you appeared satisfied half a year ago, as you assured me you would not constrain me in my choice of a profession —I cannot think that this decision can be so utterly contrary to you at heart that you would reject every explanation as quite indifferent to you. For was it not you who so often rejoiced over my talent, and urged it on, and even brought it forward as the *noblest* in me, when you were vexed with my conduct or opinions in other things?

Therefore do be kind enough to fulfil my request. It is of such great consequence to me to know your decision, because I must be ready to order all my future life accordingly. That is why I send these lines so quickly after receiving your letter. You yourself expressed the wish to hear from me soon.

About my health I beg you to trouble yourself as little as possible. I have never been a robust man, nor accustomed to live without physical ailments. In the summer I shall have to go to one of the baths somewhere.

I must certainly take up my piano-practice again seriously, for, even if my fingers have not got stiff, I have no *répertoire*, and that is most necessary, whether for public playing or for teaching. I hope really before long to learn a dozen Beethoven Sonatas by heart. And I am not *au fait* in new things, modern music, as there was no music-shop in St. Gall, and I was not able to get new music from Winterthur, where there is a great deal of musical life and classical taste; all this I will now retrieve. As regards composition I shall also have to yield to circumstances, and probably first to write pieces that will sell. Existence and consistency to one's convictions occasionally contradict one another. But I shall not lose courage; God forbid!

Farewell, dearest mother : try to love me again.

EDUARD TO ERNST VON BÜLOW.

[*May* 1851.]

Hans has been with us for the last four weeks, well and bright, for a rest after his veritable musical campaign in St. Gall. His labours there have ended with honour. He has gone through a schooling such as no other young musician of his age would easily do, and is now in a position to conduct any orchestra. He is just now composing a string Quartet, and intends after that to compose a Symphony to Aeschylus' ' Oresteia,' which he is studying in the original for that purpose. In a fortnight he goes to Munich, and thence to Liszt at Weimar, with whom he is to live.

Thus young Bülow started for his new destination, Weimar, which, in the person of the honoured Master to whose guidance he now gave himself up, contained all his hopes for the future. In spite of his apparent cheerfulness and freedom from care, which he knew how to assume, a great earnestness lay in the depths of his soul.

He writes to his sister before his departure from Ötlishausen :—

How my future will shape itself is all in the dark. After all, the words of your book-marker remain to me : "Aide-toi, le ciel t'aidera." And not heaven alone, but all its storms and tempests too. Happy the time when one still wishes them near, until—and that is also a blessing —one is struck down by the lightning in the strength of one's youth. A certain humour will remain to me, and it is *not* mingled with bitterness, thank God !

WEIMAR

CHAPTER VI.

WEIMAR.

TO HIS FATHER.

WEIMAR, 17th June 1851.

DEAREST FATHER,

I have now been about a week in Weimar, but have not written to you, because I had not yet got things into order. Houses for people like me, *i.e.* furnished rooms, were not to be had, so I was obliged to stay at the hotel, until at last, through Raff's persuasion, I took up my quarters in Liszt's house on the Altenburg. There, in the second storey of the adjoining building, I have four beautiful rooms at my disposal, but content myself with two—properly speaking, with one—in which, close to my bed, stands a very fair piano. Liszt himself is away, gone to Eilsen in Bückeburg, where Princess Wittgenstein is lying very ill. When I arrived here Liszt was expected back at the beginning of July; but the latest tidings are different, and Liszt has had all his clothes sent on to Eilsen, a proof that we must not expect him back yet awhile. He has been informed of my arrival, and of my taking up my quarters in his house, and has written fully about me to Raff, who at present fills his place towards me. Liszt's plan is that I should first of all prepare myself for the career of a virtuoso; and, as it is very desirable that I should speedily be able to earn for myself, I shall probably, after a couple of months' requisite practice here, go to some of the neighbouring towns and smaller Courts in order to make my public appearance as a pianist, and indeed as a pupil of Liszt. So, *for the present*, I agree to do this, and renounce any will of my own, in order to give myself up to "the school of the école de Weimar," as Liszt writes to Raff. I have already begun, and practise eight to ten hours a day. Thus I have in these few

F

days drummed into myself a tremendously difficult Trio of Raff's, one with which even Liszt had to take no end of trouble, and tomorrow evening I shall play it before a small audience on Liszt's good piano with Joachim and Cossmann—I have never yet had two such capital players to play with. Amongst the audience will be the democrats, Professor Stahr and Fanny Lewald, who have both taken up their abode here for a long time, and who, in spite of their different opinions, visit a good deal at the Court. I am extremely delighted that people are so democratic here, as one will not be obliged to parade one's opinions, because they are quite without danger, and therefore without merit, and people don't get in a rage and excite themselves for nothing.

With regard to composition, I am especially to learn to write some pieces for my own instrument and for my own capabilities, i.e. full of individual difficulties, designed for me specially. I have not yet been able to write a piano piece really suitable for the piano; and Raff says that is just the reason I must learn to do it here. Well, as I said, I have given up my self-government for the present, and am letting myself be be-Weimared : but naturally I shall keep enough of my " ego " left to be able to judge of the experiments which are being tried on me. I also want very much to be able to speak with Liszt personally, but just at present that is impossible ; for Liszt, away with his sick Princess and his head full of other things, is not in a mood to trouble himself with outside affairs, and one would gain nothing by writing. But to continue about what I began to say. The string Quartet I began at Ötlishausen I am now finishing, and it will then be played. And then, after I have thoroughly studied the pieces I now have in hand, I shall begin Liszt's first pianoforte Concerto (still in manuscript), and when there is an opportunity of an orchestral rehearsal I shall try it with them : Liszt has not yet played it here himself.

Now you see, dear father, what I am doing and working at at the present moment. I get up about six o'clock, and sit down to the piano in a very négligé apparel (the popular costume of the future), and set to work at my hammering with a calm and peaceful soul. Liszt's cook makes my breakfast in due form—I think it won't be too dear ; Liszt's valet cleans my boots and my clothes. Till one o'clock I stay at home ; Raff comes to me every morning for half an hour to see how I am getting on ; as yet he has only spoken favourably of my compositions. At half-past one I dine at the 'Erbprinz' ; this one must do, so as to be seen in good society in Weimar, and to get to know other musicians, singers, etc. After dinner I kill time by taking a walk for a couple of hours. Towards four o'clock I generally go back to my hole again, and work till near nine, when I go to supper in the town. By half-past ten I am usually back at home again, and extemporise on the piano by moonlight or otherwise—it makes no difference. As there is no second house-key, I have to climb up into the courtyard over a tumbledown wall, and to get into the house through a window which I can open from outside.

I shall probably continue living in the way I am doing now. I shall not go to see Frau von X., because there is no good in doing so; and if one wants to kill time, if the *utile* is wanting, there must at least be the *dulce*. I have got to know Stahr and the Lewald. The former asked after you, and spoke of your earlier novel, and of the classic novel of the fat sculptor. Did not you once tell me that Stahr wrote a good critique on your writings? He has been writing lately about Wagner's 'Lohengrin,' and since then he has also corresponded with him. I like to listen to him, for he talks very sensibly, and no 'young-German,' but like a man. But whether he is a great light I can't yet say. Joachim, who often looked at me rather askance in Leipzig, is very pleasant to me here—in short, it does me no end of good to be amongst my own sort again, who value me as far as I deserve it. I cannot tell you how that everlasting *knowing that one was undervalued* has embittered me and then made me flag.

I have not yet been to the theatre; on the 28th is 'Tannhäuser' (a free performance), and very soon, *i.e.* before that, 'Don Juan.' Herr Moritz is here with his wife, *née* Röckel; she is starring it here, and as she is liked she will probably get a permanent engagement.

Raff hopes to obtain the post of Secretary to the Goethe Institution, or to the Musical Department of the Library, and to draw a small salary.

Now I must go back a long way, and tell you about my journey.

So first Munich: I stayed there six days and looked about me, and, with the exception of some tedious hours, I enjoyed myself.

After describing the sights of Munich, he continues:—

He [Dingelstedt] wants to bring out 'Tannhäuser' next winter, but Kapellmeister Lachner * will oppose this, who cares for none but the classics (with the exception of himself). Altogether they are twenty to thirty years behindhand in musical matters here; whereas, in the north, people are already beginning to sift the works of Mendelssohn and Schumann, and to give them their acknowledged place. They have not got so far in Munich as even to know them in a superficial manner. Plenty of old fogeyism, but on the whole very little musical feeling; the

---

* Franz Lachner (1803-90). From 1836 Hofkapellmeister [Court conductor], and from 1852-68 General Director of Music in Munich, composer, master of counterpoint.

music-shops are in a fearful condition. Speidel, himself a bit of a fogey, is, properly speaking, the only pianist : he gives four to five hours' lessons a day, has earned a little capital, and in the winter goes to Paris, there to profit his soul a little. *Then I could really very well take up the orphaned pianos and amateurs there, and find something else to do when Speidel comes back again.* I am curious to know what Liszt will say to such a thing ! I am quite in favour of it, and think it would be practicable, and I should not set myself up in opposition to Speidel. This is the result of my visit to Munich. In my hotel I met five Englishwomen from Stuttgart, and gave them ample opportunity of misusing the French language. At a piano shop I played to Speidel and other young artists, a violoncellist Goltermann, and others, and thus put myself in a proper position of respect.

As regards the route of my journey, that by Coburg is the shorter, if not also the pleasanter. I stayed the night in Nuremberg, which seemed to me the best plan ; but of this another time.

For today farewell, best father ; keep me up in the Ötlishausen news, even if the most historic fact is the purchase of a goat.

TO FRANZ LISZT.

WEYMAR, 29th June 1851.

MY DEAR AND ILLUSTRIOUS MASTER,

I should have taken the liberty of writing to you long ago, if I had not thought that your time was too full of sad preoccupations just now, and this, consequently, an ill-chosen moment to speak to you of my personal affairs. Nevertheless I should not have delayed expressing my lively gratitude for the generous hospitality which Mr. Raff has offered me in your name, if I had not felt the almost certainty, or at least the hope—so ardently shared by all your friends in Weymar—of your speedy return, a hope which has fallen through for the moment, to my great regret.

I was far from expecting the gracious reception you have given me in your letter, which gives me the opportunity of explaining frankly my situation, and the intention with which I have come to Weymar.

It is a feeling of absolute confidence, both in your superiority and experience as an artist, and in your former kindnesses to me, which has brought me here ; I have come to beg you to judge of my musical powers, and to advise me as to the best career for me in which to develop them, and thus to secure for myself a more or less honourable position in the artistic world.

This resolution, which met with the entire approbation of my parents on the one side, and, on the other, of our mutual friend, Mr. R. Wagner, whose help I enjoyed last winter, and towards whom I feel many obligations, was not however followed by any fixed plan on the subject of my future career. I repeat, I have come here to place my fate unreservedly in your hands, and to proceed in the direction that you may advise, without obtruding any preference or decisive sympathy for one branch of a musician's career over another. I am only too happy to have shaken off the yoke of a profession which was repugnant to me for a thousand and one reasons, and from which I cannot regret having withdrawn myself, except for the bluntness which I then considered indispensable towards my mother, so worthy of my filial respect; and therefore I do not mind what road you may map out for me. I am resolved to devote myself with all possible ardour to whatever career you may deem suitable, as I place my whole confidence in the clearness of your judgment.

I want, moreover, to profit by all the advantages which the town of Weymar, made illustrious by its modern hero, can offer to a disciple of art, and I hope to be able to stay here till I have in some measure attained my object—either by the help of my mother, to whom I do not despair of reconciling myself entirely, or else by earning the means by my own activity. For—to omit nothing in this confession which might have a special influence on my future destiny—my father is not in a position to help me with his own fortune.

This, in few words, is my present position. Whilst awaiting your return I will still take advantage of your hospitable kindness by cultivating my piano-playing at the Altenburg, neglected in Switzerland for the business of conductor at poor theatres, an occupation which, although it has not been altogether useless for me, would not suit me again in similar circumstances.

Last night I heard 'Tannhäuser.' O how we missed your magic wand, the breath of life, the soul of this inanimate body !

Whilst begging you to continue to me your valuable protection, of which you have given me fresh proofs, pray accept the respect and gratitude of

Yours most sincerely,
HANS DE BÜLOW.

In a long letter to his father on the 6th July he writes :—

I have been corresponding with Liszt for some time. He first of all welcomed me by letter, and invited me to live at the Altenburg, and to consider myself at home there. His plan is as follows : he wishes me to remain a year in Weimar, and to drum into my brains, principally, the *newer* works of his own, the bigger Sonatas of Beethoven, the best of Chopin, Schumann—in short, to make such a *répertoire* for myself as not every pianist, or indeed no pianist, can show ; besides this, I am to study instrumentation and that kind of thing, and am specially to learn to write for the piano myself. He thinks it is necessary for me to have a Härtel grand piano (a new one) from Leipzig, as the instrument I now have is worth nothing. In short, Liszt thinks the days of real virtuosity are not over, and he considers that I shall be capable of earning my livelihood by concert-tours as his pupil and successor, for he himself has entirely given up public playing. For this I should require, *provisionally*, help (pecuniary) only until January '52. By that time I shall make my appearance as a pianist in the neighbourhood, first at the Court here, then at the Courts round about, at Erfurt, at the subscription concerts in Leipzig, etc. Finally, in the winter of '52-'53 I am to make my first concert-tour, possibly in company with Joachim, who is about my age, and first of all in Paris. He is peremptory against Munich for next winter ; he says I should learn nothing there, should not progress, and should waste my powers.

My mother seems to be fairly well pleased with Liszt's plans ; at any rate she has a great opinion of Liszt's penetration and experience. She also wrote, in a recent letter to Raff (to whom I am most grateful for his intervention in the matter), that she would provide me with the necessary assistance in my career.

I am anxious to hear your opinion about Liszt's plan for me ; I do hope that you will approve of what I am doing. I will not leave fallow the executive skill which I have already, not without labour and pains, attained. That the epoch of Virtuosi is not over—of this one has proofs every day, and I intend to do my very uttermost. Meanwhile Liszt's personal presence here is not absolutely indispensable to me—he does not return till the beginning of August—I have enough to go on with without him. With regard to the ' Oresteia,' I saw to my dismay on nearer inspection that I do not yet understand enough of instrumentation. I am doing instrumentation at present as practice. The first movement is however fully sketched out. For the rest, I am collecting and putting in order my earlier compositions, so that I may be able to make some use of them as opportunity offers ; a ' Phantasiestück ' for piano and violin will be ready shortly ; to write a good pianoforte movement is a thing I have first to learn ; I cannot do it yet. For then the "Ego" would be created.

Saturday week was ' Tannhäuser,' unfortunately not under Liszt's conducting ; it was commanded in celebration of the marriage of Princess

Auguste of Würtemberg to Prince Hermann, the cousin of the present Grand Duke. The performance was very good. The public applauded firstly the entrance of the grandees, who came punctually to the theatre and remained till the last note, and then also every single number of the opera with great enthusiasm. 'Tannhäuser' is so popular here with all classes, more so than any other opera except 'Freischütz.' Although Wagner has no melody at all, according to some people, yet one hears them whistled all over the streets. That was a tremendous pleasure for me! Now the theatres are closed till the beginning of September. The seal of the packet for Tieck was spoiled, and I had to seal it afresh. Many thanks for the Allemannian poems; the copy for Isa is going off tomorrow.

TO HIS MOTHER.

WEIMAR, 4th September 1851.

DEAREST MOTHER,

My heartiest wishes for your birthday! I could wish, for your sake, that it were over for this year, for I hope by this time next year another sort of a congratulator will present himself to you, who will be able to give you more satisfaction by some little success. I believe you when you say that you cannot yet have any real confidence in my present choice of a profession; an unfinished, "going-to-be" sort of man does not inspire confidence, and, although I cannot alter it, it often makes me angry that I am placed in a position in which I can at most lay claim to the title of "hopeful"—that is to say, not entirely hopeless. Happily the time for my patron Liszt's return is drawing near, so that there will soon be an opportunity of seeing how things will turn out. This news will ease your mind, as much as to me it is welcome news. Liszt has already started some time ago, and the day after tomorrow, or else the day after that, the musical Grand Duke will arrive for certain. Then your son's history will begin to be somewhat more interesting than it has been up to now, when I really have not much to say about him. As a pianist I must have support and guidance; it is high time for this, and, as the most important thing in my immediate future is to cultivate my powers as a Virtuoso, this must be the central point of all my endeavours, towards which I must brace myself up to special efforts. In making these efforts I see, however, that I must not overlook due care for my health. I have observed, namely, that my chest always suffers if I do an unreasonable amount of practice, such as Litolff would have, if you remember: and yet practice, as Wieck understands it, cannot in so short a time lead to the result which is at stake. Well, I follow the golden middle course, and as I lead a very regular life, and almost always get home about nine o'clock, and shall be able to continue doing so through the winter, in spite of Liszt bringing a Hungarian guest, Czertaheli, back with him, I shall not come to any bodily harm. Strange to say, I have discovered that music sometimes works upon my nerves—I who used to boast of my hardiness in this respect. If I throw the blame of this on-to the enervation of the modern musical ear in general—a fact to which I mean to give special study soon—yet I have observed that it is Liszt's compositions especially which affect my nerves most if I go on practising them long, a weakness which I must get over, although even Raff, the musical architect, shares it in many points.

Raff and Joachim continue to be my only company. I am delighted to see that they think something of me, and seem to like to have me with them. In the domain of learning [erudition] Raff is looking after me, and willingly serves as my Mentor, to teach me all that is worthy of knowing, and I see more and more that all this is *necessary* for the musician of to-day. No one can do this better than Raff, who is himself just now deep in the sphere of fore-classical antiquity, busy with the poem for his 'Samson.'

. . . .

TO HIS MOTHER.

[WEIMAR, 1851.]

DEAREST MOTHER,

I had already written to you this morning early, and with my letter in my pocket I went up to the 'Erbprinz,' where Raff gave me yours which had arrived meanwhile. I won't keep you waiting for an answer to that, the more so as there are things in it which I must frequently repeat—so please excuse the rhapsodical postscript, which I add at Raff's house directly after leaving the table.

. . . .

One point which requires a speedy answer is that about the so-called 'journalistic' business. I have not offered myself as a correspon-dent to the *Signale;* Raff begged me to undertake it for him if I did not mind. For the present I shall not do this.

On the other hand, I shall write for Brendel's paper (but for no other), first, because the paper has a dignified, well-principled, erudite attitude; secondly, because it ensures the interests which Wagner and

Liszt have in common, and because there are few people who can write well and sensibly; thirdly, because as an artist I shall belong to the public, against which, moreover, I can't write the word "unfortunately."

It is my dearest wish to pay the utmost possible regard to your desires, and to sacrifice to them any private wishes of my own, where I possibly can do so. But you will agree that, in my immediate future, I must not allow a plurality of authority to step in and settle things for me; nor do I specially like the principle of authority; but there is one authority that I shall for the present recognise and respect, and that is Liszt's, and no one else's.

My own individuality will not be lost, it remains in God's care; but for the present the only right thing for me to do is to tack myself firmly on to Liszt, and detach myself from anybody else.

I am dreadfully sorry that you cannot feel the same confidence in Liszt which I feel, for if you did it would reassure you to know that I shall do nothing without his advice or against his will. My working on *one* musical paper, which I may make serviceable to him through my own personality in several ways, can only be agreeable to him, and I most earnestly beg that you will believe that I am old enough to go to work circumspectly and rationally in my affairs.

You may be sure (I promise you this afresh) it shall be my earnest endeavour to regard your wishes about me as far as possible. I cannot do more, and cannot help it if I fail to carry out the ideas you have had for me. The lapse of years, the peculiar course of my education, all these lie in the way; I can't help it any more than I can make my outer appearance more pleasant or more important.

Please forgive the haste in which I have written.

Your grateful, affectionate son.

TO HIS FATHER.

WEIMAR, 2nd October [1851].

DEAREST FATHER,

I have today received a third letter from you, and confess that I am quite ashamed never to have responded until now to these proofs of your fatherly friendship and sympathy. You will have guessed the reason of my silence; I wanted to wait until Liszt had returned, so as to be able to write to you, as you have a right to expect, with some certainty about my future plans. This, for me, most important event has up to now been announced from week to week, but has not taken place, and

unfortunately my patience has to undergo a still longer trial, till the end
of next month.

.   .   .   .

Nothing is changed in my mode of life and the work I am doing,
and things are going on as quietly and simply as heretofore. The greater
part of my time is devoted to piano-playing; I have enough to do to
perfect my technique, as it is now a settled thing that my immediate
career is to depend upon my executive talent. Together with this, I have
written some new one- and two-part songs, with a view of perhaps publishing them pretty soon. Therefore I cannot think of the 'Oresteia'
any more for the moment, but the grand subject will certainly incite me
again at a more favourable time; I have, moreover, written out a few
sketches or ideas for it. For practice in style, in which I fully acknowledge the principal faults you point out, and for other, personal reasons, I
am the correspondent from here of two musical papers in Leipzig (the two
which are most read, the *Signale* and the *Neue Zeitschrift für Musik*),
and send in also articles of other kinds—just lately a rather long reply
to a *Grenzbote* critique of Richard Wagner's; in a couple of days will
follow a treatise on a rational performance of 'Don Juan,' one suitable
to the demands of modern opera. This I am not doing for money.

I also lately found another subject for an opera, on which I have at
once set to work. It is 'Merlin,' and it was Fr. Schlegel's 'Romantic
Poems of the Middle Ages' that led me to it. I will write more fully
about it when I have got the thing clear in my own mind; I find
it rather difficult to exclude from the subject all miraculous elements.
When the sketch is ready I will send it to you, and please give me your
opinion about it.

I have written such a lot about myself that I have only just remembered my duty, namely, to let you know about mamma's visit. This was
how it came about. I had not written for a long time, thinking that
mamma was still embittered against me, and therefore I did not know
what to do. So, in order to know something about me for certain, she at
last came here. She spoke to Raff first, before I knew she had arrived.
I then found her pretty calm; she was quite disposed to be reconciled
to me, and the past was hardly mentioned. Although, as she says, she
cannot yet feel any confidence in my choice of a profession, yet she has
several times helped me up to now. So my old relation to mamma is
pretty nearly restored.

.   .   .   .

TO HIS MOTHER.

WEIMAR, *15th October* 1851.

DEAREST MOTHER,

Today I have to announce to you the long-delayed, joyful tidings that my protector and master Liszt arrived at length last Sunday evening in good health. I was at the station both morning and noon to await his arrival; but the servants, who were sent on in advance, said he would not come till the last train, at ten o'clock. So I went quite unconcernedly to hear 'Cortez'—music so full of power and nobility, like a steel bath to be-Flotow'd ears. There he appeared suddenly and unexpectedly a few yards before me in the stalls, as though he had sprung from the earth by magic; a whisper ran through the whole house and reached the orchestra, which during his absence had run wild and gone to sleep—in their terror they played twice as badly, and Liszt got in a rage, and would have liked to seize the sceptre from his humdrum deputy, and to have made an end to the easy-going Philistine-anarchy by the despotism of his own conducting-genius, had his scruples allowed it; and as they did not allow it some one else got in a rage also, and that was myself.

Liszt silently welcomed me, and eased his mind by pouring out some of his ill-humour in my ear. After the theatre I had supper with him, together with Joachim. The Princess looked very ill, but strange to say has already got wonderfully better in these few days. She still possesses her admirable eloquence and art of disputation; I doubt if there ever was a woman of such astonishing knowledge and such quick and penetrating intelligence. I shall probably now be promoted to the office of house-disputator, as I am more accustomed to French than Raff. . . .

Yesterday evening I was again alone at the supper, and went on with a discussion with the Princess right into the night; I could not break off, but the wearied Liszt at length spared me the misery of deciding between the two-fold dictates of courtesy. I played a couple of pieces to him, in which the principal things he found fault with were a want of the necessary precision and decision in rhythm, and of a certain *aplomb*, in which, owing to my anxiety at the moment, I was more than usually deficient. The first pieces I am to study with him next week are, a Scherzo of Chopin, a Liszt-Schubert paraphrase, and Liszt's transcription of the Wedding March from the 'Midsummer Night's Dream.'

I must now hire a grand piano stiff enough to be of use to my studies; it will cost 4 reichsthaler a month on hire. Liszt has again explained to me what are his views with regard to my future career. . . .

He thinks now that he shall in any case spend the winter here, and, as the new theatre management is making polite advances to him, it seems as though he would be very much occupied for Art-life here.

Of my Doctorate work I am also thinking ; I hope to be clear about it in a year.   It will be a big work, for there is a great deal in it, and it requires deep study.

.   .   .   .

I have a lot of other letters to write today — to Uhlig, Franz, Brendel, etc.   So farewell for today, dear mother, with the exclamation " Long live Liszt ! "

TO HIS FATHER.

WEIMAR, 25th October 1851.

DEAREST FATHER,

I ought to have told you a week ago the gospel of the happy arrival of Liszt, so impatiently awaited on all sides, but especially by me ; but the very fact of his arrival has made me so busy that I have never had a quiet moment till now to write to you.   Outwardly, Liszt's return has indeed made but little change in my very simple, customary life in Weimar, for I am enjoying his hospitality as before in the matter of rooms, breakfast, and service, things which I can really accept without scruple in such a large household with so many empty rooms ; but my labours have greatly increased.   To the most important matters first.   In his first conversation with me, which took place the day after his return, he recapitulated to me again what I have already written to you. . . . He considers that music-conducting, in circumstances such as those which I have already experienced—and while I am so young I shall certainly not find any better—is a very unsuitable means for rising in my profession ; that it very seldom happens that a man is promoted from an insignificant to a distinguished position ; and hat, in order to be able to lay claim to such an one, I must first put myself into the position of being perfectly well able to do without it, and standing independently on my own merits, which it would not be difficult for me as a Virtuoso to attain.   Well, when I had gone through my piano examination with him, in which I very much pleased him by a rather happy performance of one of his most difficult piano pieces, this was pretty much the judgment that he passed upon me : he says he places positive, well-grounded hopes on me; and more than hopes indeed (he has desired me also to write and tell you this), for he says I shall, now that he has once for all retired from public playing, be able to take up again the position of a Virtuoso where he has left it. Eight months with him will be amply sufficient for my preparation—granted, of course, the necessary industry on my side; then I am to make my *début* perhaps in Berlin, or, better still, in Vienna, and go thence to Paris and London. Within three years I shall have attained my object—that is, an assured independence; I may consider him as surety for this.

I on my side, in my inexperience, not only require to seek the support of an authority like Liszt, to attach myself closely to him and strictly to follow his advice, but I also have such great confidence in his knowledge of the world and mankind that, without being afraid of the *"jurare in verba magistri,"* I have made him unconditionally the arbiter of my fate, and have told him so. So I now devote the greater part of my time, four to five hours daily, exclusively to the cultivation of my technique; I martyrise the eventual founders of my material prosperity; I crucify, like a good Christ, the flesh of my fingers, in order to make them obedient, submissive machines to the mind, as a pianist must. It is also quite right, and for the simplest reasons very delightful to me too, to be able to do something for him in return for the great kindness he shows me—he gives me regular lessons. So I am now making a copy of his excellent arrangement of Beethoven's Ninth Symphony for two pianos, which he has also promised to play with me sometime; it is certainly a laborious and minute piece of work, but meanwhile it teaches me the score by heart; I am also translating his 'Tannhäuser' article (of the same length as the one on 'Lohengrin') for the *Illustrirte Zeitung.* I also occasionally act as his secretary—but this is a secret. At the beginning of next year Liszt will introduce me at Court, where I shall in all probability play.

. . . .

If possible I shall do my Doctorate's work before my first concert-tour. The subject is—' The History of the Belief in Immortality.'

Liszt was 40 three days ago.

TO HIS MOTHER.

WEYMAR, 21*st November* 1851.

MY DEAREST MOTHER,

The letter you have just written to me after your long silence has made me very sad, for it proves pretty clearly to me that the events of the past year have greatly shaken, if not enfeebled, your love and your motherly indulgence—a fact which I liked to think was not so.

You were more prompt formerly to forgive me a hasty word spoken in an unhappy moment of wounded pride, and you were not wrong in thinking, as I suppose you did, that sooner or later I should be the first to repent sincerely. Do not, I pray, have a worse opinion of my character today, the principal defect of which is perhaps an extreme irritability, an innate fault, stronger sometimes than my will itself, and of which I have not been able yet entirely to cure myself. That is why I have been extremely sensitive to the heartrending doubt you cast on my sincerity.

Don't you remember too the definition which our mutual friend Litolff gave of my character in this respect? " He hates all kind of demonstration and display."

Nothing is truer, you may be sure of that, and if I make an exception it is because my heart is in it ; and I protest strongly against the accusation that I have no heart. I have been very unhappy about it, and it has been on my mind for many days. As you and I have the same tastes in many things, so it is with our affections. Remember how many a time a sharp and unkind letter has remained on your mind for whole weeks, and made you incapable of every more tender feeling. Well, I share this sensibility, though in a lesser degree. The thought that anyone I love, who is writing to me, is ill-disposed towards me and bears me a grudge, makes me miserable and uneasy. I assure you that your letter has made my various work, with which at the moment I am overdone, much more difficult. Let me beg you once more, my dear mother, to write to me some kinder words soon, which will show me that your anger is somewhat pacified, and has given place to the indulgence and kindness to which you have accustomed me. I appeal to your judgment, " *sine ira et studio*," whether you have not really a son too German to make fine speeches, and I beg that you will take these simple lines, full of divers Teutonisms, as a piece of justification.

I am very glad to be able to give you today two pieces of news which, I hope, will not vex you, although they tend to bring me more into publicity.

1. On the 2nd December I shall appear for the first time as an artist-pianist (up to now it has only been as an amateur-pianist) in the second of the Quartet-Soirées that Joachim, Cossmann and other musicians have begun to give to the Weimar people, at a price unheard of for Weimar, but fixed by Liszt at one thaler per concert, or a subscription ticket of three thalers for the four. Consequently only the best society frequents them, but in pretty large numbers ; the entire Court

and the Grand-Ducal family also come. I shall play Schumann's Quintet, not a particularly brilliant piece, but one that makes a sure effect, and is easy to understand.

2. On December 7th, on the occasion of the performance of Shakespeare's 'Julius Cæsar,' Liszt himself will conduct an Overture and a March composed, but not yet completely instrumentated, by *M. votre fils*, hater of demonstrations, but who, in spite of that, would not be displeased with an encouraging demonstration on the part of the public on this occasion. My Overture is tolerably original and interesting, according to what Liszt says. You may well imagine that I am burning with impatience to see this memorable day arrive. With regard to Reissiger, I do not recollect the slightest incident which could have sown discord between my ex-ideal and me (from the time when a holy flame filled my soul, greedy of quavers and sharps, for the unhappy 'Adèle de Foix,* ma foi, une fois,' etc.).

As to my relations with Liszt, I have every reason to be satisfied. I have the most sincere attachment for him, and I endeavour to prove it to him. This attachment is not merely based upon gratitude, but also comes from a sympathy which is quite involuntary, for the mere sight of his noble and expressive features rejoices and expands my soul. I need not describe to you in detail the healthy and encouraging influence which his presence exercises in so many ways on all those around him, and especially on a pupil who enjoys his more intimate friendship and protection. Enough that, although beset by work of all kinds, he regularly devotes two consecutive hours a week to my development as a pianist, and I find every time new matter for admiration of his genius; and as my intelligence, thanks to Nature (which has been less stingy to me in this respect than to many others), is not very slow in divining his hints, I flatter myself that my musical education does not go much against the grain with him. Apart from the lessons I see him almost every day, either in the afternoon in company with other artists or with strangers, or else at the family supper in the evening. In a word, Liszt does far more for me than just fulfil his promises. I am happy to be able to do some small services for him, such as copying his manuscripts, or doing some of his commissions by correspondence.

You would rejoice if you could hear me practising for some hours a day at Czerny's School of Virtuosity with a *sangfroid* and tenacity which even astonish me. *Apropos*, I had to pay rather dear for this work, as well as for some other pieces, Studies of Chopin and Henselt and Schumann's Quintet, which cost a good deal. Although I try to

---

* Opera of Reissiger.

spend as little as possible—I have not been to the theatre for a month—living costs me more here, in spite of all the advantages I enjoy, than in any other town living alone. The piano, the tuner, washing, correspondence,—all these devour more of my allowance than in Berlin, to say nothing of the shoemaker, who is especially favoured by the bad pavement here. The other day Ziegesar* invited me to a small party at his house; Liszt played a Trio of Beethoven, and enchanted even the musicians themselves, which means a great deal. The Hereditary Prince also put in an appearance for a short time.

I am so busy that I don't know what to do first. The tidings I have just received from my father are pretty satisfactory. I should be very much obliged if you would send me shortly, with a few lines in reply, Chopin's separate Studies, which are at home. Farewell.

TO THEODOR UHLIG † (DRESDEN).

WEIMAR, 29th November 1851.

MY DEAR FRIEND,

At this moment I am engaged on work at home, that is to say, with the composition of an Overture and March, and possibly also other music, to the 'Julius Cæsar' of Shakespeare, Schlegel, Laube and Genast. This music or unmusic (Unmusik) is to be given on the 14th of next month in the theatre here, and I am longing to hear my first great score. I instrumentate rather slowly and deliberately, so that this egotistical occupation takes up all my time. The work is rather a long one, heavily scored and difficult; and written somewhat in the rude style of the 'Rienzi' Overture, without its grand ideas. If it sounds at all decent, perhaps I'll send it to Dresden.

Next Tuesday I have to play Schumann's Quintet at the second Quartet-Soirée here—two débuts pretty close together. My friends in art must be glad about this, for by these public performances (provided they don't go badly) their party gains in me, who until now appeared only as a decayed nobleman, with something of the amateur still clinging to him, and only just good enough to run alongside of them. So pray for me!

.   .   .   .

---

* The theatre manager at that time.

† Theodor Uhlig, a gifted musician and writer, well known as one of the friends and warmest champions of Wagner. Died in 1853.

For Brendel's paper I have found no time to work lately. I have
got him a Berlin correspondent, so you see I have not been entirely
egotistical.

I fancy that you will prefer to read the enclosures rather than my
unreadable scrawl. This reminds me of the necessary explanation :—

1. I send you herewith the first article you wanted, which the
" martyr to truth "—but no, he appears to be really a very decent sort of
man—declined to take. The red-pencil marks are his; if you can make
any use of the best jokes in it, pray do so.

2. In case you have not yet read Heine's ' Romancero,' I send you
a selection, which I have copied for you. So he still remains the German
Aristophanes (as Stahr calls him), until a greater one appears.

3. You will find the letter you wanted from Robert Franz. * He
has begged me not to disclose the secret of his authorship. So, if you
have it printed, please keep it anonymous, i.e. without Robert's name.
Perhaps I can persuade Franz later on to withdraw this prohibition.

I have been able to do as yet very little—don't scold me—at the
translation, and I shall not be able to finish it before New Year. If you
can find someone else who can do it quicker, do give it to him; but if
there is time, then have patience with me.

In confidence: the time which Liszt devotes to me, the hospitality
which he has shown me,—these make me very anxious and happy to be
able to do anything for him in return. I know you will agree with me in
this. The limits which this sets to my time appear but a small sacrifice
in comparison with all I have received.

In the *Gazette Musicale*, which Liszt takes in addition to the
France Musicale and the *Diapason* (a Belgian paper), nothing has yet
appeared about your capital adaptation of Roger. I don't need to tell
you how much I rejoice in all your articles, and how fully I agree with
you. With regard to Schumann, his later works—that is to say, for
many years past—have been quite antipathetic to me on account of the
humdrum, narrow-minded good-citizenship that prevails in them. A
laudable exception to this is the very beautiful Overture to the ' Bride
of Messina,' which Brendel unfortunately has not fully appreciated.

As you are aware, even longer than I am, that there is nothing to
be done with ' Siegfried ' in the immediate future, as Wagner wants to
write a Trilogy, and has altered his whole plan, it leaves us some hope

* Printed in the *Neue Zeitschrift für Musik*, 26th March 1852, No. 13, page
142, signed by Robert Franz.

for the 'Flying Dutchman'; the Princess is tremendously in favour of it,
and has long been urging Liszt to do it.

Please kindly excuse haste.

TO HIS FATHER.

WEIMAR, 14*th December* 1851.

DEAREST FATHER,

        I have chosen to write to you the day after
rather than the evening before a great event; it is only a pity that the
surprise comes so late, for I should so have liked to give you this
amusement on your birthday. You will be impatient to learn without
more ado what this said great event can be; I refer you to the enclosed
theatre-bill, and add also that it is *my first public appearance as a
composer.* During the last month the ambition and impulse to produce
something suddenly seized me. 'Julius Cæsar' was shortly to be acted,
and the idea, which had once seized upon me at a very immature period
of my life, to write music to it, took hold of me again. I read the
tragedy through again, and it really inspired me to a task which I have
carried through with industry and love; . . . twice lately I have had to
work by night in addition. Liszt was exceedingly pleased with the
sketch of it, and encouraged me throughout. He studied the rather
difficult Overture with great care, and conducted the performance
himself. So my *début* as a composer was in no way *mesquin,* and it
conduces no little to my pleasure that I have not disgraced my father
thereby. Don't laugh at me if after my first success I am a little elated
and jolly, and express to you quite simply my hope that in the eleventh
edition of Brockhaus's 'Conversationslexikon' I shall have a little corner
after you : by that time I think I shall achieve the distinction. To
return to our starting-point : the Overture was received with lively
applause, only I was vexed at the noise, at first rather loud, in the
Galerie noble, for whom my rather serious and long Overture was not
adapted. This noise did not cease till the very prominent trombone
Recitative "Et tu, Brute," followed by a bar's rest—*captatio benevolentiæ*
to you—at which those "candidates for the lantern"* were alarmed
when they heard their own voices. A War March between the fifth and
sixth Acts,† conducted by Stör, was also very successful; it sinned less

---

    * Meaning 'aristocrats ;' the occupants of the *Galerie noble.*

    † Evidently an *arrangement* for the German stage, probably by Genast and
others, which would account for a sixth act.

against modern taste than the Overture. The theatre music and a well-thought-out melodrama for the appearance of the ghosts also made a good effect. For the second performance I shall also write the prescribed battle music in the orchestra during the change of scene; then they will put on the bill "Overture and Incidental Music by," etc.

The performance of the tragedy, as a whole, was very bad, except the decorations and scenes with the populace, which went excellently.

Last Tuesday I also made my first appearance in public in Weimar as a pianist. For I had already been heard at certain large parties, which I could not get out of, as Liszt took me to them. The occasion of my *début* as a pianist was the second concert of the Quartet-Academy—we have here a most excellent Quartet—at which modern chamber-music was to be produced. The first was set aside for the usual trefoil of Haydn, Mozart and Beethoven; the last will give three Quartets of Beethoven from his different periods. The choice was not a thankful one for the piano, but opportune for me. It was a Quintet of Robert Schumann—one of his early works, full of freshness and spirit, and generally of a lively character. I am sure it would have met your approval if you had heard it, and your lasting approval too, not a passing one, such as you felt for the 'Waldscenen.' In short, the piece pleased quite tremendously for Weimar, and I earned the most unexpected and brilliant praise for it.

With regard to my present occupations, I have first of all to work for Liszt and for the Brendel paper, especially to write articles on piano-composition in the spirit of Liszt. Then I am also getting ready a couple of new books of songs (for eventual publication), a couple of pieces for piano and violin, and a Trio. Before I set to work on a larger dramatic subject I want to write a good deal of specific music, so as to get thoroughly into the routine of it. I am so happy that for once and away I have done something well, and had a success. It will make the work go all the quicker now.—One humble question: Could you, without having any further trouble, ask Tieck to give his protection to my 'Cæsar' Music in Berlin?

TO FRAU RITTER (Dresden).

DRESDEN, 26th December 1851.

DEAR MADAM,

Do not be surprised that these lines have to take the place of a call upon you, on which I had been so much counting, and which I am obliged with bitter tears to renounce. No doubt you know all about me ; your son, my dearest friend in all the world, will probably have told you about the time we spent together in Switzerland. You have probably also heard about the turning-point of my career there, since my mother's generosity enabled me, in spite of her deeply-rooted and unconquerable aversion from my adopting an artistic career, to carry on my studies, under Liszt's guidance in Weimar, to the desired end of a complete material independence.

My mother, who has really suffered very greatly through me, and who most earnestly desires a reconciliation between us, invited me to spend the Christmas holidays with her in Dresden. When I arrived here, the first *indispensable condition* of pardon for the wrong I had done my mother was that I should avoid all intercourse with the dearest friend of my youth, your son. Dreadfully hard as this sacrifice is to me, bitter as are the tears that this decision has cost me, and little as I would have undertaken the journey to Dresden had I known of this beforehand, yet I have not the courage to go against this first indispensable condition of a reconciliation with my mother, however inexplicable it may in some ways seem to me. A sentiment of reverence, which I think you, dearest Madam, will be the first to appreciate, makes me feel that it it is my duty, at any cost, to bring about this reconciliation.

You will pity me if you reflect how sad and unhappy it must make me to think that tomorrow I shall be so near to my beloved Karl, and yet not daring to enjoy the longed-for happiness of seeing him again. I wish I could run away, for I do not know how I shall bear it. Happily the misery will not last long, as in 2 or 3 days I return to Weimar. But at the beginning of January, somewhere about the 7th or 10th, ' Lohengrin ' will be given. If Karl would come and see me then, and perhaps his dear brother with him, it would make me endlessly happy, and make up for these miserable days now.

I hope that Karl's just pride will allow of this ! By what I know of you I do not feel afraid that he will be hurt by this letter. Beg your sons—I appeal to your motherly love—to continue to like me which will bind me to them for ever.

Farewell.—With most sincere respect,

H. G. v. BÜLOW.

Forgive the evident signs of an emotion which I could not master.

TO HIS FATHER.

WEIMAR, 21st *January* 1852.

DEAREST FATHER,

I have so many things to thank you for that I am quite puzzled where to begin. And since I received your Christmas letter so much time has elapsed, that I must go back a long way in order to tell you everything. Luckily today I have time for this—until now I have tried in vain to get several consecutive free hours in which to write to you fully, for in paltry little notes one can't say much, and they are merely a conglomeration of news in a more or less laconic form, which, after all, requires amplifying in the end.

From the 25th December until my birthday I was in Dresden. There I received your letter, for which my warmest thanks; it gave me as much pleasure as the news of my success as a composer seems to have given you. The present you enclosed was no less valuable as a token of your loving sympathy than it was welcome in itself. I wanted to be back in Weimar for the New Year: I had given up the hope of hearing my 'Cæsar' Music, which was to be repeated there with the tragedy on the 28th December. This time Liszt did not conduct it again, as it was enough for him to have studied it and introduced me as the author by conducting it himself on the first occasion. But the performance of 'Antony and Cleopatra,' even though an arrangement of it by the Court Steward, Lüttichau, enchained me to Dresden a couple of days longer, and then a less pleasant visitor, in the shape of my headache, which recurs regularly every half-year, and which made me for several days incapable of thinking. On my return journey on the 8th I was obliged to stay two nights at Leipzig. Liszt had given me a heap of commissions to do for him there, and had also taken the opportunity of giving me the warmest and most flattering letters of introduction to Kistner, Härtel, David and others. It appears that before Liszt returned to Weimar (in October) he stopped at Leipzig, and, as he mentioned me as one of the pupils awaiting him, people told him the most awful tales about my humble self. Madame David said: " Mais il est d'une impertinence affreuse." Moscheles and his wife had the idea that I was such a mad revolutionist that it was impossible to have any sensible talk with me. Others said that I had once made a scandal amongst my relations by inveighing against Mendelssohn before everybody (not a word of which is true); that I am an eccentric, crazed fellow, who possesses the idiosyncrasy of enjoying nothing but Wagner's music, and so forth. In short, you see that Liszt's mode of procedure was not superfluous, and was very timely, as next year, when I begin my concert-tours, I must also make my *début* in Leipzig. Liszt's letter of introduction to Kistner drew from him the exclamation of astonishment: " Well, you must have cut out all the others who surround Liszt, for you seem now to be his favourite ! "

Well, when I had done all Liszt's and my own commissions in Leipzig, and got back here again, where I was warmly welcomed by my friends, I found everybody full of the preparations for a second perform-ance of ' Lohengrin,' and I also found work to do at once. I had to write about a dozen letters of invitation; and as strangers were coming from many cities, as the confederates used to come to the Olympic Games thousands of years ago, I was appointed to do the honours of Weimar to them, whereby my purse of " time-money " was pretty well drained, cer-tainly not altogether without regard " pour le roi de Prusse," whereby, on the contrary, much that is useful and necessary is gained.

After an enchanting evening of ' Lohengrin,' which I can never forget, and after the visitors had departed a few days later, fresh work awaited me. Liszt was in a great hurry for the copy of the arrange-ment of Beethoven's Ninth Symphony for two pianos, which I had promised him : I had not been able to finish this rather tremendous piece of work before Christmas, being extremely occupied at that time *pro domo*, in spite of which I often went without my dinner in order to lose no time, and for something like five to six days I did not get to bed till near three o'clock in the morning—fatigues which rather knocked me up and made me look ill, but from which I entirely recovered in Dresden by an absolute " *utile far niente.*" Now comes suddenly a charity concert in addition, for which Liszt, in spite of his dislike to mixing heathen Art with Christian " *caritas*," was obliged to do something. This something consisted in making me appear again as a pianist in public, a practice which is of essential use to me, as it is by such opportunities here in Weimar alone that I can get over that miserable nervousness in public playing, from which I have begun to suffer again for some time past. I send you herewith the programme, which you can put with the rest of your collection of trophies. I gave universal satisfaction. I must also take this opportunity of explaining to you the misunderstand-ing which my account of my first appearance here as a pianist occasioned you. The piece which I had then chosen for one of the Quartet even-ings, which are designed for serious chamber-music, answered the purpose in view, but just on that account was no virtuoso piece. Of course virtuosity was required in the performance of it, and it was no wonder that in this *ensemble* piece my special talent for execution should be made prominent. So the thing is as follows : at my first appearance I had more opportunity to show off the piano-playing *musician*, whilst at the concert that has just taken place it was rather an opportunity to show forth the technical *pianist*. Liszt was satisfied with me on both occasions, and equally so with the recognition I obtained from the Weimar public.

With regard to my studies as a Virtuoso—in the coming time these will have special attention, though not quite exclusively so. Liszt's opinion, that through the career of a pianist I shall, in three to four years, attain a material independence, which must be the first aim for my future, has become strengthened in the course of the time which I have passed with him, and he expressed this to me only yesterday in a long talk with me, somewhat in the following manner : " I might make use of you here as I could of no one else, to help me in my post of conductor, and might also help you to a position in the Institute here in a short time ; but I consider that this would be an injustice to your future, as, by the other road (the career of a Virtuoso), you can attain the same end in a more brilliant, more favourable, and even a shorter way. *Now* you would naturally take a subordinate place (possibly as second music-director), and perhaps you would not find it so easy to get out of it : but in any case by this (what I may call bureau-cratic road) you could never rise step by step to a higher position as conductor at, say, Berlin, Dresden or Munich. Posts such as these one gets all in a moment, for one is appointed to them ; wait, therefore, for such an appointment as this, when you are materially independent and set on a firm footing by the results of your career as a pianist, for which, *then*, you will not have to wait so long."—Perhaps he will write to you himself. Your letter, for which my best thanks in his name and then in my own, has pleased him. He sends his best remembrances to you, and is very sorry that just at this moment he is not able to answer you —that is what he said to me a fortnight ago—as he is uncommonly busy. The first four months of the year he always devotes entirely to the opera, as it is the custom always to give a new opera every time there is a Grand-Ducal birthday, all of which fall in the months of February and March. On the 16th February Berlioz's opera 'Benvenuto Cellini,' which made a half fiasco in Paris a long time ago, is to be given ; the composer probably to be present at it. I am delighted to think of making his acquaintance. Although I don't at all like the course which Berlioz pursues—anti-Wagnerian, pseudo-imitation of Beethoven—yet his genius, which stands forth in so many departments of his art, interests me, and to it the later development of music has much cause to be grateful for its rich technical acquirements, especially in regard to instrumentation. Berlioz has taken the initiative in many innovations, and has shown the right practical application of them. He is certainly a Frenchman through and through, and his brilliancy rests on externals. That Liszt produces his opera is due, in the first place, to his personal friendship for him ; and, secondly, to the motive which, if not altogether an unqualified one, is nevertheless very meritorious, of doing justice to a man who is almost more misjudged in Germany than in his own country. Another motive is also that of raising singers and orchestra (of the nation which stands foremost in its indolence and ignorant arrogance) to a higher level, by making them undertake difficult and unaccustomed tasks. This French and Italian rubbish which, since the July Revolution, has made its way on all the German stages, has really done incalculable harm. These composers are obedient slaves of the singers, to whom they leave absolute freedom, in return for which the latter, it is true, push on their rubbish, only, with success ; and the singers are so spoiled by them that they will not any longer submit to the yoke of a correct declamation and dramatic expression laid upon them by Wagner and Gluck, and even hardly trouble themselves to fulfil the very moderate demands of Cherubini and Spontini, or of Weber, Spohr and Marschner. Liszt alone cannot put an end to this scandal, but the sight of a living conductor—indeed the only really active one—undertaking, and successfully carrying through, the work of a radical regeneration of opera, so far as such a thing is possible under present political and social conditions, may perhaps wake up the rising generation. Amongst other important novelties in art we are to have Byron's ' Manfred' in March—I don't know which translation—with Schumann's music. Liszt is very much intercepted in his great plans just now by Beaulieu, the Intendant of the moment. Next season, however, Liszt's friend, Herr v. Ziegesar, who is now quite well again, will resume the reins of government, and then Wagner's 'Fliegender Holländer,' and Gluck's ' Iphigenia in Aulis,' with Wagner's arrangement, will be resumed. I myself take a deep personal interest in the change of Intendant : under the present one, who is very stingy with free tickets, I cannot get any ; I almost had to pay to get in to hear my own music ! So I go very little to the theatre now on that account, and indeed my former passion for it has greatly diminished ; sometimes, but only very occasionally, Liszt orders a free ticket to be given to me. The editor of the official paper, a Dr. v. Mangolt from Dresden, lately appointed here, a man of pretty liberal opinions—for there is still some individuality in opinion here—even he has received no free tickets ! Under Ziegesar I am certain to be thought of.

Next Monday Sontag makes her appearance here, and vouchsafes the artistic performance of a forty-eight-years-old soubrette in the

'Figlia del Regimento'; the following Wednesday she will sing once more, either Martha, or Rosina in the 'Barbiere.' I confess that I am not in the least anxious for this treat; and added to this I should never call Sontag an artist in the true sense of the word, on account of this wretched choice of hers (always excepting the 'Barbiere'). The prices, which will be trebled—for one evening she is certain to receive one hundred louis d'or—would also further restrain me from satisfying my curiosity, but Liszt has managed to have a place kept for me.

Amongst other things I have the bad habit of hopping about from one thing to another in my letters, and because my pen cannot catch up my thoughts, in which there is occasionally a dearth, owing to a musical idea coming into my head between-times, I make the most extraordinary leaps in all directions in what I write. It is all very well for me to determine to write a proper letter; in the most favourable case it only results in a larger and more careless note. I can't fix my mind on a continuous chain of thought, and wander about in a sort of anarchical way, from innate propensity.

I will now tell you briefly my plans for the immediate future, my studies, and the work I am doing. The principal thing for me is of course to work as hard as possible at the piano, and to prepare an extensive *répertoire* for my concert-tours. Liszt has decided this himself, and also that I should make a successive study of the pieces selected. As regards composition, I am now doing an Overture to 'Romeo and Juliet,' the musico-philosophic plan of which—not of course after Gervinus and Flathe—is already prepared, and some definite ideas are collected: at the same time I shall work at a Pianoforte Trio, a work in which, in consideration of its specific musical basis, there will be less of the virtuoso element. A new book of songs, dedicated to our best singer, Frau v. Milde, with whom I am on good terms, will be ready immediately. At the beginning of February I am also to blossom forth as a schoolmaster. A young *pianiste*, Fräulein Soest from Goslar, daughter of an officer, is coming, I believe, to take lessons from Liszt. Liszt has no time for this, so will only overlook her once a month, and I am to take his place by giving one hour's lesson a week for one thaler. I don't know what I shall look like when I receive the money; I believe I shall send it back—at any rate I have the greatest objection in my own mind to receiving payment like a plebeian—and yet I shall certainly want it all the same. Besides these things I have mentioned, the coming time will give me much to hear and to study. My work as a writer is involved with my position to Liszt on the one side, and with Wagner on the other. The latter branch of it gives me less to do than the former. I have just had a great discussion with the *Grenzbote* about both of them, and have carried it through to the great entertainment of my friends. The article about Rellstab you must have; it would be a shame if it were to be lost. I shall write to Rellstab—perhaps he has kept it—and beg for a copy.

As regards politics, I am delighted at your promised omission on this unrefreshing topic. I am the old, red Republican I was. But I think that homœopathy is no radical cure—politics will not be annihilated by politics; the primitive force of a natural element will make a radical cure, and for this I believe in the excellence of 'pyropathy,' for hydropathy will not do here. I don't read any political paper beyond the *Kreuzzeitung*. My necessary political education I get out of *Kladderadatsch*—and when anyone asks me to which party I belong, I say " to *Kladderadatsch's* party." Moreover it is the only one that has a future before it.

The great work you are now doing interests me much; and, knowing Ernst, with whom you are carrying it out, I hope much from it. I shall be grateful for further tidings, especially about the succession of the members of this 'Pantheon,' in which I hope you won't, out of excess of Teutonism, forget the French nation.*

With regard to my associates, the society in which I live, the best is —the artists. Raff, Joachim, Cossmann; the poet Frankl, whom you also know, and who has now completed a great epic, 'Tannhäuser,' which is a remarkable and talented work (comprising the period of his life until his entrance into the Hörselberg) — all these I meet daily at the 'Erbprinz,' and occasionally elsewhere also. I am now and then at Liszt's for dinner and for the evening. Every Sunday is Quartet-cultus, chiefly Beethoven, either at Joachim's or at Liszt's house. There one also sees the 'Minorum.' †

I don't go into society at all. Hofrath X., whose wife and daughters adore me, occasionally invites me, but I decline to go there any more, because he is a violent antagonist of Liszt's. If I went over to the anti-Liszt side I should soon be immensely popular. Liszt's enemies here are like refuse by the sea; for he interests himself in other things besides piano-playing—the 'Goethe-Stiftung,' etc.—and that is a thorn in the people's side. They only allow him, in fact, the right to entertain them as a pianist, which he has given up once for all.

With Wagner I carry on a not particularly lively, but continuous,

---

* Biographies of great men in history—a kind of modern 'Plutarch'—on which Eduard von Bülow was at that time engaged, the completion of which was frustrated by his death a year and a half later.

† Franciscans.

correspondence. I shall be sending him very soon my score to look through, with a piano arrangement of which, for four hands, I am now occupied.

He feels very lonely and unhappy at Zurich, although Ritter has made him safe materially through his (Ritter's) legacy (from an uncle). Wagner complains that he is condemned to live in his own thoughts, and not in a real world, and that he is worse off than deaf Beethoven—he has never yet been able to hear his own 'Lohengrin' once! I often have to write to him instead of Liszt, who is excessively busy.

I see that, if I go on in this style, I shall never come to an end, and yet I really must do so, for my letter has dragged on over several days, although I have devoted almost every spare moment to it.

On the 1st February 1852, he writes from Weimar to his friend Uhlig, in Dresden:—

In the next number of Brendel's paper you will read an article on Henriette Sontag by me. I think Brendel has entirely washed his hands of this. It is at any rate the best article I have yet written. It will create a scandal, but a scandal that is not an article of luxury, but of necessity. If you read it before you have heard Sontag you will think that it is reeking of impudence, but afterwards you will see that it is really only full of truth and moderation. What a lot of good puns I could have put into it also!

In a long letter to his sister, on the 6th February, he says:—

Early this morning Liszt suddenly paid me a visit in my room, and made me a present, which was also a great joke; a perfectly beautiful stick, most original and full of meaning—I am so ignorant that I can't tell you the name of the material of which it is made; it is brown, and looks like dark amber, is pliable, but thick, and quite of a natural shape— is it perhaps indiarubber? Enough that the one you gave me must hide himself away, and I have helped him to do this by finding a corner for him.

But now the best of the thing: Liszt had this stick brought for me by Joachim, who has just been a trip to Leipzig, because he wished to endow me with one as like as two pins to the one he carries himself, only in proportion to my height. To carry this stick gives me even greater, though just as childish, pleasure as the wearing of a cockade did in my more timid year of '48. It is to me like a badge of the order of Liszt of the Altenburg.

Liszt and the Princess also have grown fond of me little by little, and I am regarded more than formerly as the *animal domestique;* I say *animal*, because that expresses best the feeling of comfort. Thus Liszt has lately—certainly without my having anything to do with it—found out on several occasions that I am not only a less uncultivated man, but also a less ignoble and insensible one than other young slow-coaches, and that has pleased him on account of its rarity. . . .

Henriette Sontag has been here. If you have an opportunity of hearing her, don't avail yourself of it. The other day I met Eckermann, who is always tremendously friendly with me. It was pouring with rain, but he came boldly through the mud to me with his umbrella up, and had a quarter of an hour's chat with me. Amongst other things, he told me that Goethe had spoken to him as follows about Sontag: "When I had understood what kind of a creature she was, and had got sufficiently enraged over the bad taste of the public, I took both my grandchildren, in spite of their resistance, and led them, one in each hand, out of the theatre, just as Lot fled with his two daughters from Sodom and Gomorrha when his wife was turned into a pillar of salt." Eckermann has forgotten to publish this, so now boast that you know it.

She is a woman gifted with a voice *sans pareil*, and is an excellent soubrette. But poetry and passion are conspicuous by their complete absence, and therefore I should prefer her room to her company. The Lind has much more stuff in her. Liszt says: "C'est une antipathie de race." He received her with icy politeness; that was splendid. But a coquette she is and always has been. See her for yourself, and then mend your ways, or else when you are a married woman of 48 you won't look more than 24. Really and truly, Lucille Grahn,* who has been dancing here this week, has more music in her little toe than Sontag, and I much prefer her as a musician. I believe I shall meet the Grahn this evening at supper at Liszt's.

Bülow could scarcely have dreamt, when he described his impressions of Henriette Sontag in the foregoing letter, that this name would lead to such long-enduring and painful experiences for him. On the 13th February 1852 a scathing article appeared in the *Neue Zeitschrift für Musik*, in which he gave vent to his opinions on the direction Art was taking in the person of Henriette Sontag. The letter to his father, which follows shortly, shows that what he did was regarded with great suspicion, not merely by the adherents of the great star in question, but also by his parents and friends. His father, in particular, appears to have been temporarily estranged from

---

* A dancer.

his son on account of this article, and hence the very touching and pathetic letter bearing the signature, " Giovanni penitente."

TO THEODOR UHLIG (Dresden).

WEIMAR, 22nd April 1852.

DEAR FRIEND,

Do not be angry with me that I am so late in sending you the score of the ' Fliegender Holländer,' for it is not my fault. Our baritone Milde wanted to sing the great duet in the second act with his wife in public, and Liszt had lent him the score for that purpose, that he might get the parts copied out.

We, and especially I, have been dreadfully sorry, as you may imagine, that you could not come to Weimar during Passion Week, as you intended.

I am not feeling particularly grand just now—I suffer so much from sick headaches, and have a fearful amount to do. The Benvenuto Cellini articles have taken up a great deal of my time ; but I had promised Liszt (who sends you best greetings) to write them—of course the fact that I *would*, but not the *how*. The opera, that is to say, Berlioz' music, has impressed me greatly and uncommonly. I have judged Berlioz much more favourably, that is, I have ascribed much more merit to him than Wagner really does ; do you think that W[agner] is angry about this? I have not written to him for a long time, but will now do it directly. If you are writing to him before that, will you be so good as to make my excuses to him.

Liszt wanted to go lately, on Good Friday, to Leipzig with me, to hear Bach's Passion-Music, but a sudden affection of the eyes prevented him, and kept him several days in bed. Now he is well again. Joachim started for London a week ago, and will remain there, I suppose, three to four months.

Nothing much new in the way of music, though much that is irritating, such as the utter imbecility of Haslinger's ' Napoleon ' and the shallow pond of Hoven's ' opera.' There was still a third performance of ' Benvenuto.' Now we have ' Ernani ' and Schumann's ' Manfred ' in prospect; perhaps you will run over for the latter. As soon as possible we shall have ' Tannhäuser' again (as soon as the Grand Duchess comes to the theatre for the first time after the Court mourning) ; of course we shall have it in the old arrangement.

You have pretty well done for the Well-known one—Lobe,* whose identity was immediately guessed here, where he is well known—only you are a little too serious, which he does not really deserve. A review of the 'Lohengrin' pianoforte score is coming out directly 'Benvenuto' is finished, and in one of the next numbers there will again be an "opinion of the minority," entitled 'Flotow's Martha to her public.'

Ritter passed through here lately on his way to Eisenach. With me he was pretty sociable until the last, when he suddenly started off on his journey without saying a word. Towards Liszt he behaved curiously, was not at all conciliatory, in which he did wrong. I am curious to know what he is going to do; if he remains idle it would be a shame with such brains.

It is nice of you to interest yourself for the Fastlinger: and how did she please as Fidelio?

The latest news from W[agner] (indirect news) makes me rather anxious—but that is nothing. Why does he suddenly despair of Brendel? For once it really won't do.

I hope soon to read in the paper a critique by you—special edification—on Reissiger's 'Da' ('there,' pointing to the head) 'vide' (empty).†

Thanks for the programme to the 'Tannhäuser' Overture; in case you happen to have a surplus of copies of the two letters published by Hinze, I should be very much obliged for some.

TO HIS MOTHER.

WEIMAR, 23rd May 1852.

DEAREST MOTHER,

I wanted to write you a long and tidy letter for once, and that is what has kept me so long from answering your dear, kind letter with a mere word of thanks; I was always hoping to find time for this and could not. A heap of work came, one thing on the top of another; one week, for instance, was entirely taken up with copying a Liszt score for piano and orchestra; Liszt had earnestly begged me to do

---

* J. C. Lobe, musical theorist, composer (1797-1881). Uhlig had written, in the Neue Zeitschrift für Musik (No. 14, Year I.), a smart reply to the musical letters which had just then appeared, entitled, "The Truth about Music and Musicians. For Friends and Connoisseurs. By a Well-known Person."

† Play on the title of an Oratorio, 'David,' by Reissiger.

this, and he is so good to me that I always set everything aside to fulfil such wishes immediately. A second piece of work, more interesting than the first, followed, but it was one which took up more time because it demanded more thought. Berlioz' opera was to be given once more this season, and as I agreed with Liszt's opinion as to the uselessness of the last act, which only wearies people and sends them to sleep, he proposed that *I* should make the necessary cuts, as well as the slight alterations in music and text required by these ; I discharged myself of this task to Liszt's satisfaction, although this was my *first* appearance as a rhymer of blank verse.

At last it came about that the Princess gave me to understand that I might write a few words on Liszt's 'Chopin.' I have been accustomed to be a *bon entendeur*, and had therefore first to set myself to read it, for which I had not previously found time. As I have now finished with it I send you the book, which will perhaps excite and interest you more than it did me. Although I doubt whether anyone could have handled the subject more suitably, or even more poetically, than Liszt has done, yet there are many things in it which are not quite sympathetic to me, especially because they make me think that the Princess has had a hand in it. That does not prevent me from having found much beauty in it, such as Liszt alone could give to it.

I send you with this the manuscript for Isidore from Joachim. After I had complained to you in my last letter that Liszt did very little with me in the way of piano-playing, I gave myself the lie only a few days afterwards. That is often the way with me, and it makes me almost afraid to express myself definitely in letters about what concerns me ; it is like taking one's umbrella when one goes a walk. Liszt has allowed me and his other pupil (from Munich)—the third is studying musical theory at Eisenach with the organist Kühmstedt—to play a great deal under his direction ; he has made me study the great B Flat major Sonata of Beethoven, which I play not at all badly—in the Adagio Liszt praised me tremendously,—also Weber's 'Concertstück' with some added effects, and Beethoven's 'Fantasia.' Next time I shall play him the first movement of the E Flat major Concerto. My playing has lately very much changed for the better ; my fingers are gradually gaining that elasticity in which a good touch really consists, because it makes one capable of giving every possible *nuance*, and I find Liszt's method more and more to be the only truly artistic and practical one. I occasionally go so far as to be satisfied with myself, and I think I shall, in any case, belong to the better ones among pianists.

Now—the most important matter, namely to tell you about the Musical Festival, which is to be held at Ballenstedt on the 25th and

26th June. I shall have to go there a week beforehand as *ministre plénipotentaire.* Could not you manage to be present at my first great *début* as a pianist ? In addition to this, the concert and Liszt's conducting will be specially interesting in themselves. On the two days the following works are to be given : the Overture to ' Tannhäuser,' and ' King Alfred,' Mendelssohn's ' Walpurgisnacht,' Beethoven's ' Ninth,' Berlioz' ' Harold Symphony,' Wagner's ' Liebesmahl der Apostel ' (Last Supper), Duet from the ' Fliegender Holländer,' Liszt's music to a poem by the Duchess of Orleans, a Violin Concerto by David, the first Finale from ' Euryanthe,' and Beethoven's ' Choral Fantasia ' for piano and orchestra. Besides this last piece I may also perhaps play the ' Midsummer Night's Dream ' (Liszt's transcription, a solo), and the ' Tannhäuser ' Overture, which, when people have heard it by the orchestra, will be a grateful work for both Liszt and me. Once more—it would be very charming of you to give me your presence at this Festival ; do try to arrange it, and perhaps you will bring Isidore with you. Then let me know soon, so that I may get rooms for you, for there will be heaps of people. The printed song I am sending you herewith is published in an album, and appears in good company, with Liszt, Joachim and others.

The spring has made me much livelier again, and I feel better, both bodily and mentally, than in the winter months, which have this time been very sad ones for me.

I have altered my outside life here in one respect for the better, as I think ; with a sudden bold resolve I have given up the ' Erbprinz,' in spite of the fact that I can only pay my debts there little by little. I now dine at mid-day elsewhere with Cossmann, where it costs me only a little more than half what it used to do, and the fare is simpler and more wholesome. Indeed Cossmann forms my chief society now ; he is a quiet, soothing man of good French manners, clever, but somewhat apathetic. The end of the theatre season, when Cossmann goes to Baden and Liszt accompanies the Princess to Carlsbad, will probably change much of this. That time will be shortly after the Music-Festival. My trade of schoolmaster goes on pretty successfully. My two pupils are really getting on with me ; I am also much adored by them. The second is the niece of an English lady, who is a friend of Liszt, and he specially begged me to yield to the earnest wish of the aunt. The young lady, like all English girls, has a very negative musical talent, and plays wrong and out of time with true religious fervour ; so there is certainly not much to be done. The aunt has the extraordinary idea that her niece has a decided musical talent, and would be inconsolable if she were told the contrary and robbed of her belief ; so I try to do my best with unspeakable amiability.

My unpopularity here is unbounded; I rejoice in it to the utmost, because it is a sort of filial unpopularity to that of Liszt, and the saying, " qu'ils me haïssent, pourvu qu'ils me craignent " is applicable here. A caricature has even been circulated here, in which Liszt figures as Don Quixote and I as Sancho Panza.

Liszt took me lately with Cossmann and Mangold to Jena to see Stahr, who is settled there, and is very unwell.

Please write to me very soon, I do beg, or else let Isidore write. She has plenty of time and I have so little, and as she is so fond of me she should give me, with her pen, more frequent opportunity of gratefully acknowledging this.

In any case I hope to be able to have a talk with you by word of mouth before so very long. My head is so full of all sorts of different things that I had great trouble to disentangle to some degree all the things I wanted to say to you.

Liszt promised me that he would write to you; has he perhaps done so? On the other hand, Countess —— may wait a long time. " Qu'elle s'en aille au diable," were Liszt's very own words, which he uttered with comical anger when I gave him my information. . . .

Once more, do not be vexed at the long and unmerited delay, and take best thanks for your loving thoughts of me.

TO HIS FATHER.

WEIMAR, *25th May* 1852.

DEAREST FATHER,

If you have a spark of affection left for a son who, though his actions speak against him, has never for a moment ceased to think of you with the deepest love, I do beg you, above everything in the world, not to be angry with me any longer for the unhappy time now (thank the gods) past, but to forgive and forget. Perhaps, without this, the confession of all the misery I have gone through will soften you towards me. Though I was quite conscious that I owed you this confession, yet I have put it off all this time, partly from a certain timidity at having to recapitulate every little inward vexation of my own, and really also from want of the power to look at my own affairs as dispassionately as if they were somebody's else's. Once more, grant me this earnest request; do not be angry with me any longer, spare me all reproaches, for it is just these that I should find it most hard to bear,

H

and that would, by their severity, thwart all my endeavours to regain the happiness which I have almost lost.

That scandal which came to your ears about the famous (or infamous) Sontag article was undoubtedly the real beginning of unforeseen, and even almost unexpected consequences. I send you the article herewith : you can see for yourself how the momentary excitement of a lively indignation dictated it, and how entirely without calculation it was written. I can assure you that our astonishment was great when such a storm was raised against me from all sides, above all from Leipzig, when I was recognised as the author of the unexpected "voice of the minority," striking so mercilessly at one who was the idol of the hour to an irrational multitude.

Of course calumnious reports were also spread ; Liszt was accused of being the real author, and this authorship was ascribed to a petty revenge.

Had Liszt known of my intention he would at all events have tried to dissuade me from it ; but he did not see the article till it was in print, and too late to recommend me to write more moderately. As regards the calumny which touched himself he said nothing, and thereby gave me a lesson and an example of how I ought to behave towards injuries to myself. By this calm and resolute silence I have been able to preserve a demeanour that is in my favour, and I am sure I have thus avoided many unpleasantnesses. I have made a collection of the most violent attacks in the papers here, and from Leipzig, etc. ; if you were to read those you would understand in what a state of perpetual excitement and embitterment the long dragging on of these affairs has placed me ; though at the same time I did receive a few very flattering, but not very comforting, signs of recognition of my courage. Not merely people such as Robert Franz, Wagner, Herwegh, but even quite respectable Philistines, have given me to understand that they entirely approved of what I had done.

But now to the worst consequences which my venturesomeness has entailed. Sontag was foolish enough to lay such tremendous weight on my opinion that she, together with her mother, her husband, etc., had not anything better to do than to spread the affair abroad—unconscious that she was thereby making the best possible propaganda against herself. As soon as she came to Dresden she gave the reins to her anger by heaping up the strongest invectives against my humble self at all the houses where she visited. So it was not long before it came to my mother's ears from various quarters, and you can imagine that she was not particularly pleased about it. Spare me the details, the remembrance of which is even now painful to me. Only the principal thing : I should, really and truly, have had nothing to live on, had not my piano-teaching here brought me in a few thalers. I will only mention that, amongst other things, I had to do entirely without supper, and that my clothes had got into the most neglected condition. I was for the first time in real want; of course I would not borrow from anybody, because I had not the remotest idea when I should ever be able to pay back again; and besides this, my most intimate friends were none of them in a position to lend me anything. Before I would have asked Liszt to lend me any-thing—well, I really don't know what I would not have tried first! So I was obliged to pawn what little I possessed, and consequently I am so placed to-day that if anyone asks me "What's o'clock?" (a clock) I can only answer them by your joke, " a measure of time."

And up to the present time I have not been able to recover my old sense of humour, of which I used to possess a fair amount, but which, during that inauspicious time, has been conspicuous by its absence. You really cannot imagine into what a state of complete depression and despairing indifference I had fallen at that time. The feeling of wretched abandonment enervated me as much, physically, as it paralysed my mental powers, so that the work which was waiting to be done cost me immense efforts to do ; for I *have* worked, notwithstanding, and can show proofs of my industry.

The reason I did not write to you at that time was partly what I have already mentioned ; and if the necessity of confessing my position—for I was so down in the world that I could not have withstood the temptation of asking you to help me—kept me from writing to you, it was because it seemed to me that it would be the height of unworthiness on my part even to *appear* to fulfil my duty of writing to my father only when I was constrained to ask him for help.

No doubt this is all very incoherent and uninteresting for you to read, but my moral power is still so weak that I am not in a condition to arrange my confused thoughts and write them in an orderly manner, and must be satisfied with having conquered a stupidity which, I daresay, will seem less inexplicable to you when you have seen what a frame of mind I was in. I hope you will at least be willing to see, by my letter today, which I have been trying to write for nearly a fortnight, how much I long for a return to the old relations between us. You may be sure that the interruption of these has been much harder for me to bear, all alone as I was, than probably for you. In case you are angry with my letter, and give vent to your feelings, may Louise have the happy idea of making Willi use his promising lungs to drown your voice, and to be an honour to his musical brother by coming to his aid with such timely harmony.

Now to the most important things connected with my present or

my immediate future.   On the 22nd and 23rd of this month there is
going to be a grand Musical Festival at Ballenstedt, under Liszt's conducting.   I shall make my *début* on that occasion as a pianist and as a
pupil of Liszt, for the first time before such a large public, and shall
play, besides some solo pieces, Beethoven's ' Choral Fantasia,' for piano,
chorus and orchestra, a work of the composer's later period that is but
little known and that makes a great effect.

My piano-playing has latterly made substantial progress ; I have
gained in elasticity and a certain virtuoso *chic*, which was formerly
entirely wanting.   The great mastership of Liszt — apart from his
individual appearance and personality—rests principally on his marvellously expansive and manifold power of expressing outwardly what he
feels inwardly ; not merely in the perception and grasp of a musical
work, but in the way he can reproduce it outwardly, the extraordinarily
faithful embodiment of the spiritual.   Nothing is further from him than
calculated effects ; his genius as an artist consists chiefly in his certainty
of the effect he gives so brilliantly at every performance.   This point
in Liszt seems to me the most worthy because the most possible of
imitation, and I have tried for some time, and not without result, to copy
him somewhat in this.

I am very much delighted to find that Liszt intends to spend the
summer here, and will only be away at most four weeks, and that not
till August, when he accompanies the Princess to Carlsbad.   As he is
devoting a great deal of time to me and another young and rather
talented pupil from Munich, I can safely reckon on being set free next
December to start on my first predatory virtuoso-tour to Vienna and
Pest.

I have been composing very little, although I have not been entirely
idle in that respect.   But, on the other hand, I have written several
things for the musical press which are not at all bad, according to what
Liszt and others say.   My life otherwise has been of the simplest ; I
have been in no society whatever, except that of other artists.   Two
ladies whom I teach adore me, both for my talent and for my personal
amiability, in which I have made great progress.   However I don't care
about it.   On the other hand, I do care very much indeed to hear soon
from you that you forgive and forget.   Meanwhile,

Your loving son,

GIOVANNI PENITENTE.

W. Streckfuss pinxit 1855.   Gravure Meisenbach Riffarth & Co.

Hans v. Bülow

TO HIS FATHER.

WEIMAR, 28*th June* 1852.

DEAREST FATHER,

Only today have I got back, the last of the Weimar company, bodily and mentally refreshed by the glorious and never-to-be-forgotten days I have spent at the Musical Festival at Ballenstedt. The first thing I am taking in hand here is to answer your letter, which I received shortly after my arrival at Ballenstedt, when I was just in the most delightful excitement of having all kinds of things to do. I thank you from my heart for your willingness to forget the sad suspension of our happy relationship which lasted for a while, and your readiness to have some trust once more in my heart! It now lies with me to justify this trust, and I shall always be fully conscious of it. You may truly believe that, in spite of appearances being against me, I am so far from all indifference towards you that, on the contrary, I feel myself much nearer to you than I did in earlier years. I have reached an age which enables me to understand you better than I could formerly, and to find many points of contact with you which formerly were not visible to me. In many things I now have very similar views to yours ; and, where we do not have the same sympathies, I feel, with the warmest gratitude, that you come forward towards me and affectionately try to soften and to lessen the opposition, so that I feel that it is not only my duty, but also my natural desire, to do my part also. I feel the real need of communicating often with you, and I need only to follow the first promptings when they come to me. I feel so happy and pleasantly excited after the stay at Ballenstedt that I shall become much more expansive than I ever was before ; it is not in my nature to be so under depression and wretchedness, such as have been my companions here in the time that is past.

I will begin at once to tell you all about Ballenstedt. Perhaps you will have already heard from Isidore that I did meet her and mamma there. It was a meeting I very much wished for. Mamma, in the society of the excellent families v. Herder and Siegsfeld, was in a pretty forgiving frame of mind, for the after-effects of the Past were not yet extinguished, and the old mistrust of the success and the expectations of my musical career, increased as they were by the scandal I made as a writer, was still deep-rooted in her. Liszt, to whom she wrote some time ago, about the same time you did, had not wished and had not been able to answer her, and was therefore very much pleased to be able to talk to her personally at last, and to explain the necessary things to her. He has therefore quieted her all round to some extent ; at least, he has done so much that she has been tranquillized by him as she could have been by none other. That could not have been done in a letter. Liszt's personal amiability contributed its part towards this also. By his persuasion she remained for the Musical Festival, which she had at first declined to do, from motives of economy; and I had the satisfaction of seeing that my performances and their success gave her pleasure. Liszt was thoroughly satisfied with my playing at the concert, as well as at the Court, where we were invited to supper on the second day (Wednesday), through the very friendly and amiable Hofmarschall v. Siegsfeld. The Duchess and her sister, the Princess of Holstein, to whom I had been presented a couple of days before at a musical coffee-party at Frau v. Siegsfeld's,* were very amiable to me. As Liszt absolutely refused to play anything, I was obliged to come forward after supper as his official pupil, and I played for about an hour to the people, who really behaved extremely well, and listened with great interest. Liszt very much commended my sureness and unconstrainedness, and the extremely individual character of my performance, which, as he said, had surprised him, and had put before him the prospect of my self-dependence sooner than he had expected. You can well imagine that this praise has made me feel very happy and hopeful for the future. Mamma and Isidore, whom I found not looking very well, took their departure on Thursday at noon, stayed one night in Leipzig, and arrived in Munich the day after, whence, after a short stay, they will go straight to one of the German baths. I hope that the favourable impression which my *début* in Ballenstedt made on them will last, and act as a counterpoise to the other doubts and disagreements. Unfortunately I was hardly able to see anything of Isidore, for I was excessively occupied as Liszt's adjutant—that is to say, his musical adjutant—for Raff, who left a couple of days before Liszt and myself, had attended capitally to everything else. The whole Festival may be regarded as a particularly brilliant one, considering its impromptu character; for a week before it took place the whole undertaking was still uncertain. Liszt really worked wonders; in three days' rehearsals everything was in trim, and the orchestra, which was brought together from all parts, and the members of which were all strange to one another—chorus and orchestra numbered some 300 persons—was so thoroughly inducted into the work that it seemed as if they all belonged to *one* Society: Liszt's personality in conducting had inspired them and carried them away. The audience, it is true, numbered only 800 to 1000.

The *entrepreneur*, an hotel-keeper, a well-educated and very decent fellow, who was indeed quite ruined, but who nevertheless fulfilled every

---

* Frau v. Siegsfeld, a granddaughter of Herder.

duty he had undertaken towards those who were taking part, had acted rather unpractically through the whole affair, and had not chosen the right moment to try to weaken the effect of a couple of unfavourable, spiteful articles that had appeared in the paper. Such an article, for instance, had kept Stern's *Gesangverein* from coming, after they had firmly promised their assistance. Old Schneider in Dessau also played us a shabby trick. The orchestra there had promised its co-operation, and Schneider had openly placed them at our disposal; but as he was extremely indignant because they would neither perform his 'Weltgericht' (Last Judgment), nor any other composition of his, nor divide the conducting between Liszt and himself, he privately got every individual member of his orchestra to sign a round-robin to the effect that, out of devotion to him, none of them would take part in the Festival unless he went with them. So, then, not one of them came. The orchestra was composed of the Bernburg, Sondershausen, and the best part of the Weimar orchestras, and individual musicians from the neighbourhood were also pressed into the service. The vocal forces had been imported—the vocal Societies of Bernburg and Cöthen, and, above all, the Leipzig Students' Vocal Society, the *Pauliners*, who had come over under the leadership of their music-director Langer, sixty in number, all gifted with fresh, beautiful voices. Robert Franz from Halle had also brought a chorus of thirty ladies and gentlemen, in addition to which stray singers came from Berlin and Leipzig. The performances went off extremely successfully; the programme met with uncommon approbation, in spite of its very marked tendency. The second concert — I send you the programme herewith—did not take place till three o'clock in the afternoon, as the forenoon had to be used for rehearsal. In spite of the great fatigue, everything went like clockwork! The very limited time for rehearsal of the 'Berlioz' Symphony only allowed of the two middle movements being given. On the other hand, after the 'Walpurgisnacht' there was a lively demand for the repetition of the 'Tannhäuser' Overture, which thus formed the first and last links of the chain. The effect was immense. Liszt, who was welcomed both times with flourish of trumpets and applause, received at the end all the flowers of all the ladies present, which were thrown at him.

Besides playing my Fantasia, which was almost the most warmly applauded of any of the solo pieces, I had also to help in the 'Orpheus' scene, by playing the rather important harp part on the piano, owing to the indisposition of Fräulein Spohr,* the niece of the Kapellmeister, and I had also to accompany the 'Liebesmahl der Apostel,' in order to give

---

* Rosalie Spohr, afterwards married to Count Sauerma.

a little support here and there to the difficult vocal part (without accompaniment), so as to enable them to keep strictly in tune.

I also helped in the teaching of this work, and played the big drum in Raff's Overture. I nearly got in a rage about this afterwards, when I heard that Meyerbeer had once done the same service for Cherubini in one of his operas.

We had a very lively time at Ballenstedt. Kroll, Raff, Pruckner (my fellow-student as pianist in Liszt's school) and I had a nice large room, all four of us together, close to Liszt's. Of course our expenses there were paid for us, and we also had our journey there free. But the Herders and Siegsfelds did more than anybody else to make us enjoy ourselves, and they have the largest share of all our pleasant recollections of Ballenstedt. They gave us dinners and parties, and, above all, made things so comfortable for us that we felt quite at home there, because we really were so. And for me there was the special satisfaction that both ladies, who stand alone in their amiability, are democrats and Feuerbachers! Frau v. Siegsfeld sends you warm greetings. She has honoured me by presenting me with Feuerbach's latest book, which lay on her table, as a remembrance.

Liszt was unfortunately obliged to return to Weimar on Wednesday night. His mother, who had come to pay him a visit, fell downstairs in his absence, and sustained a fracture which at first appeared dangerous, but now it is considered certain that she will soon be all right again.

Kroll and I remained three days longer in B[allenstedt], as we had also promised to arrange a small private concert for Nehse, which therefore took place on the Saturday morning before a very few people. Nehse might have had an audience of 200; his great awkwardness and apathy ruined his chances.

On Thursday there was another soirée at the Siegsfelds', for which I had arranged the programme, and at which I had to do duty as accompanist to the singers, who are extremely fond of me in that capacity. On Friday we made an excursion to the Waldkater and Kessel, not far from the Rosstrappe—the Siegsfelds, Herders, Mildes, Spohrs, Schreck, etc. The weather was favourable, and it was a delightful after-celebration of the Festival.

What also especially enchained me to Ballenstedt was a small love-passion. I had not been in love for such a very long time that it possessed all the charm of novelty for me, and put me into a disposition which, if it should last for a while—which is possible—might be of great use to me musically in the coming time. As I am perfectly contented with my subjective inclination, you need not be afraid that I shall go and do something stupid; quite the contrary.

Liszt starts next Thursday for Brunswick, for the Musical Festival there, which Müller and Litolff will conduct. I am not going with him, notwithstanding that I might do it if it were necessary. I shall remain here, and try to recover by hard work from all my knocking about.

.   .   .   .

Is my style still so dreadful? I will really take pains to improve it, and am grateful to you for your warning. I can quite well bear the strongest expression of blame which comes so thoroughly from the heart.

TO HIS FATHER.

[WEIMAR, *end of July* 1852.]

DEAREST FATHER,

My heartiest good wishes and my most brotherly welcome to the new citizen of this world, who, I hope, will be as strong a fellow as Willi promises to become, and whose existence is a happiness to me for many reasons. Firstly, because I gain a new object for my brotherly-uncledom, from which I expect much honour and pleasure, so far as I may be called to have to do with him; and secondly, because the world is now the richer by two baronial democrats.

.   .   .   .

I already gave you a hint in my last letter of my present lyrical mood, so I need only add that it is happily not merely a mood, but is of a productive nature. I am at present writing a dozen songs (text by Heine, Sternau, and Petöfy, in the translation of Szarvady and Moritz Hauptmann), eight of which are already done. Liszt is very much interested in them. His criticism is of the greatest advantage to me; he discovers at once every intention, and then knows not only how to discover any chance contradiction between thought and form, but how to suggest the simplest and best means of putting it right. Hence he is, by his own experience, the best and most impressive adviser as to the observance of simplicity and clearness in the piano accompaniment—he who formerly did the most important things in exactly the contrary direction. His opinion of my songs was that they are "very beautiful, very much from the heart (*sehr innerlich*), finely conceived, and of a very original and individual colouring"—an opinion which has pleased me more, in silence, than any praise that has yet appeared in the papers.

It is, especially, a great comfort to me that he allows that I have individuality, because, according to my theory, it is only a very marked individuality, especially in Art, which as such (*eo ipso*) has a justification for its existence in respect to artistic creation. Besides the songs, I am already sketching my Overture to 'Romeo and Juliet.' About that, *i.e.* about my plan, which has been very much corrected by R[ichard] W[agner]—my first was too abstractly philosophical, too wanting in clearness—more some other time ; and I am collecting material for a big Pianoforte Trio. I have also in hand two concert paraphrases on pieces from 'Lohengrin ' and 'Tannhäuser,' which, through Liszt's mediation, will be published by Härtel in Leipzig, and, as a smaller and less taxing piece of work, the arrangement of the piano edition of Wagner's version of Gluck's 'Iphigenia in Aulis.' Had he done none other but this, in many respects, beautiful work, he would yet be worthy of the highest esteem. To learn to know the " why and wherefore " of this arrangement by a detailed insight into the score is a very great enjoyment. Wagner has left the work so uninjured, owing to his reverence for the great master, that he has, on the contrary, given the noblest and most positive proof of this. Truly the old saying, " Quod licet Iovi non licet bovi," is none the less applicable on that account. I think that, later on, in some *lustra*,* not before, I shall do the same for the 'Orpheus,' which also needs polishing up, if one would not have it become unenjoyable to the masses, and of only an occasional historical interest to the privileged few. My pianoforte arrangement is treated in a good, strong, simple style— perhaps as such it may become a model one. Certainly if I didn't succeed in such an easy task as this I should despair of myself. Whether I shall get all these things done before I go to Vienna I really don't know.

    .   .   .   .

Give my love to Louise and Willi, and a *Vivat* to the new-comer ! Farewell, best father ; I must be off to my teaching, and therefore conclude.

Hans being now extremely busy, and his letters, comparatively speaking, few and far between, a few extracts are here inserted from letters from his mother to his sister, written from Weimar :—

[*? November.*]

" Hans is well, but is looking wretched ; he is very industrious, but

---

* Periods of five years, in the old Roman days.

is in continual agitation ; he would be able to do such great things, but unfortunately he devotes most of his time to the glorification of Wagner. He is perfectly fanatical about it, and sacrifices himself entirely, placing himself and all his own aims in the background."

25th November.

" Hans was in a pretty state for the week, or rather, ten days of Berlioz' stay here : rehearsals, management of all sorts, doing the honours to strangers with and for Liszt, and on the top of all that the article on Berlioz ; never in bed before three o'clock ! Yesterday he was feeling rather out of spirits."

18th December.

.   .   .   .

" I have indeed seen Hans, but have hardly spoken to him ; he is very busy giving Spanish lessons to the little, or rather, the big Princess Marie, besides his music lessons, and a great deal of work with Liszt, and so on. . . . To-day I paid a visit with Hans to old Schwendler, who has known all possible people of interest, and remains perfectly fresh in spite of his eighty years. It amused me to see how Hans carried on an interesting conversation with as much ease as subtlety ; he is altogether very remarkable ; he has on the one side an incredible self-command, certainty, and *aplomb*, and then again a boundless imprudence, which may drag him into the worst quarrels, and there are more of such contrasts in his character."

29th December.

" On the last day we were all with Liszt, who played marvellously with Joachim (Kreutzer Sonata) ; at midnight they brought me home ; at half-past three in the morning I was again at the Arnims, and accompanied them to the station, where Liszt joined us with Joachim and Hans, and we all six started off in one *coupé.* . . .

New Year's Day to church early ; a letter from you. I dressed and went to the Princess's, where we dined with Talleyrand *en famille* but magnificently. After dinner Liszt sat with me alone for a couple of hours in an ante-room, and talked with me most affectionately about Hans ; he was very earnest, and reiterated many times, ' Je l'aime comme mon fils, je me regarde comme son père, et comme aujourd'hui ce sera en dix ans.' "

TO PETER CORNELIUS.

WEIMAR, 20*th December* 1852.

DEAR BROTHER AMONG ELEPHANTS,

The elephant is now opposite the other elephant at Werner's wine store, first floor, and we shall have a right jolly, elephantine sort of Christmas. The Arnims remain here till the New Year, and Joachim also, who is then going to be Concertmeister at Hanover—with advancement.

You are the only one wanting to our circle; there is a gap which you alone can and must fill; it is for you to complete the incomplete whole. So, without wasting words, make yourself ready, and come and be a light to us in Weimar, and that quickly, without delay.

You know you intended in any case to come back to us, and, even if it is only a flying visit, you will *never* again find Weimar just as it is now; therefore tear yourself away from the Westphalian hams and come here.

We are expecting you most positively and as quickly as possible, and will take no denial. Pack up your bundle and come; bring my shirt with you, in exchange for which you shall have your shawl, which I am meanwhile using.

You belong to a society, a league, to which you have sworn no obedience, wherefore you owe it all the more. It is commanded you to start off at once, and to come and thaw with us as soon as possible, for you must be half frozen.

You are such an unceremonious sort of fellow that I need not add another word to this letter and the order it contains. All the more, it is enough that I am in a hurry to send off this letter; for four other people besides myself are dying of impatience to see you.

The knight Franz will also rejoice to see you again; it is, it must be, of consequence to you also to meet him again at a time when things are quieter than formerly.

Let us have a line to say when we may expect you at the station. My address is " Carlsplatz 28, c/o Professor Schwerdtgeburth" (opposite Joachim). I have been settled there a fortnight as a *self-govern* * man.

It goes without saying that you will stay either with one of us or

---

* These two words are put in English by Bülow.

with the Arnims, who have plenty of spare room. You should just see the rows and disputes there will be amongst us about this.

Adieu, and to our very speedy meeting.

TO HIS SISTER.

WEIMAR, 28*th December* 1852.

DEAREST SISTER,

.   .   .   .

I have thought very often of you during the Christmas days, and I have been really very sorry that our mutual correspondence has had such a long rest. I have reproached myself very much about this, but I really *could* not help it. I have been so very much engrossed lately, mentally, and stand so alone in this ; and it would be quite a Herculean and Danaïd work to write full particulars to anyone of things which I can't always make clear to myself, and which someone else would understand still less, and would misunderstand still more.

Mamma will have written you word how we spent our Christmas evening here at the Arnims'. She herself had one of her unfortunate sick headaches, and was very uneasy at the non-arrival of news from you. She has got so accustomed to hearing from you often, and rejoices a whole week over your letters in prospective, by which you have much increased her great tenderness for you. So go on writing to her often, especially as it is a satisfaction to you to be able to express yourself freely from your heart.

Bettina has given Joachim and me each a glass on which the names of the three fairies are engraved. That was the nicest possible Christmas present to us.

Joachim goes at New Year to Hanover, where he is taking a very brilliant and important position. His departure would be a great trouble to me—and it also comes at the same time as that of the Arnim family, who have really grown into my very heart—were it not that the time I still have in Weimar myself may also be counted by days. For Liszt has fixed the beginning of February for my going to Vienna ; I am not anxious, but only curious to see how it will fare with me there.

No doubt you already know that mamma made me come down from the Altenburg, and has got me lodgings in the town. I should have been perfectly frozen up there during the winter, and should have been without any attendance and every sort of care ; and so, for a thousand other weighty reasons, I am uncommonly glad to live in town, about fifty steps from where mamma is living.

In Jena I played lately twice within a fortnight at the academical concerts, and pleased much. I tell you this because it is perhaps not a matter of indifference to you.

Do write soon and tell me what you are thinking of doing or of leaving undone for the future—how long you are going to stay at Ötlishausen, etc. I heard through mamma with great sympathy of your feelings about your stay there. Work and enjoy yourself in the solitude, which can also be a real happiness—a happiness for which I have long wished enormously.

Anyone else in my place might perhaps be quite contented with some good-will; . . . that I can't be so, with that everything is said. Things have no value *in themselves*, and they only attain it by their relation to that *for* which they exist.

May the New Year be a right happy one for you! Look to one thing alone before all else—your health—and take as much care of it as though it were the property of someone else. Then freshness and courage will return again to you, and you will be able to become something for *yourself;* and that is the chief thing. Outside ourselves we find nothing, absolutely and entirely nothing, confoundedly *nothing*.

Give my love to Louise and the two little ones; and let me soon hear from you, as I also regard this letter only as a *contre-marque*.

TO HIS MOTHER.

LEIPZIG, *last of December* 1852.

DEAREST MOTHER,

Heartiest love and good wishes for the New Year. That you are perhaps beginning it, alas! sadly and alone this time, is the only thing that troubles the happy days here, in which I am gliding from '52 into '53. Our journey was an uncommonly pleasant one; we were all in the highest good-humour. And then we still had to consider two proposals which I laid before them; the first on our early journey, the second with somewhat desperate efforts. The results are, first, that we all six yesterday, all five to-day—for Liszt started off at seven o'clock—are living together in the 'Hotel de Bavière' and the adjoining house, without any hotel scandal, and on the first floor; secondly, that the Arnims, as well as Joachim, will not leave here till early on Sunday morning. It has cost me rewarded trouble, yet trouble, to bring them round to this, and to frighten them into writing to their family to put off their journey.

I ordered the two bouquets, at one reichsthaler, quite early this morning, at the florist Rohland's, in Auerbach's Hof, and you may count on them for certain.

In the morning I went about with Liszt and Joachim, to Senff, and to Härtel, where I had to play a piece from the 'Midsummer Night's Dream;' also to David and Gade, whom we did not find at home. At two o'clock we dined together, *entre nous,* and soon after that Liszt received visits from David, Radecke,* and Brendel. Then I went with the Arnims, who had a heap of commissions to do, for the Princess amongst others, whereby I have made fresh progress in my Sardanapalisation. In the evening we went to see Kistner, then went to a party at Brendel's; but our visit only lasted for half an hour, for by nine o'clock we were with the Arnims at a party at David's, where a gorgeous supper was arranged, and where I distinguished myself still more gorgeously on a wretched grand piano. Liszt was really *excessively pleased* with me. I played with great certainty and freedom, and even astonished him, as well as everybody else. He will tell you about it himself when you see him tomorrow. We were, in case I was back in time, to dine with the Princess on New Year's Day. I am writing very hurriedly, but it is impossible to give you any news except in this broken fashion. You will rather have it than none. Yesterday evening was really an important one for me. Liszt expressed to me several times his extreme pleasure at my " confirmation " of his hopes, and was altogether unspeakably good to me.

Senff, Gade, Radecke, even David, etc., have given me high praise. Tomorrow will be an interesting concert. I shall go to the rehearsal for an hour today, because they have all invited me to it. Joachim is getting impatient, but gives you a hand-kiss herewith.

I am feeling fabulously well in every respect, and should like to extend my stay a few days longer, as I have made my *début* here so successfully and well. People come forward to me in a very kind manner.

If the Arnims were not asleep they would send you a thousand warm greetings.

The town has really become very handsome since I was last here. No doubt at the moment I am seeing everything through rose-coloured spectacles. Once more let me assure you that, from the point of utility, a few days more here would be very advantageous to me, and so do let me have them.

I will write and let you know when I am coming. Liszt will

---

* Robert Radecke (born 1830), conductor, composer ; from 1871-87 conductor in Berlin ; at present Director of the Royal Institute for Church Music in Berlin.

probably call on you, so don't be out too much. At Liszt's most stringent command, I had to get yesterday a new and very elegant hat ; the old one was too good-for-nothing, and I could not go out either with Liszt or the Arnims in it. For this expenditure of 3½ reichsthaler for a birthday present *de fait* I am therefore not answerable.

TO HIS MOTHER.

LEIPZIG, 3*rd January* 1853,
HOTEL DE BAVIÈRE 40.

DEAREST MOTHER,
Warmest greetings from the Arnims and Joachim, whom I left at six o'clock yesterday at Köthen. If the former had not spent all their money—and we tried very hard to get them to stay a few days longer—I believe they would have done so. I was going to say goodbye to them at the Leipzig station at half-past three, when Fräulein Armgart said it was so obviously impossible that I should not accompany them as far as Köthen, that I could not do otherwise. There were now two projects mooted : first, to stay the night at Köthen ; and, finally, the more bold stroke that Joachim and I should both go with the Arnims as far as Jüterbog, and then return by the night train ; but both these plans were given up when we found at Köthen that the trains fitted in so well for us all that Joachim could start for Magdeburg at half-past seven, and that I could return to Leipzig at the same moment. So Joachim and I had an hour and a half together, and could lament in common, and talk of many things in which we had a common interest. I must confess to you that I felt the parting very keenly, and today I feel rather out of my mind. I cannot come to Weimar, and also I have not yet been able to do various commissions, nor to begin to copy and correct my songs. Today I shall most likely spend the whole day shut up in my room, and tomorrow evening, or early the next morning, I will return to Weimar.

We spent New Year's Eve at Prof. Fechner's—pleasant people— whose *famulus*, with whom I was once slightly acquainted, and Prof. Weisse were the only other people there. The Schletter picture-gallery, which contains some capital works of art, the New Year concert, a kind of musical afternoon-matinée at Joachim's former teacher, Dr Klengel's, filled up our New Year's Day.

If you are ever able to think yourself into my frame of mind you will understand that I cannot venture at this moment to come back. I am feeling too unhappy to do so. Today I shall, in perfect quiet, pre-

pare my songs for the press—I shall hardly get them done—since I cannot accomplish this quickly in Weimar, as is necessary.

I hope you have begun the New Year happily, and without headache, and that you have received the bouquets and seen Liszt.   Before
my departure I have still to see David, Radecke, Kistner, and others, so
that the time still remaining to me here is quite filled up. . . .

TO HIS FATHER.

WEIMAR, *8th January* 1853.

DEAREST FATHER,
                       Today, the 8th January, I have spent my birthday until
five o'clock this afternoon in bed, very unwell, full of sad and gloomy
thoughts on the one side, and on the other with the fatalist's resolution
of resignation to the inevitable, and to the lot assigned to me.   The New
Year has begun very sadly for me, with the sudden death, a few days
ago, of Theodor Uhlig in Dresden, an old friend of mine whom I deeply
loved and respected.   Nevertheless today I have finished with many of
the old things, and have made many plans, the fulfilment of which is all
the more sure as they are called forth by my own free will, and neither by
religious nor moral introspection.   I am conscious that this New Year just
begun is the *Va Banque* of my life,* and I look steadfastly, though
also without undue exhilaration, at the shaping of my future.

You have yourself so often described your position towards me as
just that of my best older friend, and have thereby abdicated the throne
of traditional parental authority in favour of a much nobler and more
beautiful one.

It has been an unspeakable grief to me to get an answer from you
to my letter for your birthday—in spite of my earnest request—an answer
which was more miserable than I could have foreseen when I opened the
letter in fear and trembling.   If you had not written, I could have
accomplished, in a succession of letters, what I had no heart for after
your reply.

And whilst I should have endeavoured in this manner to bring myself nearer to you again, I should have followed my real inner need ; it
is indeed only according to the measure of your love for me that you can
expect to enter into my position and frame of mind, which are of such
an individual and special nature that they can only be understood by one
who is with me, and cannot be judged by someone hundreds of miles
away.   I am sure I am one of the least egotistic men that can be, but

---

* Meaning " The die is cast."

I

it is only natural that one should be more disposed at the moment to rely on those who are near at hand, to give support to a man in process of development, who does not yet stand on his own feet, who is not yet independent, such as myself. I break off, because I have abjured all bitterness of heart with the coming of the New Year.

One thing which makes it ever so much easier for me to lay aside this bitterness of heart, as well as many other inborn self-tormentings, is the acquaintance and intimate intercourse I have had through Liszt with Frau von Arnim and her daughters. I have so very much to thank these delightful people for, for they have done me ever so much good in all sorts of ways, and their coming, and the being with them in Weimar, forms one of the brightest spots in my existence. Without exercising any injurious influence on my personal liberty, much that is hard and uncouth in my outer self has been smoothed and softened by them, for my own good alone. The truly rare sympathy, the manner in which they singled me out, and the regard they showed me, have increased and strengthened my faith in myself—a thing so absolutely necessary to me in the time when I must come out into publicity and into life with my own individuality—and have helped me indirectly to concentrate more firmly my often absent mind, and have certainly also kept me from many a stupidity or foolishness, into which my misanthropic and belligerent temperament might otherwise have led me, without their *Deus-ex-machinâ*-appearance. With Fräulein Armgart—upon whom my interest was concentrated from the very beginning—especially, I have struck up a friendship which stands foremost in the inventory of my present feelings. Unfortunately my antipathy to correspondence will not allow me to keep up an unbroken intercourse with these delightful people. . . .

I hope by the end of this year to be able to congratulate you on the year and on myself : at the beginning of next month, somewhere about the 8th or 10th February, I am leaving here (at Liszt's desire) to give at once my first concert in Vienna, which, by Liszt's mediation, will be announced and arranged for me before my arrival by the music-publisher Haslinger, whom I got to know personally last year in Weimar.

Liszt prognosticates a great success for me   He will write to you quite fully about me before I start. He has really not had time as yet, and also he could not write anything so definite before, as he now can ; he wanted first to know me better, and to be able definitely to gauge the hopes which he has formed of me. He is extremely attached to me, and assures me of this constantly ; he does more, he proves it by his actions. What has made me the more dear to him is not the understanding I have for him and for Art in general—not my talent, which is distantly related to his—but my heart, and unegotistic, ready perception, which I showed, for instance, on the occasion of Berlioz' visit to Weimar, when I tried in every possible way and with the utmost zeal to be of service to him, both by writing and by action. My relations to Liszt are altogether different from, and much less disturbed and much clearer than, those of any other pupil or of any young artist patronised by him.

The manner in which I went through the rehearsals for public performances (after Ballenstedt) this summer at Erfurt and twice at Jena, where I made my *début*, but always without payment ; the certainty with which I also recently made my appearence as his pupil at an evening party at Concertmeister David's in Leipzig, and on a rather poor instrument— all this confirms him in his hopes for me. My first tour will conclude at latest by the middle of July. I shall only give concerts in the Austrian Monarchy — principal points, Vienna and Pest,—and then I shall return to Weimar until something fresh is settled. Liszt thinks I shall " earn " a clear profit of 2000 gulden, or even more.

But in order that I may start on my career comforted and happy, I must be at peace with all those nearest to me, with whom any misunderstanding makes me wretched. My mother, on whose frame of mind in general, as well as on whose attitude towards me, the Arnims have had the happiest influence, appears quite reconciled to me, without any looking back or any remains of old antipathies. Will you not be the same, and believe in my devotion and love ?

In my next letter I hope to be able to send you a printed copy of my songs published in Leipzig as Op. 1.

TO HIS FATHER.

WEIMAR, 27*th January* 1853.

DEAREST FATHER,

My warmest thanks for your kind letter, which has lightened my heart of a heavy burden. Also for the enclosed assistance for my journey, which I have likewise thankfully received, and mainly used in paying a few remaining debts. It pleases me immensely to have you again—even if bodily absent—present as a spectator of my future successes and failures, and to reckon you among those interested in the racing of my fingers. I hope often to be able to send you reports —and good ones—from Vienna. Happiness makes me as happy to write as it makes me talkative, and only when in a bad humour and despondent do I forcibly give myself up to isolation and retirement, because when the *ne plus ultra* of loneliness and wretchedness is reached, there *must* be a change for the better.

You will get a very discontented note from me today ; but for some weeks past I have felt my brain in such a state of tumult that I have had to give up thinking. My piano and my landlord can both testify to this ; they have both suffered during this interregnum of my piano-hammering hands. I practise about eight hours daily, and in the way in which I do it—the only one by which I can get any results—it is pretty irritating, so that I dare attempt nothing further except the care of my bodily health. In about ten days I shall be ready for my journey. I must first get several manuscripts of Liszt's copied which he has lent me to take with me, which will be a most interesting addition to my *répertoire*, and of great value to me, and I must then study them as quickly as possible. Among them is, for instance, one of Weber's Polonaises, instrumented and arranged for orchestra ; a Fantasia on Beethoven's ' Ruins of Athens,' for piano and orchestra, and another on Hungarian themes ; all these are by Liszt, and perfectly new, not even known by name. Then, indeed, before I am really absolutely ready to start, there is only the unavoidable necessity of having my passport made ready. May I ask your help in this matter? To enable me to get to Vienna without hindrance, my passport must at any rate have the *visé* of the Austrian ambassador in Berne. I should think there will be as little difficulty in getting this in Berne as Berlancourt has made in giving me a *visé* for the Prussian States and the Grand Dukedom of Baden— the latter without my even asking for it, out of extreme Christian human kindness. Will you then be so very good as to relieve me of this burden of citizenship, and to get the official to be quick. Be assured of my thanks beforehand. I wait here, of course, till I get the passport back, *viséd* or not, and will at once let you know of its arrival and of the date of my departure.

I have long since determined and prepared strictly to follow your advice, to keep a sevenfold seal upon my lips and their guardian, my heart, not only as regards politics, but in other matters also. Just as I would not think of packing in my luggage one of Proudhon's pamphlets concerning 1848, so I do not scruple to leave many of my opinions, wishes, plans, sympathies, and antipathies behind me. As regards politics especially, I have for a considerable time belonged to those people who are indifferent from a feeling of disgust ; and little by little a number of protecting membranes have formed round the still dark-red heart of my political and socialistic bulb of opinion. I have for a long time resolved and prepared to draw a curtain over my most secret inner being, aspirations and endeavours, which, should it happen to be open for ventilation, would close automatically at the sight of black and yellow barriers. My exact intention in going to Vienna consists in this, to make as much money as possible; for a peaceful independence is absolutely essential to me for the life and activity of an artist, such as I wish and hope to become. Of course (and in this you will certainly trust me) I can never be tempted to become a traitor to my artistic Confession of Faith, or to renounce the unalterable and plain principles which I hold here. Liszt will pretty nearly arrange beforehand the programme for the four concerts which I am to give in Vienna, and will also specify in what private circles or *salons* I should or should not play, etc. In addition to his own letters of introduction I shall also have some of a very different kind from Frau v. Lüttichau, from Noëls (at Thun), from the von Arnims, Fanny Lewald and others, so that I shall have opportunity of making myself sufficiently known.

Your letter was, alas, somewhat laconic; about yourself, Louise, and Isidore, of whom I should so gladly have heard something more through you, there was not a single word, nor about Willi and Heinz. I hope and beg much that you will make up for this next time, so that I may not feel myself so much of a stranger in the family circle at Ötlishausen.

It will, besides, not do for you to write to me in Vienna about your literary and poetical work, in so far as this is connected with the present time and its occurrences—this one remark will show you that I am on my guard; and I have not only forbidden any suspicious subjects to be mentioned in letters to me there, but have especially declined to receive letters from friends who are at all notorious. Liszt wished you would sometime make him a present of your works, at any rate of your original work, your novels, etc. Please do so when you have a suitable opportunity. My Spanish pupil—the young Princess Wittgenstein—reads Manzoni's ' I Promessi Sposi ' with the assistance of your translation. I had got on so well in Spanish that the Princess did me the honour to make use of my knowledge of it for the benefit of her daughter, who, not possessing any particular social talents (such as music or drawing), was to be made a linguist. This has taken up a good deal of my time, but its loss was made up for by an equivalent which enabled me to repay part of my debt to the Altenburg, to improve myself in knowledge of the language, and to make the better acquaintance of the amiable and clever young lady. We have read together ' The Faithful Prince,' ' Zenobia,' ' The Physician of His Honour,' and the ' Devotion to the Cross,' pretty quickly and without any assistance in the translation.

Frau von Herder and her son Alexander have been here several weeks, and will probably remain here for some time. We see her occasionally, though not often. I have, alas, not time enough to form a nearer acquaintance with Herr von Herder, which I should much like to do. They send their best remembrances to you. I shall write a few lines to Isidore, if possible, when I come back from Liszt, who will give us, his pupils, a lesson again today for an hour or so.

It would be a great pleasure to me if, after a successful result of my journey to Vienna and Pest, which will end just in the best travelling time of the summer, I could visit you in Ötlishausen, where I should possibly still find Isidore.

My mother will feel rather lonely after parting with me. She intends to spend a week in Jena, and then to go to Dresden, which is always a much pleasanter place of abode for her, when I am not with her, than Weimar.

It must have been shortly after receiving the above letter that Eduard von Bülow wrote one to his cousin Ernst, from which an extract is given below, not only because it is the last letter of his extant, but, above all, because it is satisfactory to see that, so short a time before his own death, he was entirely at one with his son's profession and development.

EDUARD TO ERNST VON BÜLOW.

[1853.]

. . . "Hans has completed his musical education. His first composition is just coming out in Leipzig, and he is now going off on his first great concert-tour to Vienna and Pest. If he is fortunate, we shall soon hear things publicly to his honour. Liszt has the *highest* expectations of his success, and has earned Hans' deepest gratitude by having entirely reconciled his mother to himself and his vocation. I am thoroughly satisfied with him in every respect, both as regards the development of his character, conduct, learning and art. He is happy and contented in the latter, and will, as I confidently hope, do us honour.

In his political principles he remains unchanged, for which God be praised ; but he has learnt to control himself and to be silent—until better times. You will perhaps smile at the rosy colour of this letter, but I assure you it is real ; and, should Heaven sooner or later afflict me with the reverse of the medal, well, I must bear it too." . . .

Franziska, writing from Dresden to her daughter at Ötlishausen, on the 4th March 1853, says :—

" At a quarter to ten on Wednesday night Hans started for Vienna, where I earnestly hope he has safely arrived. He has six letters from

Liszt—letters such as he rarely gives.   Amongst other things Liszt writes :—

'Je réclame tous les services de mes amis pour lui comme pour moi même, et les considérerais comme rendus à ma personne, car je le reconnais comme mon successeur légitime, comme mon héritier de par la grâce de Dieu et de son talent.'"

AUSTRIA

CHAPTER VII.

AUSTRIA.

SPRING—SUMMER, 1853.

TO HIS MOTHER.

VIENNA, *Palm Sunday,* 1853, 12th March.

DEAREST MOTHER,

You will have been anxious at hearing nothing from me for so long. I am extremely sorry about it, but I did not want to make you *positively* unhappy for no good, and that is the reason I did not write. I wanted to wait till I had given my second concert, at which a change for the better in my fate was possible—this second concert took place yesterday (Saturday) evening at half-past 9 o'clock. Now my patience to bear my unlucky fate is quite exhausted. I am writing this to you in bed ; I have no strength to get up, and I only wonder that my disgust with life allows me to write at all.

My first concert, apart from expenses, which amounted to 133 florins 16 kreutzer, brought me in 28 florins—I have all the receipts, so that I know I have not been cheated. So that I had 105 florins to pay ! With this amount to the bad, I had bought the privilege of seeing my name cut up in the most nonsensical manner in more than a dozen papers. Ignominious existence ! I have fretted about this comparatively little, but it has disheartened me nevertheless, and made me unhappy, in spite of the success which I enjoyed with a free-ticket public. None of my introductions have been of the slightest use. Stockhausen, Dietrichstein, Thun, Könneritz,—not a man amongst them came to either of my concerts. Liszt's letters have been of just as little use to me. No one has shown the slightest interest in me, except Haslinger, who did so "ex officio," looking after the business arrangements for me—if I had

done it alone it would have been more economical—and Dr Liszt* and
Löwy.† You have no idea how lonely and dreadfully forsaken I feel !
Living here is immoderately dear.   I did not remain 48 hours in the
hotel, yet they reckoned it as 3 days by the dates ; by great good luck
I found some lodgings in the inner city, on the second floor, for 15
florins a month without attendance.   That is tremendously cheap for
here.   My address for the present is, Spenglergasse, ' Zum Auge Gottes,'
c/o Herr Landrath von Bujan.   In a suburb I could not possibly have
lived ; it would have been too far away, and the mud in the 37 suburbs
is so thick that one might spend a whole day in getting from one road
to another.   I am as much exhausted as my purse is from the constant
running and driving about.   In spite of the utmost economy, one spends
more here in a single week than in three weeks anywhere else.   If Liszt
had not lent me 200 florins, instead of 100, I should have had nothing
to live on after I had paid for my first concert.   I can give you proofs of
my carefulness if it interests you, as I have kept an exact account of my
expenditure from day to day.

If only you knew how hard it is to me to go on writing ; how difficult it is to me to conquer the deep loathing that my present experiences
in Vienna have given me, in order to tell you how things have gone with
me, and what a pitiable state of mind and life mine is at present !   As if
I had not had enough unhappiness up to now !   What will happen to me
next, I have not the remotest idea.   Thus much as a preliminary : the
costs of my second concert, which will run up to about the same sum as
the first, I cannot pay, even if I left myself without a farthing in my
pocket.   Possibly someone will lend me the money ; perhaps Löwy, but
perhaps also not.   Perhaps His Majesty *Chance* will help me, if misery
gives me a letter of recommendation to him.   I am on the right road to
become a great man, according to Napoleon's judgment.   Moreover the
inauguration of the proletariat is not enjoyable.   Today my strength
feels quite shattered ; perhaps tomorrow I shall recover it.   For once I
shall experience the piquant situation of living not merely from day to
day, but from hour to hour.   Perhaps tomorrow I shall say quite truly
" I have rested my hopes upon nothing."   But, alas, that is impossible,
as my hopes are already resting on less than nothing.   But I have not
told you anything about yesterday.   I practised the whole day like a
madman.   When, late in the afternoon, I learned that not a fifth of my
expenses would be covered, when I saw that the wretched weather would

---

* Dr Eduard Liszt was the younger step-brother of Franz Liszt's father ; Liszt
was accustomed to call him his cousin.

† Löwy, a banker, and friend of Liszt.

probably keep away the few people who *did* intend to be present, such a state of stupidity and overpowering despondency took possession of me that I became quite unsusceptible to any applause, and played the last piece (Midsummer Night's Dream) almost badly. (Don't imagine that the lateness of the hour was a stupidity on my part—here you cannot do otherwise—no concert takes place while the theatre is going on, and people like best to come on to a concert from the Italian Opera.) There was only one feeble call for me at the end, which is here equivalent to a fiasco. You have no idea how I felt; I should just have liked to break off in the middle of my playing and hurl a few chairs at the public, and improvise the most utter rubbish on the piano—the critic will inveigh against me in any case, I thought to myself; in any case I have *not* the wherewith to pay the expenses! Last night I was in a perfect fever, and could not sleep; perhaps I shall have a downright illness.

Of Vienna itself I have seen very little. Before the result of my concerts I have been to no theatre, and would not go in for any pleasure of any kind. If only I knew what will become of me now, and what I must, or rather can, attempt. For today I can stop in bed and not trouble myself about anything;—but tomorrow? Curses on my coming to Vienna! I should have done better to accept the post Frau v. Lüttichau offered me, through you, of accompanist or chorus-director in Dresden, than to pay for the chase after a shadow by the loss of all happiness in life.

On the 3rd April I am to play Bach's Triple Concerto at a *concert spirituel* with the pianist Dachs and Professor Fischhoff, who, although I had no introduction to him, has received me in the most friendly manner. The invitation is an honourable one, but of course I don't know how much longer I shall stay here. Probably nothing will come of it. I understand now the expression, "forsaken by God and all the world."

On you, dear mother, I would on no account—do you hear, on *no* account—be a burden any longer. If however there could be anything done with regard to the accompanist post in Dresden—I should not like to come to grief here ignominiously. Nowhere do I see a way out, nowhere does a rescuing hand show me such a thing. And my superstition that I shall not die before September 1855 forsakes me, as that in Liszt's ring* and some other superstitions have already forsaken me.

I, fool that I was, thought that I should find roses in Vienna, my hands still bleeding from the thorns of earlier days! *Spine senza rose!*

---

* Liszt lent Bülow a ring as a talisman.

That also applies, because the two Spinas,* to whom Liszt introduced me, have done nothing whatever for me.

If I see any prospect of the slightest improvement in my position, I will write to you at once, so as not to keep you longer in suspense. I promise you this by all the love and gratitude I feel towards you.

.   .   .   .

The poor mother, at home in Dresden, passed through a long and weary time of waiting, till at last, after receiving the first letter from Vienna (the above), she wrote to her daughter :

"From Hans I have only heard once, and that was bad news ; I am hourly hoping for better tidings. Liszt, with whom I am in correspondence, does certainly not lose hope, but, much as I love him, that does not comfort me. Everything that I foresaw, when he took that unlucky step in the autumn of 1850, has come to pass literally. God forgive those who led him to it."

LISZT TO FRANZISKA V. BÜLOW.

WEYMAR, 26*th March* [1853].

MADAME,

Before receiving your letter, for which I beg you to accept my best thanks, I had received from various quarters news of your son, who, up to the present time, has not written to me. Upon the whole, I am far from judging his actual position at Vienna to be as bad as he seems to have described it to you. The losses which his two first concerts have occasioned him can easily be made up, and I am going to write to him directly, to recommend him in a friendly spirit not to give way to a despondency or ill-humour which would not be at all in season. The experience I have gained in these matters allows me to tranquillize you as to the final result of his journey to Vienna, which, I am persuaded, will appear more favourable to the interests of his talent, his career, and even his purse, than you imagine possible at this moment. The only thing necessary is that he must not let himself be discouraged, and that he must preserve a little *sangfroid*, in order to profit by the means which will continue to offer, of conquering step by step the ground to which he has a right. The bitter and onesided tone of the newspaper critic ought not to make him in the least uneasy ; he must learn to bear his part in these things quietly, like a man of sense and talent : chances of this sort must not be considered as sinister, and have never prevented anybody

---

* Music publishers in Vienna.

from taking his right place, as our friend Hans will be able to do, be it a little sooner or a little later.   During the months of April and May I advise him to remain in Vienna, except for a short journey to Pest at an opportune moment, about which they will be able to advise him at Vienna.   It is probable that he will earn some money at Pest, and perhaps at Pressburg; but, in order to attain this end, I consider it indispensable for him to take a more permanent footing in Vienna than he can do in a fortnight.   As he is extremely intelligent, and possesses all that is needful to make a good and fine career, it will be best to leave him entirely free in his actions and movements during these two months, and simply to help him to bear calmly the ill-chances which are inevitable in this profession.

My cousin, Dr Eduard Liszt, will remit to him the 100 florins which he wants at once, and he will hold another 100 at his disposal later on.

Pray believe me, Madame; there is really nothing to be anxious about, still less to lament over Hans in regard to his two concerts in Vienna, and I hope you will soon get news which will help to make you share the security and confidence which I continue to hold.—Pray believe me, Madame, with every expression of respectful friendship, yours sincerely,

F. Liszt.

TO HIS MOTHER.

Vienna, *27th March* 1853.

Dearest Mother,

A thousand thanks for your dear letter, which has done me no end of good! Certainly if there ever were a time when I needed it, this letter is a convincing proof that I have no cause to feel myself alone and forsaken! I have had to go through much here up to the present time—vexations enough for a whole year, and all compressed into scarcely three weeks. Passion week, at the beginning of which I wrote to you, brought me so many unpleasant experiences. The severe influenza from which I have been suffering, and which is now over, gave me an opportunity to rest a little, which was no small advantage to me, after the nervous excitement into which events now past had thrown me. Much as I missed the care which would have enabled me to throw off my severe cold much sooner, yet I was comforted for the want of it by the thought that you could not hear the dreadful concert my cough made, which forcibly reminded me of the happier days of my childhood. However I hope to be better in a few days than I was when I arrived in Vienna, ready to carry on my career with new and fresh energy, with the feeling of having got back to my old self again, since you advise me to do this, and will not forsake me.

Liszt has been already fully informed of the unfortunate results of my first two concerts, and of the non-success of his letters of introduction, etc.; of course not by me—that would not have been proper—but by Löwy and Haslinger.

Let me give vent here to my anger about one of the wretched things that happened to me, of which I have gone through so many; I am certain you won't misunderstand my feelings about it.

That rich Councillor *X.* (the composer), for whom Liszt has done so much—he has given two of his operas in Weimar, having touched up his last score *à la Voltaire*—and to whom he very specially introduced me, did not go to my first concert, although I had already played in his salon one evening. One morning he is at Haslinger's, making an offer to their publishing firm, when I accidentally come in; I praise his songs and his opera with the unfeigned wellwishing of impartial irony, and express the wish to utilize some of the motifs out of his last opera for a piano piece —that very morning I had made up a combination of them in involuntary reminiscences at the piano—and am now really taken up with doing this, as he naturally brought me the opera at once, the other day. He was visibly touched, and when, later on, Haslinger reproached him for not having gone to my concert after I had already played to him, he took 3 reserved stalls, but did not pay for them at the time. And I saw him at my second concert with his wife and child—the concert-room man has been to him several times to ask for the 9 florins, and was dismissed the last time by *X.*, who said he would pay me the money himself. As *X.* has sense and also knows me a little, you can well imagine that he never intended for a moment to commit any such insolence. But he did commit that of asking me the other day to meet Dreyschock, who was to play at his house. Although I was ill, of course I went, in order not to give occasion, by my absence, to any misconstruction. Except for this, *X.* is sensible, amiable, and a most decent fellow!

One who stands out as quite an exceptional man, not only in himself, but also towards me, is Eduard Liszt, cousin, or rather, young uncle of the real one. A most excellent man, one in whom one might have absolute confidence, without any repeated solicitation. He advanced me some money also lately on his own authority, when I told him in what want I was placed.

A few days ago Liszt wrote to me and begged me to do him a service. It is a diplomatic-musical mission to a Hungarian Count, who has a property in the neighbourhood of Ödenburg. He has given me the necessary 30 florins for the journey. I shall start in a few days' time if the weather improves a little : we have had such a severe winter here as has not been known for years in Vienna in March, the snow lying as deep as it was in Weimar when we left, and the railway connection checked by little delays. I shall take the opportunity of playing in the Ödenburg theatre (where at any rate I shall have no expenses), in order to go a step further in breaking myself of the lamplight fever,* and to get accustomed to playing Hungarian pieces, on which I am principally reckoning for Pest, where the outlook is a much more cheerful one for me. Of course I must first let Dreyschock get his visit over; he is at present here, but wants nevertheless to get to Pressburg and Pest before me. Dreyschock is an *homme-machine*, the personification of absence of genius, with the exterior of the clown. For the rest, we have no personal acquaintance with each other.

I have a clear conscience that I have not got into bad society. Sometimes I have not any at all, and then I gladly give the waiter a tip, at the coffee-house where I sup, simply to hear a friendly " Good evening."

I like Fräulein Paoli very much; † I have been to see her a couple of times; she has too small a connection to be able to be of use to me, and I don't want to have to thank her for little "nothings" which try to make believe that they are "something." In spite of her being unmusical she went to my concert; I had sent her tickets; and she said the very same thing that Fischhoff afterwards said to her of me—that if there were any fault to find with my playing it was that I put *too much* thought into it. That is true, and it is also true that it is a fault, because it leads into a fragmentary and unintelligible rendering. Fischhoff, to whom I had no introduction, has nevertheless been most friendly to me all the same.

The Laubes, to whom I sent tickets for my concerts, of which they made use, invited me lately to supper. They were most kind to me. Bauernfeld, Dawison, and Baron Stolzenberg (the real Duke of Dessau) were there. If Frau v. Lüttichau would still send me a line to Laube, I should be very much obliged to her; perhaps then he would let me have the Burg-theatre for nothing.

I would write more to you, but it tires me so; I have really been very unwell; the thanks, which I wanted to express to you warmer than ever this time, are silent, but deep and lasting. Your letter really warmed my heart, and if I again feel myself a man it is chiefly owing to you. I shall write to my father directly (to Ödenburg). How is Isidore, and, above all, how are you yourself? The Milanollo ‡ is here now, and

---

* Meaning, playing in public.

† Elisabeth Glück, 1815-94, an Austrian poetess and writer, who took the name of Betty Paoli.

‡ Teresa Milanollo, 1827, a firstrate violinist.

absorbs every interest.   I shall not give my third concert before the
24th April, which is a Sunday, the only day when a concert is well
filled.   Anyone who thus gets a Sunday is really a "Sunday child," for
these days are few and are generally secured a year in advance.

I came here much too late, was also announced too late, and thus
gave my concerts under the most unfavourable circumstances imaginable.
After well considering everything I see that I *must* try to make my way
here, in spite of all hindrances, or even *because* of them.   If I give my
concert on the 24th April with orchestra the expenses will be considerable,
but I think that it is just by my playing with orchestra that I should have
a success : the trite 'Concertstücke' of Weber and Mendelssohn were
what made Dreyschock's success.   After the way I have begun, I cannot
draw back from the position I took up at my first *début*.   How sad and
discouraging everything here was for me !   Even people of the most
subordinate talent find here and there someone to give them a lift on, or
a *sincere* and kindly-disposed criticism; I have found *nothing* of all this.
Not a soul has done anything *con amore* for me !   And how careful I
have been to be everywhere courteous and cautious ! . . . My introductions !   I wish I could cut all the letters of this word out of the alphabet
for ever !

As I lay in bed for several days from 7 o'clock in the evening till
2 o'clock the next afternoon, I comforted myself immensely by reading
Balzac !   Never could it have been more suitable than in my present mood,
and nothing could have suited that mood better !   At the same time I
instrumentated my Cæsar March afresh out of my head, so that it might be
played by Johann Strauss' son, who is a true successor to his father ;
his orchestra is firstrate and his Waltzes most piquant.   I have also
begun a couple of little drawingroom pieces.   Now I am getting an
unconquerable thirst for some sort of amusement !

I want to ask your advice once more about my concert.   There is
still plenty of time.

Next Sunday, this day week at mid-day, I am to play Bach's Triple
Concerto with Fischhoff and a local (good) pianist named Dachs, and
orchestra.   That means *certain anticriticism ;* at the same concert there will
be a Beethoven Overture and a Mendelssohn Symphony—it is considered
the most artistic (also really the best) Concert-Society that there is here.

The only official Vienna paper speaks decently of me, but on the
other hand gives free vent to its rage against Liszt (*revers de la médaille*).
. . . So of course I can't send this criticism anywhere !   My friend of
University days, Herzfeld, has been very nice to me, inviting me to a
very pleasant party at his parents', and, although I sent him plenty of
tickets, he also took some more, as I afterwards learned.—It is 11 o'clock ;

by this time I have been already asleep on other nights. I am tired and weak; I have written at such length in order that you may not be anxious any more.

A thousand thanks for all your love and kindness! Good night.

TO HIS MOTHER.

VIENNA, 14*th April* 1853.

DEAREST MOTHER,

Just returned from my 6 days' stay at Ödenburg I find your letter here, the third which Frau Bayer delivers to me. I reply at once, to give you good news which will make you happy—it is not that my position has, outwardly, materially improved in any way, or allows of anything more than mere hopes, but it is that I feel myself morally and physically pretty well and brisk. The little excursion has done me a great deal of good. I have breathed again. The commission I had to execute for Liszt I believe I have done to his satisfaction, and the days passed pleasantly for me. This was how it was. I found a couple of amiable, cordial men, at whose house I generally spent most of the day, like Litolff with us. Quite by chance I had a letter of introduction offered me to a well-to-do Hungarian family, v. Lenhard, who shewed me such kindness and sympathy as I have never yet experienced. The only outlay which they expected from me on my side was that I should give a few music lessons for nothing to their little girl of 13, who was very talented and intelligent in music, though a fearfully spoilt child. As I wanted to breathe for a few days far away from my thoroughly detested Vienna, I improvised a concert in the theatre (half to kill time), by which I paid my expenses and my stay. I was in an excellent mood, although the piano was not up to much, and I made an unprecedented *furore.* I had a small, but a very select, audience, almost all in the boxes, the entire Hungarian *haute volée*, such as the Erdödy, Pallavicini and Festetics families, Count Montenuovo (son of Marie Louise), etc., people who otherwise never go to the theatre. The ladies applauded madly, and discovered in my face a great deal of likeness to Liszt. . . . I began with the Volkshymne,* a *captatio benevolentiæ* of the garrison, and was called forwards ten times in all. I had to play the Hungarian Melodies over again, and I should have had to repeat the last piece also if it had not been for a cabal of the servants of the theatre, who were tired of the music, and prevented the curtain being raised the third time.

---

* Popular hymn.

. . . I am very glad to have had this little general rehearsal of Hungarian pieces, because I now feel quite sure of my things for Pressburg and Pest. I am at present waiting for an answer from Hunyadi, whom you got to know at the Arnims in the elephant,* as to when I am expected there.

Dreyschock is giving concerts at this moment at the above cities. Count Leo Festetics, the Intendant of the Hungarian National Theatre, a friend of Liszt's, has already placed his theatre and a third of the net receipts at my disposal—whereas he has refused Dreyschock's request for it. Whenever I come back from Pest I think I shall again give a concert at Ödenburg, as I should then have quite a full house—this time the concert was a too hurriedly improvised one. The afore-mentioned family have raved about me to such a degree that they will come to my concerts here also, and have made me promise to sit to a painter there for them.

Now to the most important thing. I have not yet announced a concert, but I must do so at once. As I stand here at present, I slink away from the scene of my first deeds like a thief—and, besides *all* else, honour is also lost. Liszt has strengthened me especially in this respect, by his decided wish that I should make myself a firmer footing here above everything. This I must do before the end of the season, or I shall throw my whole career back a year. I must therefore now give a concert that will make its mark, and therefore it must be with orchestra ; I hope, I am convinced, that I shall then succeed. But, as I said—the money ! The expenses of such a concert will amount to 180 thalers ! Although I am certain to make the half of this sum, yet I must first possess it, so as to have no anxieties of such a material nature, if I would come out in a manner worthy of myself and of Liszt. Freiherr v. Münch-Bellinghausen,† who called upon me, said to me, " Orchestral compositions of Liszt would have tempted many unmusical men, that is, men lazy about concerts, like myself." . . . If I give a concert with orchestra, that is, a concert in which I have such immense expenses, then I could ask the Bayer to take part in it; but if I ask her to help in quite a simple concert, then that looks like sending the hat round, and in saying that I have said everything. . . . At this moment the Milanollo is mistress of the ground, being the fashion, which she deserves to be, for it is worth *very* little ; she gives on Monday her 6th concert, and then, I believe, half a dozen more. . . . Of course I must let her get out of the way first. And by that time it is to be hoped that Spring

---

* Refers to some private joke or nickname. See letter to Cornelius, page 124.
† The poet Halm.

will no longer be here, all the more so, as today the thermometer was below freezing point.

This very day I will write to Liszt about the concert, and will beg him to give you his opinion about it, as he does not yet appear to have done so. . . . It would have been much the best if I had ventured to give my first concert with orchestra. I cannot tell you how much of my heart's blood and of my life I would give to gain a victory, and I shall never need one as I do in this decisive year. Perhaps I can go to Pest beforehand, and save there as much as I shall require to give a concert here. This would have to take place on the 28th April or the 1st May, and I must decide it a week beforehand. Don't you know anybody who could lend me a portion of this sum? The trade I am now driving has truly no *shadow*-side, but only a side of dark night. It is horrible! To have to buy the means to authenticate one's existence as an artist!

But I am writing to you confusedly and vaguely—perhaps I shall receive the long looked-for letter from Pest, so that I can go there at once, where I will risk everything, so that with the motto "*Liszt et mon talent*" I may rout the Bohemian musician from the field!

Thun has inquired many times how things were going with me; today I will thank him for it. As I said—*fi des lettres de recommendation;* should this mark of sympathy move me to tears, or can it pay my way for me? I have both courage and energy now, that is true, and I am also *en train* to play—(this in answer to your last letter but one, which I have just read through again); only give me a room to play in, and some sensible, artistic people in it!

As regards my social behaviour, the most adverse critic could find nothing to carp at in it. I am conscious that I have spoken and acted everywhere prudently, worthily, as a gentleman, and, what is more, as an honest man. I have never derogated from my own dignity, and was so far an aristocrat that I have never been to excesses or over-loud. Don't laugh, for I must have *something* to be satisfied with, and as I can't be with other people I must be so with myself, *faute de mieux.*

Of Balzac I have read 'Histoire des Treize,' 'L'Interdiction' (splendid), 'Honorine' (ditto), and I know not what besides; but I know of nothing more inciting, nothing more calculated to take the bitter edge off irony, and to settle all its elements of fermentation down into a non-effervescent humour.

I lately praised Betty Paoli very highly in my diary. The next time I saw her she did not please me. I have a right to feel superstitious— it always does me harm, regularly and without exception, to praise the day before the evening has come, the week before the Sunday, or the month before the first of the next has arrived.

And as regards my feelings today I must say, *Unberufen !**   Be at ease about me, for I continually feel once more that I shall not so easily lose my energy again, nor let my desire to fight with or against the world fade away.

I lately saw the Bayer in Grillparzer's ' Hero.'   (She had sent me a ticket.)   You cannot imagine anything more beautiful.   She is a true artist, and more than highly gifted—she does not need to make herself appear so. . . . She cuts up Saphir, and has paid him neither with money nor with compliments.

Above all else do write to me now something about yourself, your life in Dresden, and how you are.   If this careless style of letter is of any interest to you, I will often write to you.

TO HIS FATHER.

VIENNA, 20*th April* 1853.

DEAREST FATHER,

Up to the present time I could only have given you the worst possible tidings about my first journey and its experiences and results, and on that account I have left it alone altogether.   It is only now that my good humour and freshness and inborn energy enable me, by God's grace, to raise myself to a more cheerful and hopeful mood, from the disconsolate and pitiable state in which my first endeavours after distinction had placed me—it is only now that I turn again to you, who are, alas, so far away from me, and whose paternal sympathy I cannot, from political circumspection, ever dare to beg for by a direct letter.

Bad luck has followed me here in Vienna with a pertinacity and steadiness which never seem to belong to good luck.   I came here with absolutely no sanguine illusions, but fate has even surpassed my worst fears.   My first two concerts, on the 15th and 19th March, have left me " down " both in purse and spirits, and richer only in bitter experience. I have learned too late that in our day it is not enough to have a talent, but that it is impossible to turn one's talent into fame and money unless one first begins by an outlay of money.   I also came here at an unlucky moment ; Dreyschock, who has been giving concerts for 15 years, and who has thus attained great certainty, routine, and European fame of a kind, was just making a . . . got-up furore. . . .†

---

* The nearest English equivalent to this much used German expression is ' low be it spoken.'

† Here follows a full description of his experiences and state of depression, the same as in the letter to his mother.

To this utter depression in the literal sense of the word it was but natural—at least according to my nature—that a reaction should follow. I am now with pride and joy in the reactionary state, and have hope and courage once more. I will now tell you the principal things. . . . I am now daily awaiting tidings from Pest as to whether this is a favourable moment for giving concerts there—shall then write to Liszt, who has promised me letters of introduction for Pest, which will be sure to be of more use to me than those to Vienna, as Liszt's name is revered in an almost fanatical manner in Hungary, whereas in Vienna they seem to wish to revenge themselves, by their indifference, for having formerly been so fascinated by him.

. . . .

I cannot write anything of my impressions of Vienna. I keep aloof from everything ; the people I have got to know are of the kind of whom " distance lends enchantment to the view."

I am writing a couple of piano pieces, am instrumentating my Cæsar Overture—Johann Strauss plays the March from Cæsar at his soirées with great *éclat*,—and I trouble myself about nothing. Write to me soon something about yourself.

TO HIS FATHER.

VIENNA, *7th May* 1853.

. . . .

I have given two concerts in Pressburg.

I cannot think about a third concert in Vienna till after my return from Pest ; and that only if it does not appear too risky.

My first book of songs has appeared in print. The second will follow in a fortnight at latest. I will take an opportunity of sending them to Louise, if she, in her amiability, will not be discouraged by the trouble, from seeking out their beauties. At this moment I am writing a Fantasia on one of Verdi's operas, ' Rigoletto ; ' his best, which really shows traces of great talent. Haslinger will publish it directly it is ready. If the orchestra wishes to be paid, it must submit to the wishes of the pay-master. Forgive me this headachy style and medley.

TO HIS FATHER.

VIENNA, 21st May 1853.

DEAREST FATHER,

    I had promised you to write again before starting for Pest—
for I presume you received my last letter, in which I thanked you for
your prompt help, and begged you for speedy tidings about your health,
before you left for Stuttgart. Well, I am pretty well (low be it spoken)
in body and spirit, and intend to start for Pest tomorrow morning early
(Sunday, 22nd May), the city which I have long regarded, perhaps too
hopefully, as a Canaan after the Desert of Vienna. Liszt wrote to me
a few days ago, sent me a heap of letters of introduction, and advises me
to stay there as long as possible, and to give as many concerts as practicable. Here in Vienna it would be madness to risk another. The
charlatan Therese Milanollo has become the fashion here; the perfectly
unrecognisable disguise under which Dame Art nowadays travels about.
Her old father has been on the watch lately, on account of the incom-
petent sale of tickets.

    Herr v. Zedlitz has most kindly given me a passport from the
Weimar Embassy for three months; he inquired after you, and I do
ditto herewith in the superlative degree, by begging you to let me know
as soon as possible how you are progressing in your convalescence,
whether your accident has had any bad consequences, etc., and whether
the Spring now beginning is doing you good?

    I cannot write much to you today, as I am busy with packing, letter
writing, and putting my things in order, for I am leaving part of them
behind me, as I shall come to Vienna again on my way back from Pest,
before I perhaps go to Liszt again in Weimar. If any of the Hungarian
nobility should invite me to spend a couple of weeks with them in the
country, Liszt has told me to accept the invitation. I shall play in Pest
the first time in the Hungarian National Theatre, during the entr'acte of
a comedy; after that Count Leo Festetics will make a contract with me
for further performances. As I have a lot of Hungarian pieces by Liszt
in my *répertoire*, it is best for me to address myself to the national
public.

    Yesterday I went to see Thalberg, and heard him play. Liszt had
most urgently desired me to go and see him, and I was very much
rewarded by the real pleasure it gave me to hear his exquisitely poetical
and thoroughly finished execution, although he really was only making
little musical jokes. He is an out and out aristocratic, blasé, and hard-

living man of the world, who subsists on his property. Of course he lives here in the palace of Prince Dietrichstein.

Isidore really ought to write to me again ; I do beg that she will. She must excuse me, because I really have not time, and also, what is not quite synonymous, that I am not in the mood for it.

TO HIS MOTHER.

Le lendemain de la première victoire.

BUDAPEST, *2nd June* 1853.
ERZHERZOG STEPHAN HOTEL. 78.

DEAREST MOTHER,

It would have amused you to be present yesterday evening at my triumph in the National Theatre. The shouts of " eljen " are still ringing in my ears, and they sound rather better than the German-Italian " bravo " ! They tell me there has not been such a fuss made about a virtuoso for a long time. Dreyschock, my latest forerunner, has been completely conquered by me in Pest, which has given the lie to Vienna in a brilliant manner. We will now wait and see what the critics say ; I daresay the German ones will find fault because I played in a Hungarian theatre (just as though Pest were a German town !), and here such a petty rivalry-swindle about nationality obtains. I am going on further today (3rd June), as I was yesterday interrupted by the fathers of my friends Joachim and Singer, who came, together with a lot of other people, to wish me joy of my " triumph." It was an unparalleled triumph, according to what everyone says.

I have not the presumption to imagine that this triumph is my own work. The greatest share of it is due to Liszt's name, to his divine compositions—the Hungarian piece with orchestral accompaniment, and the ' Rondo alla Turca ' on motifs from Beethoven's ' Ruines d'Athènes ' (also by him). But, on the other hand, I did not play badly ; there was fire in my playing, I felt more sure than I have ever done before, and of course I played by heart (for Erkel wanted the score to conduct from), and with perfect freedom and security ; every *nuance*, every *accelerando* or *ritardando* was so thoroughly understood and followed by the superb conductor and the splendid orchestra, that it was a pleasure to listen to such an accompaniment. How quickly the public took it up, you have no idea ! The boxes and galleries were full to overflowing ; the pit empty—none of the *bourgeoisie*. I was perpetually interrupted by applause—not *applause*, but wild cheers. I was compelled to repeat the

Frischka * of the Hungarian Rhapsody. . . . All the people I have seen today, both ladies and gentlemen, are still overflowing with enthusiasm for Liszt and myself. That such a public still exists—this has given me enormous encouragement both for my playing and composition.

4th June.

I have so many letters to write to-day.

The two brothers Doppler, conductors, composers, and superb flautists, are making a short pleasure trip to Germany. I am sending them also to Lipinski—they are Poles by birth. If Frau v. Lüttichau can work it for them to play at Court she should do so for their sakes.

The Magyar press is full of enthusiasm; they call me *great, highly gifted*. No criticism; enthusiasm. The official paper praises me very much, speaks at some length about Liszt and myself, and hopes that I shall play again soon and frequently. And yet, in spite of Liszt's letter of introduction, Count Festetics has never been to see me again, and postponed the day of my *début* arbitrarily, without letting me know a word about it, letting me run backwards and forwards all that long way to the theatre-offices about the arrangements ever so many times, and so on. I expect he will treat me just the same about the money matters—I had a feeling of scruple that kept me from mentioning this matter to him, because Liszt had introduced me to him. With Liszt's introductions I have very little luck. Herr v. Augusz has started on a circular tour through the country with the Archduke, and will not be back till next week. He was most kind on my first visit, and spoke to me of Liszt's letter, which gave him great pleasure, and in which Liszt introduced me as his *héritier et successeur*.

The Archbishop of Pest, to whom Liszt also gave me an introduction, has meanwhile become a Cardinal, and lives at Gran. Herr Guido v. Karàtsonyi, a great lover of horses, a tall, handsome young man, but very stout, and who has lately become a millionaire through his wife, has been very pleasant to me. Yesterday I dined there with Capellmeister Erkel. Very agreeable. I cannot play at the *Némzeti szinhàz* (the National Theatre) before Monday week. So meanwhile a private concert must be arranged. At the 'Hotel d'Europe,' where Dreyschock gave his concerts, the Chinese Chungakai, etc., are going to appear, so I must try to get the Lloyd salon. Dr. Ungar, the barrister, and correspondent of the *Augsburger* (an intimate friend of the Stirnbrand

---

* The 'Frischka' is the quick, lively second movement that follows the slow movement, or 'Lassan,' in the Hungarian gipsy music.

family, and therefore knowing me already by hearsay from Stuttgart), will help me to get this room : I shall devote a portion (a third) of the net proceeds to a female institution founded by ladies of the aristocracy here.

The concert will be announced beforehand for Wednesday noon, or else half-past four. . . . I think I shall then give a portion of the receipts of the fourth concert to a national institution, the Conservatoire here. Well, I will not anticipate too far beforehand.

Today I dine with Dr. Hunyadi, and tomorrow with the violinist Ridley-Kohne. In the evenings we (a few young people) generally go and hear the gipsies, and it amuses me as much as it teaches me. Occasionally I go to the circus or a summer theatre, and not merely for opera, but also to hear plays. I then take a translation with me, and delight myself in the innate nobility of the people, and the way they seem to be no mere *actors;* or else I go to hear the lady pianists here, or go to Dr. Ungar, or Hunyadi, etc.

I get up at 6 o'clock in the morning, if not at 5, practise and write ; at night I don't go to bed later than 11 or 12 o'clock. The climate is as healthy as the Vienna one is ruinous. I have felt well since the first moment I got here. The city is not merely beautiful, but enchanting in the highest degree : the hilly portion, Ofen, is joined to Pest by a grand chain-bridge over the majestic river, and, from the fortress there, one has an entrancing view at sunset of the palaces at Pest, and its immense squares and broad streets. This place is the comfort of youth, just as Vienna is the convenient place for old age. Here I should like to stay, and I could do so. Pest is a point won for me. If everything else failed, and I liked to establish myself here as a pianist, or thought of becoming Intendant of the National Theatre, you might congratulate yourself as much as if you had brought a daughter happily to a husband.

Yesterday I met Törös János, the editor of the *Pesti Naplo ;* he came up to me, pressed both my hands very effusively, and assured me that I was a second Liszt.

Thus much is certain, that next winter I am to come here again, at the most favourable time, when all the aristocracy is still here, and then I shall be able to make money, whereas now it is too late. It is to be hoped that I shall make up a part of my expenses here, for I am terribly in want of money.

I pay 1 gulden 24 kreutzer a day for my room, which is, comparatively speaking, not too dear ; the room is a large one ; the piano I have for nothing, a good grand by Tomaschek. At the concerts I play on a Streicher.

Now don't expect any more long letters from me, if things go well, but little notes frequently. I received your letter sent on from Vienna directly after my arrival here ; I cannot answer it, as I have no time just now to read it through again.

If only living were not so dear, and people did not cheat me so ! I hope you are well, and that you are pleased with me and about me. *Enfin !*

Farewell for today ; I kiss your hand, and am,

Your grateful and loving son,

Bülow János Guidó.

TO HIS MOTHER.

Le revers de la médaille.

Pest, 15th June [1853].

Dearest Mother,

My triumphant eight-page letter, which was somewhat very *blé en herbe*,* was finished long before the receipt of your last, but I did not want to send it off until I could add a consoling word about the rest of the episode of my first, and possibly also my last, virtuoso wanderings in Pest.

20th June.

The hopes I then formed have not been realised. I am more than ever disheartened, not with regard to my talent and its ultimate worth in the eyes of intelligent people—musicians as well as the papers always speak of me in tones of the highest esteem—but with regard to my outward success, and the chances of my ever being able to make an independent position for myself by my profession, or even to keep myself. So that this prospect makes me really disgusted with life. Such special, constant ill-luck follows me, hanging over me like a curse, that I must allow that the utmost exertion of my powers will never bring me to the result which a hundred-times less talented *blagueur* and charlatan attains by his playing.

I have vainly tried as yet to write to Liszt in a calm manner, for at the end of this miserable journey I have earned nothing but the most bitter experience, too late to be salutary,—the knowledge that I am too good, too honest, to be a Virtuoso; and this the wife of the Postal Secretary at Weimar also thought.

It is most odious to me to have to go back to what is past—but

---

* Premature.

I must and will tell you all about it, so that you may not misunderstand me, or imagine all sorts of indefinite things.

I have again had real bad luck with Liszt's introductions. The Intendant of the Hungarian theatre has not once shown me the commonest civilities.

. . . .

He further sent me word that I could play in the theatre immediately on my arrival : instead of keeping his word he lets me wait twelve days, incurring all sorts of unnecessary expenses at a dear hotel, where I am stuck fast.

After my first extraordinary success, which ought to have been taken advantage of at once—he could have done it, it would have been the making of me—he refuses me the theatre, and says I cannot play again before the 13th June, on account of *répertoire* and other trumpery excuses. The press speaks enthusiastically of me, but the public does not believe in my success, because I don't give a second concert. I must now make up my mind to announce a private concert. . . . No room to be had for it. All the large places were burnt down in the Revolution ; there was no choice for me but the room of a Merchant Company of the Pester Lloyd, who have often lent it for similar purposes. Although I offered to play for the benefit of the pension-fund of the Company, yet they refused me the room—perhaps and probably because I had played in the National Theatre and not in the German one. But I was obliged to give a private concert, and to let people hear pieces which I could not give in the theatre ; I therefore gave, or rather I bought, a concert in an unfavourable and expensive room, the salon of the ' Hotel zum Tiger,' which had not been used for concerts before that time. . . . The Magyar press, without exception, made an outcry against the inhospitality of the Lloyd people, and took me up with the greatest warmth. It is impossible to tell you what this arrangement cost me in time, trouble, expenditure of good temper and energy in all these wretched little trifles. . . . Impossible to do every individual thing one's self, and enormously expensive to get anyone else to do them for one. I will never give a concert again without a valet or a secretary, perhaps not even with one, or rather, certainly not. How many hours I have been running about, how many disagreeables I have encountered, to find, at the end of it all, that two singers who had promised to sing for me left me in the lurch ! Enough. . . . I played, and played Liszt's Lucrezia and Patineurs (and I played quite alone) with an energy and bravura that astonished myself. Criticism was again most favourable. And yet the National Theatre was not full on the 13th June, and Festetics put on the programmes "utolso" (for the last time) without asking me. I had the arrangement of the Cæsar March played, which was liked, and I played the Beethoven E flat major Concerto for the first time, but as though I had played it I don't know how many times before, and I had a very grateful and attentive audience (rather remarkable for a classical piece of music in a theatre!), and was interrupted with tremendous applause in the Adagio (a thing which has very seldom happened anywhere). On the other hand Liszt's Fantasia from the Prophète did not please, on account of the great similarity of the motif of the Hymn with a song that is not popular in Pest. Chopin's Polonaise also fell flat, whereas a Hungarian Rhapsody of Liszt's quite excited them.

People advise me to give one more concert in the 'Hotel d'Europe,' when the Chinese are gone. The expenses would be too great. The "friends" of Liszt don't trouble themselves about me. What heaps of people (and chatter) I have had to put up with, who call themselves acquaintances of mine, and who worry me with their advice, their tales, their self-adulation and pretensions, to the very utmost limits of a *restrained* impatience! And before me the prospect of undisguised misery, the sense of the strongest need of help, the certainty that, sooner or later, I must come to grief,—I with my talent, intelligence, and knowledge!—I feel a hell, a perfect hell, around me and within me. If only a gleam of hope did not come now and then, convulsing me afresh by its flicker—if I could at last regard myself as dead and buried, and let myself slowly die away, I know not how, offering a passive resistance to fate of every kind! But I accept, when an invitation comes which lays upon me the duty giving pleasure to others by my playing. Dr. Hunyadi asked me lately to play the Trio (dedicated to Liszt) by a German named Volkmann. This I did, and enchanted the people. No one had played the last movement with the passion and energy with which I filled it (with Liszt's performance of it in my mind); the composer was surprised at the effect of his own work; people admired my playing, the papers noticed it; and yet all this does not bring me the least help, but only fresh envy, slanderers wherever possible, enemies. What would I not give to be in some little village, with some green before my window, a piano in my room, some unwritten music-paper, a few not ill-natured people and a faithful dog about me, and peace, and a respite from these constant irritations!

I have read part of Carus' " Symbolism of the human form." It is capitally written, and he seems to be very clear on the subject. The contents are firstrate and very practical.

Pest is marvellously beautiful, the neighbourhood is lovely, and I must enjoy some more of it at all events if possible.

Farewell, I am talking rubbish—and have sighed myself tired.

TO HIS MOTHER.

[Pest, *July* 1853.]
Grosse Brückgasse. 12.

Dearest Mother,

It was not possible for me to thank you sooner for the nobleness and touching goodness which you have once more shown me by your comforting letter and the help in money which I so greatly needed. What with the removal from the hotel, with all its little attendant troubles, the hunting for a *chambre introuvable*, and all the work I had to do in preparation for another *début* at the National Theatre, to say nothing of the fearful, tropical heat, and the continual and violent recurrence of my headaches—my poor overworked brain was confused to such a degree that I was absolutely incapable of thinking or writing. My *début* took place yesterday, Monday, and was an even more brilliant success than the previous one, but from a pecuniary point the result was equally *nil*. I got your last letter just before the concert, as I was dressing !

Wednesday.

I was just going to sit down to my writing-table again, when Dr. Hunyadi came, bringing me your letter to him, in which you begged for tidings of me. I beg pardon a thousand times for being such an anxiety to you. It grieves me to the heart that you have so little satisfaction in me ! And, on one side, I make myself many reproaches and conscience-pricks that I have cost you such a lot of money (for it is hard enough to earn it), without any immediate prospect of being soon able to attain an independent position ; whilst, on the other side, the consciousness of my *more than ordinary* talent—I can even say this, after the bitter experiences and the great discouragement I have had—gives me courage and hope once more that I shall eventually be able to attain money and a position.

Please don't mind if I jump about from one thing to another, and write just as my dull, stupid brain dictates.

To begin with, my address is now—Pest, Grosse Brück-Gasse No. 12 (3rd étage), c/o Herr Marastoni. He is an Italian, and is the founder and head of a School of Painting, and his wife provides attendance and looks after me, and in case I were ill I am certain of being well taken care of by her. My room has only one window, but it is not a small room, has a fair amount of light, and good furniture; the window, a good big one, looks into the courtyard ; the house is one of the finest in the inner town. The shady side of the picture is—insects at night, and piano-playing in the house the whole day, but, as I have plenty to do, and the sun shines bright, and I think I shall again learn to live comfortably, I have already done somewhat towards throwing off the evils of both day and night.

Through your kindness, which enables me, after paying every debt, to live on another fortnight free from care, and to become once more at ease both in body and mind, I shall arrive at the point of writing to Liszt again one of these days. He strongly advised me in his last letter to reconnoitre and examine minutely every chance here, to see whether this would suit as a permanent residence, and whether, after giving some more concerts in Vienna at a more favourable time, I could establish myself here next winter as a music teacher, and try at the same time to obtain some post in the Hungarian or German Theatre. There is much to be said for this idea, and I think that, if I should still be alive then, and no favourable change had taken place in my life's destiny, it would be the wisest thing for me to earn my living, and save something, by spending a couple of years here, and travelling round about in the country giving lessons, or otherwise working as hard as I could.

Baron Augusz, the vicegerent, has invited me to play after all in the German Theatre. This the Government would like, because they regard the theatre as one of the principal means of Germanizing the capital of the country.

The Germans, represented by Lloyd, behaved badly to me at first. On this point I shall, moreover, also have my revenge. *Augusz*, that is to say, the highest civil authority, has only to give a hint to the society, and they *must* lend me their room, in which I will then arrange an invitation concert, and will play the Trio (dedicated to Liszt) by Volkmann the Saxon, who lives here, and who is a young composer of great mark; I will also play Beethoven and Bach; in short, I intend to earn a grand musical success.

I am jumping now from extreme to extreme, from the most calmly inconsolable apathy to the most versatile schemes—and all because I am again in possession of a few gulden, and therefore of the possibility of living without anxiety as to the wherewith.

How can I thank you for your love and kindness, and for your belief in me and in my future as an artist, when I myself was near despairing about it! Have not papa and my sister received any letters from me in the middle of last month? I cannot understand their silence. Tomorrow I will send them news of me, to the address you have given me. As soon as I know anything more definite about myself I will write to you at once. If I receive, by Augusz' help, a suitable pecuniary offer from the

German Theatre-director, say about 100 gulden guaranteed, then I shall play in any case.

Meanwhile I am thinking over the advice that has been given me, to give concerts at some of the Hungarian Baths, or in other Hungarian towns. If I do this, my piano playing shall be by no means a game of hazard [a hazard playing].

For Armgart [v. Arnim] I am writing six songs, entitled 'Die Entsagende,' by Karl Beck. If only I had a publisher! Possibly I may also have an opportunity of publishing some pianoforte pieces here (without any Opus number), without payment.

Perhaps, with all your love for me, it will do you good to see that I am again so active and industriously disposed. As regards the piano I assure you that you have no need to be ashamed of

Your very loving, grateful son.

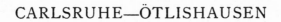

CARLSRUHE—ÖTLISHAUSEN

CHAPTER VIII.

CARLSRUHE—ÖTLISHAUSEN.

AUTUMN 1853.

WHILST Bülow was writing cheerfully to his mother about his father (on the 19th September 1853), the latter had already passed away from this mortal life three days previously. The apoplectic seizure which he had had half a year before was, in spite of the apparent gradual return of his physical powers, a precursor of his coming death.

Eduard von Bülow was spared a long illness, and on the 16th of September he was called quietly and suddenly to his rest. He was taken away whilst in the midst of a great work at which he was labouring indefatigably—the biographies of great men from all epochs of history.

A whole week elapsed before poor Hans, free from all sad presentiment, learned the tidings of his irreparable loss ; as his family, not knowing where he was at the moment, were unable to communicate with him. The overpowering grief which seized him when the sad tidings reached him, shows that the son realised the full depth of the loss that had come upon him. The next letter was written while he was still unconscious of what had befallen him ; but the ones immediately following show us Bülow's utter despair.

TO RICHARD POHL.*

CARLSRUHE, 20*th September* 1853.

DEAR FRIEND,

You are just now being regularly bombarded with letters from Carlsruhe. Yesterday your friend W. Kalliwoda† will have written to you; early this morning Liszt has been settled at his writing-desk for

---

* Richard Pohl (born 1826), a writer on music. Under the *nom de plume* "Hoplit" he was a constant contributor to the *Neue Zeitschrift für Musik* during the fifties ; and he was one of the earliest partisans of the Wagner-cultus.

† Wilhelm Kalliwoda (born 1827), Kapellmeister in Carlsruhe.

you, and this evening I take up the pen for the first time here, not to give you any news, but simply to tell you how delighted I am that Liszt will see his wish realised, of inviting your wife* and yourself to the Musical Festival, and also to beg you to turn your back on Dresden and your face to Carlsruhe as soon as possible. Your presence here will be not so much "utilis" as "dulcis" in the highest degree. We shall have to scratch the backs of the Carlsruhers a little, that is to say, in an insinuating and *Pohl*-ish manner. The artists-without-art here, specific musicians, are still rejoicing in such a paradisiacal simplicity, such an utter immovability by the Ninth Symphony, Tannhäuser, &c., that it is high time that they should be instructed in this specific music by the *unspecific* musicians. The only thing which Carlsruhe has set forth of itself, but also the *one, unique* thing, is Gluck's Armida, which will be given here on the 30th. Well, I fancy you will come a little sooner than that. Yesterday we were in Baden. Liszt has engaged Frau Heinefetter for the arias, chosen by her, from 'Titus' and the 'Prophète.' Joachim will play his own Concerto and Bach's Chaconne. In case your wife would like to know exactly what is allotted to her harp, I can tell you at once briefly,—the Overture to 'Struensee,' the Bridal Song from 'Lohengrin,' and a couple of numbers from Berlioz' 'Romeo and Juliet.'

Kalliwoda and Will, the first violin, are likewise rejoicing at the thought of your speedy arrival. With regard to the programme they hold some prejudices, as somewhat exclusive devotees of a worn-out Mendelssohnianism. As Liszt was away at Mannheim and Darmstadt, they honoured me with their confidences on this point—Kalliwoda, who is a charming man, less than the other.

TO HIS MOTHER.

CARLSRUHE, *25th September* 1853.

DEAREST MOTHER,

I am quite inconsolable. Nothing could ever have affected me more deeply ; *never* could a blow be harder than this, unexpected as it was, indeed not even feared.

I was so infinitely happy in the prospect of travelling with Liszt in

---

* Johanna Eyth, afterwards Frau Pohl (1824-70), a celebrated harp-player ; was engaged at Weimar, and afterwards at Carlsruhe.

Switzerland after the musical festival, and of then visiting him who can never know how truly and deeply I have loved him. So without a farewell—for ever! His fatherly look, which since yesterday has been constantly in my mind's eye—dust!

It is terrible. As yet I can scarcely realise it. So many hopes shattered for ever! That of your reconciliation, lost;—that of the intercourse which I now first thought to begin with him, over;—I myself an orphan, deprived henceforth of the father, whose happiness, would that I could say together with yours, would have compensated me for my past and probably future misfortunes!

My father's love—I recognise its immeasurable, unique value, just as it is lost to me for ever. The sacred connexion between him and me broken—no father for me any more!

No one in the whole world who from the depth of the heart so determined to be, and was, " *my best friend;* " that he exists no more for me, I, no more for him, I dead to him—yes, that also is a death!

It is terrible, and so quickly too, so entirely without warning!

Could not Death have waited a year longer, and have given him and me the joy of meeting after our long separation! And even if this happiness had ever after been associated with the pain of the last parting, his last look thus engraved upon my heart would have remained with me all the rest of my life.

Perhaps, also, he hardly thought about me with his former interest— he neither knew nor believed how truly, how heartily I loved him. All complaint is useless, all hope vain. My decision cannot waver; I must, if possible, once more kiss the dear one, at any rate see the place where he died, see his wife and children, who received his last smile, his last word and look.

I learnt it yesterday afternoon from the *Allgemeine Zeitung.* Liszt had received your letter the day before, and said nothing to me; had taken it to Baden, where he stayed two days; and only on his return yesterday evening did your few lines give me the unanswerable sad confirmation of what I had hardly been able to believe from the printed paper, so sudden and bewildering was the blow.

I hope to be at Ötlishausen tomorrow, Tuesday, evening—Liszt expects me back here early on Saturday. I have promised him to play one of his compositions on Wednesday, October 5th, and I will do it; I shall have recovered myself by that time.

How does Isidore bear it? May she soon find peace and resignation, and not give way too much to her natural grief. We, the survivors, have time to lament the dead; we cannot all at once bear that which breaks the heart bit by bit. Meanwhile farewell, dear mother! I shall pray daily on my knees that you may be left to us, you who are our only support and protection. Love us for him, as we would still love you for him.

Your deeply-afflicted son,

HANS.

TO HIS SISTER.

ÖTLISHAUSEN, Sept. 28, 1853.

MY DEAR, BELOVED SISTER,

        I am too violently shaken, too painfully smitten, so stupified, I might say, in mind and strength, that I am unable to answer your beautiful letter (which I just received as I was leaving Carlsruhe) as it deserves; to give you, or rather to return to you, anything like what you have given me. The tears which flowed down my cheeks as I read your sad words had so relieved and strengthened me that I was able to take the very fatiguing journey in my overwrought condition, without injury to my health.

Your tender sisterly love will well imagine what my feelings here must be; how each of the countless memories of him whom I loved as deeply—though he doubted it—as I honoured him, and how the picture of our lost one, must awaken the most poignant grief at his absence. . . . I should have been so glad to have you and Mamma here—to be all together would have been such a blessing to our hearts, as you cannot now have at all, and I only in part. Louise, as well as our two little brothers,—of whom Willi, as often as he saw me give way to passionate weeping, ascribed it to Papa's absence—has helped me very much, not out of the sorrow, but in the sorrow itself. The blossoming life of the little ones, the sudden, painless death of our dear father, do not accentuate that dark thought of death, that horror which may otherwise mingle with the cry of despair at the visible removal of our dearest from us. . . . I did quite right indeed to come down here. . . . I arrived late yesterday evening, and early tomorrow I travel back, without stopping, to Carlsruhe, where it is my duty to be, both on account of Liszt and myself, and of my ever dear father, who lives henceforth for ever in my heart.

He would really have had much happiness in me; I pictured to myself our intercourse after the Carlsruhe festival as so delightful, so soothing and enlivening for me—for I was quite determined to surprise him then by a pretty long visit. . . . I should have told him minutely of all my joys and sorrows, small and great; he would probably have listened to me gladly and patiently; I should have collected all the printed signs and traces of my first artist-journey, which were of but little value to me; to please me he would have played the rôle of Virtuoso-Papa.

I have no sympathizer like him, for all my future life—*he* alone could be that, not merely as my father, but as a man and as a character, as my truest, best, and (O had he but known it) my *dearest* friend!

Just as it has been good for me physically to make this tiring journey, which at the same time somewhat distracted my thoughts, so was it absolutely necessary to my heart to be near him once more in his home and family; to see his room;—I will not go on giving way to my grief.

I have today arranged his books and completed the catalogue, ready for Mamma, if she stays here with you for a few days on your return journey, as I most earnestly beg of you both to do, with Louise, who longs for you very much. She quite expects you both, according to Mamma's promise.

If you believe of him that he now no longer sees through the dim lenses of biassed mortal judgment, but with a pure, penetrating, direct look into our hearts, you will feel constrained to come here, will go to the altar of his room, and will bring to him and his wife the offering of full and unreserved reconciliation.

In his *Novalis*, which, like his whole *secrétaire* with everything on and about it, remains just as he left it, a letter copied by Mamma is still lying. He read *Novalis* much in the last part of his life, and often made notes on it : there is no doubt he had Mamma's letter in his hand, and, though the feelings of his heart were perhaps painfully mistaken, there can be no doubt they were noble and pure. . . . Then, as I have not been able to be with you here, do come quickly afterwards to me. Willi and I have become great friends. I hope he at any rate will be attached to me—he looks so like Papa.

If such a thing as personal consolation can be mentioned here, I have it from these brothers whom I shall always love, and you will too, don't you think so? I have not yet been in the little chapel—we are going this evening. Louise and I are agreed about two things which must be done whilst I have power to assert my own will : first, we must put a wire fence round the chapel and its ground, and secondly, we must insure the possession of the chapel by the eventual purchase of the castle, a very advisable thing for Louise to do.

I think we ought also to get a lithograph done from the daguerreotype. I will take steps about it, as also for a proper announcement of his death. I shall write about this the day after tomorrow to Gutzkow.

I hope to keep well. I play in Carlsruhe on the 5th of October. Liszt made me promise this before he let me go.

Perhaps I shall play elsewhere soon after, so as to earn a little money.

God alone knows where I shall decide to make my home. All these cares oppress me, and embitter even the quiet time of mourning, to which I ought now to give myself up for my own good, since I can now never look forward to the quiet happiness of living with my father as I hoped to do.

Could I but know and see how you both are, weep with you, and, in that mourning which we owe to the deceased, seek to find a serener courage.

You can give me no greater pleasure than by letting me see you soon in full fresh health.

Do not think it a want of tenderness if I write to you seldom. The anxieties for myself—and they are now pressingly severe—leave me no time to pour out my heart to you. I must first be or become something myself; then I can be something to both of you.

I shall still probably write to Mamma this evening, and post the letter early tomorrow in Romanshorn, or perhaps not till Carlsruhe, for I really have not much superfluous strength.

Joachim, whom I saw again after a long interval, Liszt and Pruckner, who were with me at the first shock, have behaved most beautifully to me.

There are such countless, boundless recollections that could make my heart bleed afresh, that I must pilot the dark ship of this more silent and sacred sorrow, with the foresight and careful thought which befits it, through these dangerous rocks.

Farewell, dear sister: once more my heartfelt thanks for your beautiful letter. Think lovingly of

Your deeply-stricken brother,

HANS.

TO JOACHIM RAFF.

ROMANSHORN, 29th September 1853.

MY DEAR FRIEND,

I have just left the house of my late father, the place of his death, whither I had been summoned from Carlsruhe by an alarming message as deeply painful as it was unexpected, and of which I had no apprehension.

It was a hard, a bitter stroke of fate, and I have as yet scarcely succeeded in gaining that necessary composure and resignation which enable one to bear deep grief. After a long separation I had most ardently hoped to spend a few weeks in his company, as soon as the musical festival came to an end; to dedicate myself entirely to him, and to enjoy together the benefit of renewed intimate and intellectual intercourse, for myself especially necessary. We had so much in common, and had, partly by my fault, and to some extent again without any fault of mine, become so much estranged. Relentless iron necessity has prevented my seeing him again, and he had to depart without farewell, without having given me his blessing. He died quite suddenly and without pain at 8 o'clock on the morning of September 16th. A single sigh betokened his instantaneous end, which no one had expected or thought of. A malady of which he had taken little notice caused the sudden stoppage of the heart, and brought death without any deforming demolition, beautiful as a Grecian death.

I was so unfortunate as not to hear till a week had elapsed that I was an orphan and fatherless.

It seems however a profanation to speak much of a grief full of such sacred recollections.

Compassionate me, my dear friend.

I send you this sad news from Romanshorn, where I am waiting for the steamboat to take me back to Carlsruhe, and, as I much hope, to energetic activity : I am sending it from this place especially because I think of you again most warmly here. I have so much the feeling that we are both connected with this country and therefore countrymen. Your birthplace is not far from the grave of my father.

And therefore I now also beg you to let a friendly fellowship again exist between us, that former heartiness which it has pained me to feel gone. Not merely our artistic, but our social, interests and connections have something in common. Forgive me where I may perhaps from thoughtlessness, never from bad intention, have erred towards you. Be my friend again as formerly : I am assuredly very grateful to you when thinking of those earlier times.

As soon as I am once more master of my thoughts, and in condition to send a few words worthy of your 'Frühlingsboten,' I will do so in accordance with the wish you expressed to Liszt.

Farewell — may fortune soon take the most gratifying and well-deserved turn for you! My hearty greetings to Klindworth. And many thanks to you for the Psalm, which has shortened my journey and cheered me much.

TO HIS MOTHER.

CARLSRUHE, 12*th October* 1853.

MY DEAR, BELOVED MOTHER,

Since Monday I have been expecting you here in Carlsruhe, where I have received two letters addressed to you, which I now forward, and one today at last giving an explanation of your non-arrival, which made me anxious.

On Thursday we six young people (Joachim, Cornelius, Pruckner, etc.) travelled with Liszt, the Princess Wittgenstein, Princess Marie and her cousin Eugen W[ittgenstein] to Basle, where Liszt had promised to meet Wagner. You had written to me that you would come to Carlsruhe by Basle and get there on Saturday. This was sufficient reason for me to come and meet you both, and you had also commissioned me to address your letters thither, *Poste-Restante.* We had two delightful days there. Liszt drank to our brotherhood in Kirschwasser.*—Saturday mid-day we went to Strassburg, *i.e.* the Wittgensteins, Liszt, Wagner, Joachim and I. The cathedral made such an elevating and uniquely imposing impression on me that it even now makes me happy. From Strassburg Joachim and I returned first to Baden-Baden, and the others went for ten days to Paris. On Monday I came back here, and am stopping quite alone and very melancholy at the inn, going off to the station to meet all the arrivals; for, as letters to you arrived here, I must conclude there has been some slight delay, and that I might expect you any hour.

To begin at the end. As regards the plan of my journey (of which more hereafter) I make no circuitous route, nor incur loss of time (which means money) in going by way of Stuttgart, and shall therefore go there tomorrow. Perhaps I may be able to induce Gall to let me play in the theatre there, and so earn a small fee.

It is possible that I may also be able to play at the Court here; but I don't think so : Count Leiningen, Steward of the Household, on whom I called early this morning, and who seems to take an interest in me, has promised to call upon me again this afternoon. I played in the Court-concert on Wednesday evening, as well as on the morning of the second festival-concert, with the greatest success; hence I think I shall hardly have "to relight the stump of this cigar" (a saying of Berlioz).

In Stuttgart I shall be much nearer to you, with regard to the answer for which I must beg *immediately* on receipt of this letter, and can then indeed even see you both on your journey, if it is not put off too late. Therefore please address—' König von Würtemberg,' Stuttgart.

---

* A liqueur.

Liszt's plan for me is that I shall go to Paris at the beginning of next year; he will be back in Weimar on October 22. He thinks that the worst is now over for me, and he can very easily prepare the way to a position for me in Paris. But, as I said, all this has still to be talked over.

Liszt's and my next plan for me is *Dresden.* I have promised to play there at the beginning of November, in a concert which a member of the Court band is going to give with the whole orchestra, a promise which I shall certainly keep. Wagner has also given me a commission for arrangements of Lohengrin and Tannhäuser, and, by this work, which must not be delayed, I am certain to earn something. W[agner's] and Meser's disciples have now taken up Tannhäuser, and I can make the conditions, as it is now becoming a very lucrative affair. For this work I must have quiet and a neutral ground. I shall have to make my *début* in Leipzig at the subscription-concert in November. Dresden suits me very well, I was decidedly successful there; I am indeed almost astonished to read so much that is now written about me, and to see terms such as " genial " used in connection with me, in newspapers like the *Illustrirte Zeitung.*

Now what will you do? Whatever I undertake will depend upon that. I need money. Therefore be so good as to forgive me if I am doing wrong in telling you of a proposition which has been made to me, and to believe me when I solemnly declare that I could never think of accepting it without asking and obtaining your sanction.

Madame Ritter—with whom and with whose whole family Liszt is on the most intimate footing—invited me to make her house my home for a while, as she heard that I was returning to Dresden to play at a concert. Alexander R[itter] is now in Breslau as violinist, Carl R[itter] in Pillnitz, just on the point of becoming a subject of Saxony, and engaged to be married, so there really are, here also, *tempi passati;* I could thus have an excellent house, and grand piano, be undisturbed at my work, and in case of necessity be nursed.

God forbid that I should wish to influence your decision, or even think of calling in question your antipathy. But I was obliged to tell you about it, because it would relieve you for the present of anxiety on my behalf, which causes *me,* believe me, as much painful thought as it does you. So forgive, and do not be vexed with me for this.

Now having told you of my next musical plans I beg for a speedy reply to Stuttgart. I am as indifferent to it all as even my dead father can be. I do not care to speak of *him* today in this *business*-letter.

I am in myself so weary and dead that I could not be of assistance to you in any but mechanical work.

It rejoices me more than I can say that you are all together in Ötlis-hausen, and thus honouring the dear father, whose death is a great and very lasting shock to me.

Continue to love me, and forsake me not. Keep well, and Heaven preserve you! All this of course applies to Isidore also.

Your loving son,

HANS.

Joachim can perhaps get me appointed Court-pianist in Hanover. Salary 200 *reichsthaler* for the half year; but I shall be able to give many lessons as well.—Ah, *mon Dieu!*

TO FRANZ LISZT.

DRESDEN, 5th November 1853.

MY VERY DEAR AND ILLUSTRIOUS MASTER,

How much I have to thank you for the long and beautiful letter with which you have so soon condescended to refresh my mind and heart! I hastened at once to do the commissions which you gave me, so that I might be able to answer you without delay, and thus to begin to obliterate the very bad opinion which I led you to form of my qualities as a correspondent last winter.

I feel in reality terribly unhappy and vexed that I have not been able to justify, rather better, your confidence in the Berlioz affair.

Madame de Lüttichau is at this moment so unwell that she has been obliged to keep her bed for several days, and for some time to come she will not be fit to see me, nor even my mother. As, moreover, I knew by numerous experiences that her influence on Mr. de Lüttichau does not go beyond the matrimonial relations, I went bravely to His Excellency, with the very natural pretext of paying my respects to him. In the course of our conversation I touched upon the chapter of Berlioz, by remarking, as though the observation came from you, what an advantage it would be to profit by Berlioz' momentary stay in Germany, by engaging him for a concert in Dresden, which could not fail to arouse immense and universal interest, in view of the remarkable "trimming" in the opinions of the German artists on Berlioz, and his recent brilliant triumphs at Brunswick and Hanover. His Excellency's reply was, first of all, evasive, and then entirely negative:

"A concert in the theatre is now quite impossible. It could not be arranged, because every day now is a subscribers' day, and they *will* have

CARLSRUHE—ÖTLISHAUSEN.   175

theatre and not concert.   One must have regard to the public ; if the
public does not come, then the theatre cannot subsist."

Nevertheless, there would be no need to despair if the time were not
so short.   It would also have been necessary to prepare for it by means
of the press, which I could have had at my disposal through my old
connection with the University.   However, I will go once more to
Carus, who is reputed to have a supreme influence and a certain
ascendancy over the Intendant : I missed him yesterday.   I will also go
and see Krebs, and shall put before him the enjoyment of the uneasiness
Reissiger would feel at the arrival of Berlioz.   Krebs, moreover, gave
the Overture to the 'Francs-Juges' last winter, at a concert in the
theatre.   What would be still better would be for Berlioz to address
himself direct to Mr. de Lüttichau, which, as you supposed, he has not
yet done.

Pohl will dedicate his pamphlet to the Count de Linanges.   I have
advised him to change the form, from *correspondence* into *memoir*, which
would be more objective in *fact* and in *appearance*, and less *journalistic.*
As this alteration will not in the least delay the publication, he has
adopted it.   One only doubt remains to him still—whether he ought
not first to obtain the Count's permission to dedicate it to him.   We
have been very glad, and no doubt you were also, to read at last Pohl's
anticriticism in the *Augsburger* of November 2nd.   Such a rectifi-
cation in this widely-circulated paper was not only desirable, but
indispensable.

If Spina is not as negligent in replying to me as I am prompt in
writing to him, I hope to receive the precious score, which I am
impatiently awaiting, one of these next days.

I took to Hähnel the two copies of Czerny's 'Gradus ad Parnassum,'
not omitting to give him many kind messages from you and the Princess.
He was very much touched by your attention.   The parcel of music
containing your compositions he received a long time ago.   His daughter
is studying your transcription of the Beethoven Songs.   He is going to
write to you very soon, and hopes to be able to accept your invitation to
Weimar in a fortnight, by which time he expects to have finished a
presentable Karl August (according to his own idea), a quality which he
persists in refusing to recognise in his first sketch.

Singer has written to me today.   He has not yet received the slightest
sign of life from the Intendant of the Weimar theatre, and really does
not know what to do about his engagement there, which would make
him very happy.

Yesterday evening I had to listen to Chopin's Second Concerto,
materialised under the fingers of Fräulein Marie Wieck, who is going to

play it at the next *Gewandhaus* concert. Papa Wieck, who has been
pretty amiable to me, and whose vanity still enjoys, in spite of himself,
the recollection of the evening you were good enough to spend with him
in Dresden, will shortly succumb to the jaundice, which he will not fail
to catch, on account of the Trio- and Duet-Soirées which *Monsieur* Jenny
Lind is arranging, together with Schubert and Kummer.

Karl Mayer is rushing about, madly in love with a young Russian
pianist, Mlle. de Harder, a so-called pupil of Chopin, who is going to
play his 'Concerto Symphonique' for the benefit of the poor.

I should be very happy if I had in my possession, as you seem to
imagine, the score of your 'Festgesang,' for then I could have satisfied
my longing to study it thoroughly, and to let myself be influenced, as
much as possible, by the elevation and grandeur of the musical ideas
and sentiments contained in it—qualities which must forcibly touch anyone who feels that there vibrates in himself an artistic string. Ritter, to
whom I have played some bits which I remembered—for the whole of the
work is in my memory only—was so delighted with it that his eyes were
moist with joy. He begs your permission to dedicate to this work a
'*Minoritätsgutachten*' (opinion of the minority) in Brendel's *Gazette*, to
which he will add an article on your Mass. This permission, which I
ask in his name, you can of course only grant by sending us the score.
Now I have just learned from you that you are vainly seeking, among
those who are most deeply interested in it, the score that we so much
want. Do you think you have lent it by chance to Cornelius? None
of us, I assure you, would have ventured to borrow it from you "without
informing the proprietor." Possibly it is at Kalliwoda's, amongst the
other scores which have belonged to the Carlsruhe Institute since the
Festival.

One of these days I shall fulfil the promise I made you at Carlsruhe,
to write a few words on Raff's 'Frühlingsboten.' I hope to satisfy the
composer, whose warm partisan I am as regards this work.

Mozart-Brahms, or Schumann-Brahms, does not in the least trouble
the peace of my sleep. It is about fifteen years since Schumann was
speaking in absolutely analogous terms of the "genius" of W. Sterndale
'Benêt.' * Moreover Joachim knows Brahms, as well as the un-German
Reményi,† who would render me excessively happy if he would keep his
promise of coming to see us in Dresden, as he told my mother he would.

The latest numbers of the *Signale* bear pretty marked traces of my
indiscreet confidences to the editor. I had not anticipated that I should

---

* William Sterndale Bennett, the English composer (1816-1875)
† Reményi, the violin virtuoso, born in Hungary 1830.

read an almost verbal reproduction of the piquant notices I had given him. It is a good lesson for the future.

Please excuse, my dearest Master, the *sans-façon* of this letter, which I have written in haste. I hope soon to hear of you through Ritter, to whom you were intending to write shortly. I reiterate my thanks for your letter, and beg you to continue your precious and inestimable friendship to your respectfully devoted and grateful pupil.

NORTH GERMANY

CHAPTER IX.

NORTH GERMANY.

WINTER 1853—SPRING 1854.

TO HIS MOTHER.

BERLIN, *4th December* 1853.

BELOVED MOTHER,

Yesterday morning I felt in such a rage that I was over-flowing with gall. Today I am in a more peaceful mood, for yesterday evening I had a very warm reception and real success. I have shown people once more what piano-playing means. My ear is still flattered by the agreeable sound of a breathless suspense after my *pianos*. I am contented with myself and also with the world.

Although I was intending to leave yesterday, yet now I have changed my mind. Redern, who held forth pretty extensively about my Liszt style of playing, and about the execution of Liszt's compositions, against both of which he inveighed, has indeed promised to send me an invitation, in the course of this winter, to play at a Court concert at Dresden, but I don't really believe in it.

. . . .

Herewith a programme of the concert. My choice was a carefully-considered one, and justified itself in spite of the wretched playing of " die Gänze " (the whole),* who may be compared with those before whom one casts pearls. Singer's playing was wonderfully beautiful in the Trio.

. . . .

Bettina and Gisel are at Weimar. I hear from Leipzig that Liszt, Raff, Cornelius, Laub, Klindworth and Pruckner were there on Thursday for the Berlioz concert. It seems to have turned out well, in spite of many opponents. Joachim sends best greetings to you. Moreover he

---

* A pun on the name of one of the performers, a Herr Ganz.

does not write much. I have been often very sad here; but, with my passionate nature, my feelings are always running from one extreme to the other. So, if Louise has written anything to you about my fit of dejection, you must regard it only as a passing thing. Wagner's disciples will be inquiring after me next in Dresden, in order to ask me about Tannhäuser arrangements, and to hear my conditions. If therefore anybody should make his appearance, please say that I shall be back very soon. I have never found the theatre and that kind of thing so uninteresting as it has been since I have been here. I go in for very little amusement, and am delighted to think of soon being with you again.

TO HIS MOTHER.

BREMEN, 21st December 1853.

BELOVED MOTHER,

I can find very little time for writing, so I must be very laconic, and therefore take only a half-sheet for my letter, so that I may not be tempted to run on and on, as I so often do. What a lot of useless words already, as an introduction to the so-called telegram! This runs as follows: great success, satisfaction with myself and with the public. . . . I played the Concerto extremely satisfactorily; the accompaniment was exceptionally excellent, and the whole thing went with spirit and fire. No misfortune with the piano. After my two pieces in the second part I was repeatedly called forward, and had to play an extra piece, one of the 'Soirées de Vienne.' At the present moment I have just breakfasted, and am playing with double louis d'ors.

The concert-directors, very musical and cultivated people, merchants and lawyers, have been extremely kind to me in every way, up to now, taking me all round Bremen, where there are plenty of things worth seeing.

I feel so glad to have played 'Louis van's'* Concerto again once more, and to have played it well—for now I shall play it much better the next time.

Liszt writes most kindly and affectionately in both his letters to me. I submit to his advice and wishes, in spite of the opposition of my pride —that is to say, I am writing to David this very day with regard to *playing in Leipzig*. As it must be so, I submit.

---

* His familiar name for Beethoven.

TO FRANZ LISZT.

HANOVER, 23rd *December* 1853.

MY VERY DEAR AND ILLUSTRIOUS MASTER,

.   .   .   .

Perhaps you would be kind enough to read through my letter to David and see if you think it will do? I hope that the score and my arrangement of David's Overture will reach you at the same time; for you have already been so very good as to undertake to present my respects to him. As it is you who advised me to write to him, I did not for a moment fear to be wanting in dignity by following your valued advice; nevertheless it was not easy to me to write those few lines.

I am very much obliged to you for the score of the 'Caprice Turc'; but I have not yet received the orchestral parts. Would you kindly tell me which Trio of Schumann it would be best for me to play at Leipzig? I have had Schubert's Fantasia sent to me at Hanover, so that I may study it at my ease during my stay here, which I shall prolong for about a fortnight more, as Joachim has engaged me for the concert on the 7th January. If Hiller's victim [Joachim] does not arrive tomorrow I shall spend rather a dismal Christmas Day. On my way to Bremen I stopped at Brunswick, where I saw Litolff. We played the piece from 'Cellini' together *à quatre mains;* he presented me with his third Trio (C minor) which has just come out, and in which there is a good deal of lost labour and much of the "music of the past and of the old romantic school." It seems that your compositions will not be published so soon. You can well guess that I did not fail to go and see Mesdemoiselles Spohr, whom I found most amiable, and with whom I fell in love afresh in equal shares. The family is going to Paris at the beginning of the New Year, because Mlle. Rosalie requires a new instrument, and thence to Brussels. If I find Hanover too tedious, I shall perhaps go before New Year and spend a few days at Brunswick in adoration of Mesdemoiselles Spohr.

.   .   .   .

I feel very jealous of the dignity of Reményi. Would it not be possible to tack the name *of any decent beast* onto my name? Or could not you manage to grant me letters patent of "knight of the order of St. Rappo," which would first have to be created? I would assuredly endeavour to render myself worthy of such an honour.

Please excuse the haste and disorder of these lines!

TO HIS MOTHER.

HANOVER, 24*th December* 1853.

BELOVED MOTHER,

        I reached here a couple of hours ago, and, as the post is quite near my hotel ('Rheinischer Hof,' where however I shan't stay, as it is *mesquin*), I have fetched your letter, and begin to answer you, immediately after having written fully to Liszt to Leipzig, and enclosed a note for David in spite of inward reluctance. There are a good many things that might be said on this point; but on the whole it is sufficient to *think* them.

        I enjoyed myself very much in Bremen, and almost repent of having left it today, as I am suffering from headache; Joachim has not yet returned from Cologne—I hope he is coming this evening—and I shall have a melancholy Christmas Eve. Consequently I shall be just as sorry as you that I cannot be with you.

        From the post I went to a clothier's and bought myself a decent black waistcoat, very dear, but practical and elegant (3 thalers, 16 groschen). This I then made my Christmas box to myself, that is, I admired it when I got home. That reminds me that I owe most grateful thanks for the silk handkerchiefs I found in my box. May you be happier and feeling better than I . . . this evening! I shall certainly go to bed early—yet No, for at 10 o'clock I must go to the station, which however is just opposite, to see after Joachim. Warsaw tempts me but little at this moment . . . and yet why not, if nothing better turns up? I have not yet written to Liszt about that.

        So do not yet refuse it. One can certainly wait a little before deciding. And yet, on one hand, it is really an execrably Polish or Russian concern.

25th December.

        From 8 o'clock till 10 I slept. I woke up just in time to go to the station. When it was pretty nearly 11 o'clock came Joachim at last, the train being very late. Our meeting was then a very happy and enjoyable one. Today we have been playing most of the day, and called on Count Platen, who at first was rather formal, but afterwards became very friendly. Lüttichau has had me introduced to him verbally already through Kapellmeister Fischer * of Hanover, who was lately in Dresden, and was commissioned to look me up. Hanover is rather slow. A

---

* Karl Ludwig Fischer, 1816-77,

dead-alive sort of place; in the road one sees nobody. We are having it cold and no mistake, 6-8 degrees, but a healthy air. Today there is no theatre, tomorrow is the 'Jungfrau von Orleans,' and the day after tomorrow the 'Freischütz.'

So on the 7th January I shall play at the concert here; probably shortly before that I shall play at the Court, but just not in the old year. Then on Tuesday or Wednesday I am going to Brunswick for a couple of days, to see the Spohrs. When I return I shall stop with Joachim. . . . Why have you not heard the Lind? Songs she does sing well. The Bayer-Bürk warmly defended my Sontag article lately in company!

What is Isidore's publisher about? Is there no answer yet?

28th December.

Yesterday I went to see Herr von Grote, to whom Ernst introduced me. It is quite possible that he will give himself some trouble on my behalf. He is a colonel, whereas Platen is only a captain. We shall see. I don't give way to sanguine hopes in this respect, as you know. I have received what you sent me. I know not where any more letters should come from now, when I won't answer any in the old year.

One thing which attracts me very much to Hanover is the splendid grand pianos of Rittmüller from Göttingen—Erard's mechanism. Liszt himself had spoken much of them to me formerly. They are delightful to play on. I practise four hours a day on one, as I am so enchanted with their rich tone. Joachim finds it very slow here . . . he does not know a soul, and longs to be off. It is indescribably dead-alive here. He has plenty of time for himself; that is one good thing.

The Berlin letter was from Truhn; a very kind one. I would rather be in Berlin now, or else in Dresden. Ditto Joachim, of course. But we *ennuyer* ourselves in duet here!

Yesterday we were at Marschner's; such a comic, fat face, that I had some difficulty to keep from laughing. Uncommonly amiable to me, Joachim thinks. Towards Berlioz he has become quite '*rustre*' [boorish].

29th December.

Today I read in the hotel the *Hamburger Correspondent*, the chief political paper of the north, 122 years old; and in it there was a most famous critique of my Berlin success—to employ a used-up word—very long, very striking for all the many readers of this paper in Hanover, Bremen and all this neighbourhood. It pleased me especially that Volkmann was so highly praised, as also my services in having played the Trio; moreover I feel more and more that I was instinctively right in hitting on this choice, from which all "well-meaning, practical" people had dissuaded me. And, in regard to Volkmann, who lately thanked me in the most touching manner, I now stand not censured by Rellstab's trash—and that is the best of all.

Joachim will introduce me, in a few days' time, to the Court lady, Countess Bernstorff, who, according to his opinion, is the most musical, most amiable, and most *spirituelle* of all the Court plants, which I do not doubt. But . . . can Joachim do this? I mean, is it the correct thing for him to take me like that to an unmarried lady? I should be glad if you would tell me this quickly.

At New Year I have some letters to write; to Liszt; and to Raff, to whom I owe an answer to three letters. Early this morning I have been playing with Joachim to a few old ladies. He thinks I am very much improved.

Now I want to send off my letter quickly, so that you may hear from me on New Year's Day, and not begin 1854 first thing with any kind of anxiety about me, who have given you so much occasion for sorrow, and also, at the same time, for proving your unbounded motherly love! Believe me that I discern it, not with a mere look of intelligent gratitude, but with a heart full to overflowing, a thing which seldom happens, and then in secret; and that the happiest day of my life will be when you feel you can own to yourself that you have not wasted your love on an un-worthy object. What I used to write in my lessons at school as a child— New Year's wishes to parents (O my God)—this I feel today more strongly than ever in my inmost heart. No need for me to tell you *what I wish for you;* I know that the greater part of your wishes for yourself concern me; may it be granted me soon to fulfil them to some degree. The great seriousness of life has opened before me in the terrible year that is leaving us. Grief for *him* has entered my very soul; the feeling of *his* death, and, together with that, the feeling of death in general, will be ever present with me. I have matured, in carrying this feeling about with me; and if I do not let it appear, as others do, it is because it would overcome me too overpoweringly. But I dedicate to *his* memory my *best* moments.

May you, beloved mother, my nearest and dearest comforter, begin the New Year well and happily, trusting in the future for me and for thee !

I kiss your hand reverently, and am

Your loving son HANS,

whose heart belongs to you.

Thus closed for Bülow this year of 1853, so rich in events that moulded his character. It had brought forth more of importance than any year he had yet lived through : his first artistic tour with the disillusion it brought ; his first success in Berlin ; the death of his father, of Ludwig Tieck * and of Theodor Uhlig. It required all the strength of his nature, all the energy of his will, gradually to shake himself free from the paralysing pressure of these events, and to set himself with renewed zeal to the work of life.

Writing to his mother from Hanover on the 6th January 1854, he says :

I have got to know Robert Schumann's young prophet Brahms pretty well ; he has been here a couple of days and constantly with us. A very loveable, candid nature, and something really of God's grace, in the best sense, in his talent !

From Dresden he writes, on the 5th February 1854, to Frau von Milde, the celebrated singer in Weimar :

DEAR MADAME AND ARTISTE,
　　　　　　　If it is not too late, and you have not quite lost your interest in those old songs, the value of which consists in the name you permitted me to inscribe in the dedication, I could almost bless fate for giving me the opportunity, thanks to the unpardonable carelessness of the publisher, of sending you my first work myself, together with these few lines.†

I do not introduce my songs to you, according to the fashion of young composers, in order to beg you to give them an unmerited honour by your wonderful talent : I had the higher ambition of composing them for your private music-room, and not for drawing-room audiences. But if I should see you again some day, you would make me endlessly happy in perfecting one or other of them, whichever one you prefer, by your singing of it to me alone.

TO HIS MOTHER.

HAMBURG, 13th February 1854.

DEAREST MOTHER,
　　　　　　　I can only write, very briefly, the most necessary things today. I have played and won—that is the chief thing. My playing of the E flat major Concerto by heart made a great impression. It went

---

* The old friend of Bülow's father.

† 'Six poems by Heine and Sternau.' Set to music, for soprano or tenor voice, with pianoforte accompaniment, and dedicated to Frau Rosalie von Milde, by Hans von Bülow.—Op. 1. (Leipzig, C. F. Kahnt, 1853.)

well.   The applause was not exactly very *extensive*, but was of a kind
that made them ask me to give another concert, a soirée of Chamber-music,
or else to play in the theatre.   One of these two things I shall do.   On
Wednesday I shall have an answer as to the possibility (that is, the
guaranteeing) of a Trio-Soirée, or something of the kind.   I have just
written to Joachim to ask whether I could not play at Court in Hanover
at the present time, and of course I am waiting for his answer.   I shall
not write to Brunswick till later—that is to say, when something definite
is settled about what I have just mentioned ; in any case I shall ask for
my expenses of journey and stay there (reckoned at 8 louis d'or).

I am now so *fearfully* busy that I have not time to write at any length :
it is one constant ringing the changes between musical déjeuners, dinners
and suppers.   When I first came I was very much cast down, and the
journey was a very fatal one, and much dearer than I had imagined, on
account of the night-express.   Just this moment a lady pianist has been
here, who is going to give a concert in a fortnight, and who begged me to
give her some explanations and advice about one of Liszt's Rhapsodies,
which she is going to play ; directly after that came a composer, who
brought me some of his compositions for a present,—and that is how one
is set on.

I will continue after this interruption.

My stay in Berlin was too transient for me to be able to call on the
Arnims, so I left Isidore's letter in great haste at Louise's.   She was not
at home, but I kissed the sleeping children on the forehead.   At first I
had great difficulty in getting a good instrument here—one that suited
me in the touch.   At last I was so fortunate as to meet, quite unexpectedly, with friend Speidel from Munich, who helped me.   He had
been here some days, and would have liked to make his appearance here,
which I now unintentionally prevented.

The manner of our meeting was really most original.   We met at the
door of the hotel, in which we were both living, on the way to the same
lady, to whom we both had letters of introduction.   A splendid scene for
a comic opera !

It was most welcome and pleasant to me to have found a companion
and colleague with whom I get on so well, and who is prolonging his
fruitless stay here on my account.

Life here is exceedingly jolly, and not so enormously dear as it was
said to be.   Nothing to compare with Vienna.

And what a glorious city !   Really magnificent — where I live it
looks quite Venetian !   And this delightful climate with the balmy sea-
air—so that one is not freezing, in spite of the excessively piercing cold,
which has come back again.

As soon as I have finished this letter I must go to Altona, to call on some of the musical authorities—Marxen,* Böie and others; on the side of the musicians I have been met with great esteem—low be it spoken—and am treated as a "*quelqu' un*," not as a "*quelque chose*," which is good. But unberufen, unberufen, unberufen! [Low be it spoken.] Otherwise the next thing will be, I shall have to eat my words, as it has always happened before.

As I said, I cannot at once give you a definite answer, but must wait for what I mentioned at the beginning of my letter. You will see from this that I am trying to be not unpractical, but tolerably expeditious, and also cautious in a negative sense, by not immediately rejecting anything that might offer.

W.'s letter got me a free ticket for the (reserved) pit. It won't do anything more for me, so set your mind at rest about that.

I have made the acquaintance of Kapellmeister Ignatz Lachner, through Speidel, and we frequently see each other.

If you did but know how *driven* I am today; to bed at half-past twelve, up at seven, and innumerable, unavoidable calls already by eleven o'clock.

I would send you back the money for my journey today with best thanks, if I could get it changed into notes; but the waiter has not got them by him, and time fails.

Farewell, and be ever especially good to me.

TO HIS MOTHER.

HAMBURG, 24*th February* 1854.

MOTTO : *Unberufen, unberufen, unberufen !*

DEAREST MOTHER,

I must say my head is very bad, and I have some trouble in recovering myself sufficiently to be able to give my concert this evening at the theatre, and after that to rejoice a big musical salon with my presence and my playing. But I have still a free moment, which allows me to write a line to you. Yesterday I gave my musical matinée—see programme. It was brilliant! All that Hamburg contains of the most elegant and distinguished met there. My clear profits amounted to about 20 louis d'or. I send you five herewith, as a reimbursement of a small portion of all the money I have cost you for my pianistic travelling expenses lately, and am paying, with another five, various debts. On the 1st March I must support Glasbrenner's concert as I have promised; on

---

* Eduard Marxen (1806-1887), the teacher of Johannes Brahms.

the 6th is my soirée at Altona; on the 11th I have to play in Brunswick, where Joachim has promised me his collaboration. It would be mad to come back to Dresden just now; I shall still have to be away a good fortnight longer. These are my present plans; it is possible that there may be alterations, but, in that case, you shall hear from me at once. I did not write sooner, because I wanted to be able to tell you the results of my concert, and to give you good tidings.

What a constant alternation it has been for me of soirées, suppers, dinners and déjeuners; how I have been fêted and made much of in the salons—it is impossible to write all this, or to reckon up all my acquaintances. I am the darling of all the well-to-do, and also of the aristocratic and best society; they fight about me; the musicians—the artistic ones—like me very much, and will not hear of my going until I have promised to come back in the autumn and arrange some soirées. With all this there is so little social constraint; in short, up to the present time it has been perfectly delightful here, more so than ever before, or anywhere else. Count Redern has sent me a letter to his brother-in-law—otherwise nothing has been said with regard to the Court concert—which I have not yet been able to deliver.

I am playing a great deal—because I must; I must have my whole *répertoire* in my head, and be always ready to play any favourite Trio of Beethoven, Mendelssohn, etc., at sight.

If only things will last for a while, and go on as well as they are doing now!

How are you? And how is Isidore? Write soon: I myself really have not time.

    .   .   .   .

Meanwhile farewell.

Your loving son

HANS v. B.

Best love to Isa of course. What has Max Duncker replied?

The Press praises me with fabulous respect. I am quoted as an authority; "Master," "full of talent," — these are now quite trite expressions.

TO HIS MOTHER.

HAMBURG, 7th March 1854.

DEAREST MOTHER,

      I am so glad you have written to me, that is, that I have got a letter from you this morning, for I was intending to write to you as soon as I was up, even if it were a disjointed letter, which is all I can manage nowadays. I am dreading Dresden after your description. Yet I must not stay here very much longer now, where I have been so happy. For many reasons I *must* leave. In the first place Lacombe (a really firstrate pianist and musician and a delightful man) is giving concerts here, and, before he has finished, will follow the Clauss,* who has been engaged by an *entrepreneur* here to give four concerts in eight days. Fräulein Wilhelmine was at my concert at Altona yesterday evening, of which Böie had undertaken the arrangement in his (beloved and well-known) name. It was very pleasant. The results are destined to buy me a new pair of patent leather boots, a hat and an overcoat, and also to fulfil Isa's desire of a novel. In spite of the fatiguing night-journey from Berlin here, she (the Clauss) remained till the end, and was very complimentary to me at the conclusion. She is not pretty—for the rest I am curious to hear her play, and shall call on her today. She is a great favourite *here* from previous visits. . . . This evening there is a party at Schuberth's, the brother who represents here the business of the well-known music-firm, the head of which now lives in New York. Fritz S[chuberth] has been, up to the present time, most agreeable to me, and I am the same to him. Tomorrow is Quartet-soirée in Altona (which is only divided from Hamburg by a narrow trench which one can jump across). After an hour at the opera I must go on to this. Thursday early is Lacombe's matinée, in the evening is the Clauss concert, from which I must hurry on to a monster-soirée to Hamburg's monarch, Senator Jenisch. On Friday I won't travel; consequently I shall leave on Saturday, going direct to Brunswick, where I give my concert in the theatre on Tuesday the 14th.

Then possibly to Berlin, but more probably (as far as I know at present) back to Dresden. So please address the next letters, *poste restante*, Brunswick, or to the '*Deutsches Haus.*' Kiel I have given up.

I read in the papers that Livia had been singing in public concerts in Wiesbaden with great success, especially in songs of Mendelssohn.

Would you send me three copies of Rigoletto to Brunswick?

After the concert we went yesterday to a Madame Petersen in Altona, a very cultivated amateur and pleasant woman.

Life here has been very bearable : of course there was no lack of small miseries, partly of my own making.

A dilemma does one good occasionally, and is wholesome at my age; and emptiness of mind is certainly not so sovereign in the circles I frequent here, as elsewhere.

---

* Wilhelmine Clauss (1834), a pianist, afterwards married to the writer Szarvady.

The news from Weimar would have affected me more, had I not become *blasé* of ill news by the much sadder tidings which I heard a few days ago, and which have shaken me terribly—the tragic end of Schumann. He threw himself into the Rhine a week ago in a fit of mental derangement (he had latterly been constantly seeing apparitions); he was rescued by some boatmen, but has since then been placed in an asylum at Bonn, for he is quite out of his mind. Joachim is quite inconsolable, and has gone at once with Brahms to Düsseldorf to see the poor wife. I had so rejoiced at the thought of approaching this rare and noble artist-mind, a pleasure which Joachim had lately assiduously endeavoured to bring about, so that, through his mediation, Robert Schumann had asked me to go and see him when I had an opportunity. Life has again lost something for me. Of course Joachim cannot think of playing in public just now, or of coming to Brunswick on my account.

.　　.　　.　　.　　.　　.　　.　　.　　.　　.

TO HIS MOTHER.

BRUNSWICK, 14*th March* 1854 : 10 P.M.

DEAREST MOTHER,

So it seems, after all, you have not received my last letter from Hamburg (with an enclosure for Thode)? I begged you in it to send me an answer quickly, so that I might find a few lines awaiting me here. I have been waiting for them in vain since the day before yesterday, so that, in the first place, I don't know what to do. I left Hamburg on Saturday the 11th, and look back on the time I spent there with the most unclouded happiness. I remained about 24 hours in Hanover, where I had a very pleasant time with Joachim and Klindworth, and heard a very good Quartet at the house of the former.

Here, on the contrary, it is perfectly horrid.

My concert in the theatre is just over. The best singers were hoarse, and the interest was centred in myself alone. The room was pretty empty; the audience pretty cold, except in the Beethoven Concerto;—and, to be brief, I am very much dissatisfied. Before all else I want now to know whether I can stay in Dresden : my room is given up, so where shall I go? At present I don't feel much inclined for Berlin. There I should have to submit to be cheated at the hotel, and I don't exactly feel disposed for that.

They let me give my concert here at a very unfavourable moment. The impending arrival of Pepita,* who has not yet been seen here, was

---

* A dancer.

advertised a few days ago, and has aroused the local curiosity to the highest pitch, so that nothing else is talked of. It seemed as if everything had conspired against me here. The piano was very bad. Rittmüller had promised me a splendid one of his own; he came with me himself from Hanover, and we both waited in vain for the promised piano from Göttingen; now it has arrived—a couple of hours before the concert, consequently too late! The Duke, also, is absent, travelling.

Yesterday I had an awfully slow time at Herr v. Y.'s, with three other lieutenants and the tenor S. I had to accompany his musical bluestocking of a wife in a couple of dozen songs. She is rather Austrian, but somewhat more passable than her husband. By tomorrow evening I hope to have received a letter from you, and to be able to start for Dresden. If not, I shall go to Hanover, in spite of Ida Spohr's kindness, to stay a couple of days with Joachim. In Hanover at any rate one feeds a little better than here: here it is bad beyond all description. Wretched tea, wretched coffee, wretched dinner, no porter, no Chester [sic] cheese—everything miserable; when one comes from Hamburg it is enough to drive one to suicide.

Now I observe for the first time how well I was, physically, in Hamburg,—my digestion especially. I could become sentimental in thinking of it! A healthy material life means a great deal: long live materialism!

Rosalie Spohr is just now giving concerts in Holland. Of course I often go to see Ida; she is very amiable. But that " does not go far," as the post-office wittily wrote on my Berlin friend Kolb's letter. I have got immensely spoiled by Hamburg. Next Thursday I ought to have dined with Jenisch, but how! I am not joking when I assure you that the tears are in my eyes. . . . Such a Hamburg luncheon! Long live Krebs! Down with Hoplit!

Next Saturday or Sunday a parcel from Hamburg will arrive for me in Dresden. Amongst other things it contains some excellent tea for you, so please open it. There will be a letter for Schuberth in the parcel. I hope I shall soon get a letter from you.

Adieu; I am sleepy, and very, very sulky. Farewell. Compassionate me!

DRESDEN—CHOCIESZEWICE—BERLIN

CHAPTER X.

TO FRANZ LISZT.

DRESDEN, *30th April* 1854.
DOHNAISCHE STRASSE 3/II.

MY VERY DEAR AND ILLUSTRIOUS MASTER,

As I like to push my conscience, as your pupil, beyond purely musical limits, and as I know your aversion to useless conversations—an aversion which I share—I have not ventured to trouble you with a correspondence which would have deserved to be placed in that category, since my last letter, in which I discharged myself of some little commissions I had done for you.

My "*faits et gestes*" in Hamburg etc., as you are pleased kindly to designate my recent poor attempts as a pianist of the third order—attempts which have perhaps been a little happier than those of my late *début* in Vienna last year—seemed to me, on my return to Dresden, so paltry and still-born, that I thought it would be childish and inexcusable, and therefore impossible, to resuscitate them by a posthumous account of them which would have made you smile.

I should doubtless have ventured to write to you about myself, if I had had anything serious to tell you, such as the results of Berlioz' concerts at Dresden, and I should certainly not have delayed replying to your very kind letter, for which please receive my warmest thanks, if I had not thought it essential to wait till after the third concert, which took place last night, and which promised to be the decisive one.

Well, it is a very happy moment for me to be able to give you the best possible news of an event which you cannot have more at heart than I, who have felt my enthusiasm for Berlioz increase at each concert. Last night's concert was one of the most brilliant triumphs that Berlioz has celebrated in Germany. A full room, overflowing with all that there is of the most choice, of the most " æsthetically" elegant in Dresden, received the composer with the utmost warmth on his entrance. The audience underlined every piece on the programme by their repeated applause, by *rinforzandos* unheard in Dresden since Wagner's flight; they encored the third number of the mystic mystery, and clapped with frenzy when a laurel-wreath was thrown from one of the boxes in the second circle, and fell at the composer's feet. In spite of their fatigue, the orchestra surpassed themselves in their performance of the last piece on the programme, the Overture to 'Cellini.' An ovation, quietly prepared by the younger generation in the orchestra, terminated this memorable evening in the midst of the wildest applause of the audience. (Reissiger and even Lipinski had opposed this in the morning; for the rest Reissiger has behaved very well in regard to Berlioz, but his enthusiasm freezes when it reaches envy-point.) Mr. de Lüttichau immediately begged the artist to favour them with a repetition of the " last" concert, and it will take place tomorrow, Monday. Thus, four concerts instead of two; and the almost certain prospect of the performance of 'Cellini,' to which the playing of the two Overtures to the opera will have contributed not a little. The perfidious criticism of Mr. Banck has disturbed the revival of 'Faust.' At the second concert there was not a large audience, but it must be added that those who were there belonged to the *élite* of the public from the musical point of view, and that they showed themselves very demonstrative. The remarkable *crescendo* in the numbers of the audience, which gave the lie yesterday in so brilliant a manner to the "press," would have been evident at the renewal of 'Faust,' had it not been for those villainous insects, the critics. The whole orchestra and the singers are plunged head over ears in enthusiasm. They are happy at being able to estimate at their just value their own talents and capacities, by means of this incomparable conductor, who makes them feel the disgrace and sterility of the five or six last years; and they all, beginning with Mr. de Lüttichau, who is *beaming* up to a point of which I should never have deemed him capable, would like to keep Berlioz at Dresden as their conductor. One may be satisfied with everybody, and the best feelings reign everywhere. After the first rehearsal Mr. Berlioz had destroyed every germ of opposition, converted the most refractory, and God only knows how many of these there were! In short, your predictions, when you were in Dresden last year, might very well soon come to pass. Mr. de Lüttichau has already come forward with more than hints to Mr. Berlioz; he has asked him, amongst other things, to get up Gluck's 'Orpheus' and to conduct it, Mr. de L. intending to stage it next season. To Mr.

Berlioz' remark that there was not a spare place in Dresden, all being very well filled, he replied in these pretty clear words : " Who knows ! "

Just fancy ! a week ago Krebs, at the Catholic Church, bitterly reproached and seriously reprimanded the orchestra for having played so magnificently under the conducting of a " foreigner." What a public humiliation for the local conductors, under whose direction the orchestra had never succeeded in showing so much zeal and ardour ! This sounds like a made-up story, and yet it is not so in the least. Krebs has the instinctive feeling that something extraordinary is preparing, which might very well turn against himself. In spite of this, he is so stupid as to make an unequivocal opposition to the sincere and cordial admiration which Reissiger has from the first moment shown, and continues to show, for the works of Berlioz. The other day, at a dinner at Mr. de Lüttichau's at which I was present, Krebs shone in an unaccustomed manner by his absence, accentuated by the presence of Reissiger, Fischer, Lipinski, Schubert, Dawison, etc. At this dinner, given in honour of Berlioz, the minister of Zeschau was also present.

Mr. Berlioz will probably write to you himself this morning and give you his impressions, and tell you how far he is personally satisfied ; I have therefore nothing to add to this chapter, reserving to myself always to keep you *au courant*, if your hopes should receive a positive or approximate affirmation.

I hope you have still a sufficiently good opinion of me, not to doubt that, during Berlioz' stay in Dresden, I have done all I could to be of service to this Master, whom I admire and revere with all my heart, whilst remembering with gratitude the origin of this admiration. I have not been able to do anything much ; for instance, I have only been able to write one preparatory article in a paper, the editor of which did not accept my offer of writing the critiques of the concerts gratis, for fear of wounding the susceptibility of his regular critic. On the other hand, I enrolled under the banner of Berlioz, without any ostentation, some enthusiasts among the artists, and especially among those of the orchestra. At a given moment it would perhaps be well to remind Mr. Berlioz that the first and the warmest friends he has found in Dresden in the orchestra and the audience, belong to the Wagner party, and have long belonged to it. The words I have just written—useless perhaps—have suggested themselves to my mind by the remembrance of some of Mme. Berlioz's chatter on the subject of Richard Wagner, which has irritated me a good deal. But she is, on the whole, an excellent woman, with just the failing of being rather a chatter-box, and of telling a lot of tales to which it would be wrong to pay any attention.

Ritter is enthusiastic about Berlioz. Although he is suffering from the effects of an operation, he seconded me at the first performance of 'Faust,' by taking a box with me for sixteen people, to which we invited our friends and acquaintances, all the best people there are, such as Blassmann, Hähnel, etc.

A thousand thanks for the score of the 'Künstler' chorus; I have had to get gradually accustomed to the rhythmic alterations you have thought well to introduce. The '*alternativa*' is, to me, the most sympathetic part. It is sublime, and I had already felt it to be so at Carlsruhe.

You are very good to think of me, and to wish to make known to me your new compositions for the piano. As to the piece on 'Cellini,' I played it at Brunswick. It was tantamount to a *fiasco* for me—which increased my pleasure all the more, a pleasure shared by Litolff, who was present at the concert as audience. He has given me the corrected sheets of your *chef-d'œuvre* of a Scherzo, and I have already been studying it for a long time.

I will send you very soon the article of Mme. la Princesse Wittgenstein, which I have translated for Brendel. As to the signature, I had to invent one, as I was firmly convinced that you were not the author of this polemic.

I present you my most humble excuses for the "flatness of W. J." It is through my hands that the correspondence of Singer passed, and I had the unjustifiable caprice of leaving in it my paw-mark. I will only add that I acted in this *bonâ fide;* I remember that there was a time when insinuations of that kind did not altogether displease you. But as it is otherwise now, I am the first to retract, and I will beware of a repetition of the offence, all the more as I am sick of the pen—of criticism. I will leave to Hoplit the care of making himself illustrious, and even of getting himself canonised as "*santo*" and "*chiaro*" by this means.

The very sound of "Weimar" or "Leipzig" is enough to throw me into a fever and a passion. Those wretched people go on everlastingly persecuting and illtreating me; I have sworn that I will pay them back one day all I owe them with interest. I regret bitterly that I was so weak towards David, who has known how to take advantage of it! These people now think they have a right to despise me as a man without any character, on account of my "inconsistency."

I shall have great pleasure in being present at your rehearsal in Leipzig. This little journey will also give me the opportunity of giving my opinion to Doctor Härtel, which I am resolved to do.

I am awaiting, at Dresden, the result of the steps I have taken, in the hope of putting an end to my civilian uncertainties. I must, before all else, have a passport *en règle.* I am very much afraid that my most earnest wish to leave Germany and to bury myself at Warsaw, as a pianist "in the service of" a Russian General—and that as soon as possible—will now meet with rather serious obstacles, and that this project will prove entirely abortive.

I have not yet got any decisive news, and that is why I have not spoken to you about it before.

I would not cover myself with ridicule by sending you the pieces of which you speak ; they were the merest trifles which found by chance an *imbécile* of a publisher. But in case I should soon finish a musical daguerreotype of my own (an orchestral work), I should venture to lay it at once before you.

TO FRANZ LISZT.

DRESDEN, *6th May* 1854.

MY VERY DEAR AND ILLUSTRIOUS MASTER,

. . . .

At the present moment I am enjoying to the full the echo of the intoxicating music of Berlioz, in which I have passed three weeks which I should be very sorry to see erased from the programme of my life. Of the barometer of my admiration and sympathy for the works of this Master I am able to judge now that I have a perfect understanding of them. I understand and appreciate his music in all the unity of its individuality ; and the many flights of his genius, which had struck me at first, do not shine any longer in the darkness, for that is dissipated.

You do not yet know the two last parts of ' Faust.' Ah ! how I envy you ! The fourth part especially is magnificent in imagination, sublime in originality.

I have promised Mr. Berlioz to arrange the first Overture to his ' Cellini' for the piano *à quatre mains,* so that it may be incorporated in the piano score to be published, like the operas of Spohr, for example ; as I have time just now, I should like to set to the work without delay. But where should I get the score, unless you would have the great kindness to lend me yours for a fortnight at most ?

If a publisher could be found, I would write a pamphlet on ' Cellini,' as a preparation for the opera at Dresden. If you know of one, and if you invite me to do it, I am ready to do so. Of course it is understood that I shall not expect payment for it. Mr. Berlioz has had much pleasure from my translating of the article I enclose herewith from a Dresden paper, which does great honour to the spirit of its author. It is at his instance that I send it to you.

. . . .

And, writing again to Liszt from Dresden, on the 29th June, he says :

My future is now certain for a pretty long time to come. When you know how, you will not think I have been over-dazzled or enchanted ; but, since it is settled, I am less uneasy, and I am not suffering too much from frustrated ambition. I have just accepted an engagement which has been offered me by a rich Polish Count—Mycielski—who will take me off with him towards the beginning of September, to be music-master to his three or four prodigies of daughters, at his country seat which is situated between Posen and Breslau. I shall have four hundred crowns a year, and of course my living, and all that is necessary to enable me to fulfil my daily task, which is, to give three or four lessons a day, and to amuse the people in the evening with my playing. As the family is living in Dresden at the present moment I have already begun to work a few weeks ago, by giving lessons. I shall have plenty of time, when I am there, to work by myself just as I like ; to compose Trios, Symphonies, etc. *à la* Rubinstein, with or without inspiration ; and I shall also have the advantage of forgetting and ignoring everything in the musical or unmusical world which might vex me or irritate my nerves, and also of strengthening my health by a stay in the country, whilst strengthening at the same time my apathy and my disgust at a good many things—a kind of well-being which I have begun to enjoy lately, and which would not even be disturbed by the otherwise agreeable news of the downfall of one of my *bêtes noires*.

Please excuse the unrestrainedness of these intellectual rambles, which you have so often tolerated with indulgence in my epistolary conversation. And now let us speak of other things than the internal and external tribulations of my more or less defective career. I am not in the least neglecting the piano ; I am studying Bach's Preludes and Fugues, your 'Études d'après Paganini,' and Beethoven's 33 Variations, Op. 120, for which I have a most tremendous weakness. I am just in the midst of a Fantasia for orchestra (in B minor), in the style of my friend Raff ; I have just re-instrumentated and entirely corrected the Overture to ' Cæsar ' ; and I am making successive transcriptions from ' Tannhäuser ' for four hands, which are slow in coming out.

Wagner is so good as to give me news of himself from time to time. He has promised to send me his first opera of the ' Nibelungen,' as soon as he has made a fair copy of it, so that I may make the piano score from it. To my great regret I was unable to accept his invitation for the Festival at Sitten. But the one who might very well have done it, and who was wrong in not wanting to go, was Joachim. I have just heard, I don't know from whom, that my friend, who is so terribly luke-warm as a correspondent, is gone to Vienna, to spend his summer holidays, as I was told. Is it true?

. . . .

Hans spent the summer months of this year with his mother in Dresden, and some of the family letters written during that time show that he was on friendly terms with some of the Polish aristocracy, especially with the Countess Kamienska and her daughter Helene, who had their fixed home in Dresden. As these two ladies kept up a very pleasant house, and were much visited by people of their own nation, it was very likely *there* that young Bülow made the acquaintance of Count Mycielski. The latter begged Bülow to give his daughters lessons in music as long as the family was in Dresden; for, like many other noble and wealthy Polish families, the Mycielskis were in the habit of spending a few months there every year. Bülow agreed to do this, and shortly afterwards the Count made a proposal that Bülow should take up a permanent position in his house, as master to his daughters and pianist to the family. In spite of Bülow's urgent longing to be able to stand on his own legs pecuniarily, the independent spirit of the young artist would with difficulty have submitted to taking such a post, had it not been for the thought of Paris, and the wish—which the Master Liszt had excited and kept strongly before him—to take his chance there as soon as possible as a public player.

He therefore resolved, by giving up for a time his freedom, to earn for himself the means to defray the expenses of a *début* in Paris.

Writing to his friend Alexander Ritter from Dresden, in the early part of August, he says :—

I have not very consolatory news from Zurich. HE is very much out of spirits, and discouraged enough to shoot himself. HE must be in very precarious outward circumstances : Liszt spoke of an exchange. Try to warm people up a little, so that—perhaps through Johanna*—HE may be helped at least for the moment.

. . . .

As the attempt to procure Bülow's letters to the French Master, Hector Berlioz, has proved unsuccessful, and as in all probability they do not any longer exist, the two following letters *to* Bülow may fill this gap :—†.

HECTOR BERLIOZ TO HANS VON BÜLOW.

28th July 1854.

It is a charming surprise that you have given me, and your manuscript is all the more welcome as Brandus, the publisher, who is at this

---

* Johanna Wagner (1828-1894), the celebrated singer and actress, and a niece of Wagner's.

† These two letters are taken from the 'Correspondance inédite de Hector Berlioz (1819-1868),' by the kind permission of Monsieur C. Levy, in Paris, the publisher of them.

moment engraving 'Cellini,' had already chosen a somewhat obscure and sixth-rate pianist to arrange the Overture.

Your work is admirable; it has a clearness and fidelity which are rare, and is as little difficult as it was possible to make it without altering my score. So I thank you with all my heart. I shall go and see Brandus this evening, and take him your precious manuscript. I have done a great deal of work since my return from Dresden; I have done the first part of my sacred Trilogy 'Le Songe d'Hérode.' This score precedes the embryo which you know under the name of 'Fuite en Égypte,' and, together with the 'Arivée à Saïs,' will form a complete whole of sixteen numbers, lasting altogether an hour and a half, including the *entr'actes*. It is not at all wearisome, as you see, in comparison with the sacred wearisomenesses which overwhelm one for four hours at a stretch.*

I have tried some new devices: the melody of the 'Insomnie d'Hérode' is written in G minor on the following scale, designated by I don't know what Greek name in the Plain-Song:

This induces some very sombre harmonies, and cadences of a certain character which seemed to me appropriate to the situation. You were very taciturn when you sent me the parcel of music; I should have been so pleased to have a few lines from you!

Your sister passed through Paris lately, but so hurriedly that, when I received the card she had left at the house early one morning, she had already started for London.

Will you please give my best compliments to your mother. Shall you not come to Paris? I am starting in a few days for Munich, where I shall stay three weeks. Later on, towards November, I shall come to Germany again, and perhaps I shall see you in Dresden.

Remember me to Mr. and Madame Pohl, and give a hand-shake to that excellent Lipinski.

HECTOR BERLIOZ TO HANS VON BÜLOW.

1st September 1854.

I was delighted to get your kind letter, and hasten to thank you for it. I did not go to Munich, for, just when I was about to go, a post

---

* A play upon the words 'assommant, assommoirs, assomment.'

became vacant at the 'Académie des Beaux-Arts' of our Institute, and I remained in Paris in order to take the necessary steps imposed upon the candidates. I resigned myself unreservedly to the terrible visits, the letters, and all that the Academy inflicts on those who desire to "intrare in suo docto corpore" (Molière's Latin); and Mr. Clapisson was appointed.

So now it is put off for another time. For I am resolved to go on presenting myself until death ensues.

I have just been spending a week at the sea-side, in a village in Normandy, little known; in a few days I shall start for the South, where I am expected by my sister and my uncles for a family *réunion*.

I do not expect to return to Germany till the winter. Doubtless Liszt is right in approving of your having accepted the position which was offered to you in Poland; in any case, you must not lose sight of your journey to Paris, if you can undertake it with perfect freedom of mind as regards the financial result of the concerts. I long to be able to make you acquainted with all our friends of art, whose qualities of mind and heart might render their acquaintance agreeable to you.

You know French so well that you will be able to understand Parisian; and you will perhaps be amused to see how the world of writers loves to play with phrases, and those who presume to call themselves philosophers ride [on the hobby-horse of] their ideas.

I shall be quite at your disposal on my return, and very anxious to see the orchestral compositions of which you speak. My score of 'Cellini' could not possibly find a more intelligent and friendly critic than yourself; allow me to thank you for having thought of doing that work about it in Mr. Pohl's book. For the rest, this work is certainly unlucky; the King of Saxony gets killed just as they were going to give it in Dresden. . . . It is the fatality of the ancients, and one might say of this what Virgil said of Dido : "Ter sese attollens cubitoque adnixa levavit : Ter revoluta toro est."

What a grand composer was Virgil ! what melody and what harmony he had ! It is to him that belongs the dying exclamation : "Qualis artifex pereo !" and not to that poser of a Nero, who had but one inspiration in his life—the setting fire on one night to the four corners of Rome ; a proof that a mediocre man may sometimes have a grand idea.

The opera reopened yesterday. Madame Stoltz made her reappearance in the *rôle* of the Favorita. When I saw her make her appearance on the stage, I really took her for an 'apparition.'* Her voice has also suffered the irreparable outrages from the ravages of time. The new administration of the Opera had made a *coup d'état* by taking from the

---

* A play on the words ' apparition' and ' réapparition' in the previous sentence.

journalists their free entrance, so that the poor Stoltz will have made her *rentrée* in vain.   There was a council of war, in the *foyer*, of all the most powerful (goose) quills, and we unanimously decided that we must declare to the Opera a " War of silence."   Consequently not a word will be said of the reopening, nor of the *début* of Madame Stoltz, until the management returns to better sentiments.

I am working at a long '*feuilleton de silence*' which will appear next week, and which bothers me much.   Adieu, the writing to you has somewhat refreshed me.

Writing to Liszt from Dresden, on the 26th September 1854, Bülow says :

In a week at latest I shall have left Dresden, and started for Chocieszewice near Kröben, in the Grand-Duchy of Posen.   Possibly I shall make a trip to Berlin in the month of November, especially if my solitude weighs too heavily on me.   I am, alas, one of those weak and rather passive natures that cannot do without the society of others, nor without all sorts of impressions and emotions, in order to be encouraged and inspired into productiveness, and even into the most simple intellectual activity which requires abstraction.   This feeling of isolation, which might easily become fatal to me, in spite of its advantages of which I am fully aware, will probably be redoubled by the surroundings of Chocieszewice.

.   .   .   .

TO HIS MOTHER.

CHOCIESZEWICE, 10*th October* 1854.

Præscriptum: You can read the letter without any anxious beating of your motherly heart ; it is in no way impregnated with my mood of the 7th October.

DEAREST MOTHER,

I wish and hope much that you are feeling better and more comfortable than I am at the present time.

Last night's sleep has not yet fully restored me, after the two previous miserable nights of unsettled locomotion.

The journey from Dresden to Breslau by night is horrible—an hour and a half's stop at Görlitz, and three quarters of an hour ditto at Köhlfuhrt.   Breslau is, as a whole, a really beautiful town, but the population is perfectly disgusting.   Palestine, and no mistake.   Elegance without taste.   Predominating types of Jewish faces, which form complete variations to the tune of Judaism.   The upper half of the face sometimes beautiful, the lower half very ugly and of a repulsive colour.   I went to see Hesse (the organist), a friend of Spohr's, and the pianist Karl Schnabel, but did not find either of them at home. Old Mosewius, the music-director of the University, and well known through his analysis of Bach's Passion-music, was however very much pleased with my visit, and took me to the University, where he showed me the '*Aula*' and another concert-room,—in which Liszt had formerly played,—the musical library, etc. He had been well acquainted with General Bülow-Dennewitz, and told me also about his compositions.

I also went to the pianoforte manufactory of Bessalié; he makes very serviceable concert-grands, and was very pleasant to me. Henselt was there a few weeks ago, and had written to him his approbation of the sounding-board.

At the theatre I saw 'Robert le diable,' and indeed a very decent performance, both by singers and orchestra, including the conducting. A very good theatre, both inside and out, and situated in a splendid square. Very well lighted; began at 7 o'clock, of which I was very glad, as I did not know how I should have killed time till the departure of the mail-coach for Rawicz at 11 o'clock at night. I alighted at the 'Weisser Adler,' in order not to be left sticking in the road, and I found it good and cheap. On the other hand I had to pay such an immense deal for overweight of luggage from Breslau to Rawicz, that I found I was drained pretty dry for the extra-post from Rawicz, where I arrived at 6 o'clock in the morning. After many difficulties, which this state of things occasioned me, I at last succeeded, thanks to the special friendliness of the directress of the Post, in getting them to provide me with the necessary means for continuing my journey, on my assurance that Count Mycielski would make it all straight with them on my arrival. A contemptible journey, which I shall not forget. A horrible road, fearful cold, a Bürgerwiese * hurricane; I finally arrived at Chocieszewice about half-past ten o'clock, feeling myself gone all to pieces. I am so little satisfied with the treatment I have met with up to now, that, if many things are not radically altered when the Count returns, I shall not endure these horrors more than a month. He went some days ago, with his constellation of daughters and the governess, to visit some relations; and, though he is expected back daily and even hourly, he has not yet arrived. For four weeks I can and will bear the horrors. The castle is grand; the dining halls and salons, royal; of fabulous size and height. But it wants a Slavonic temperament to be able to endure this cold, against which the warming of one's inner man is not a sufficient counter-

---

* An open space; in the *outskirts of Dresden* at the time when this letter was written.

poise as long as the cold lasts. *My* room has suffered in its walls through the inundations—still it is not so very damp. It is as large, in itself alone, as the two rooms in which you are now living in the Reitbahngasse, and a bit over. They assure me that the stove is sufficient to warm it thoroughly. A monster sofa, a monster table—both extremely homely and inconvenient, although new; a writing-table without any pigeon-holes, a chest of drawers, a night-table, and an equally un-ideal bed; these, together with four chairs, constitute the furniture, which, in the enormous size of the room, is completely lost. I invite you herewith to house all the furniture you have not room for with me.

A dirty old Polish valet, who understands very little German, looks after me; his service is maintained on a level with the functions of a prison jailer, both as regards quantity and quality. In this respect I am considered exactly the same as my neighbour and "colleague," a certain Herr Schreiber from Dresden, a very good-natured, but very moderately educated young man, a painter, whose room is separated from mine by a little corridor. Yesterday being my first day, I have had no opportunity as yet to protest against this. I must wait for everything till the Count comes back.

The scenery round the castle is beautiful—it is laid out like a park, and reminds one a little of the corner to the right of the pavilion in the public garden in Dresden. " O Hünerfürst ! " * But then, all around, one has the most truly Polish peasantry—a lot of villages inhabited by the veriest blockheads of Poles, and where not a single syllable of German is spoken. One is thus entirely cut off from intercourse of any sort. On Sundays a travelling cobbler goes round the neighbourhood, and to him is entrusted the restoration of coat-buttons, and the constitutional reparation of chance holes in garments.

Whether I shall be able to find a barber is as yet shrouded in mystery. But that won't trouble me very much, for in this cold weather a beard would help to warm me. But there are many other things that I want dreadfully. First a few thalers to pay for any letters which come unstamped, for it seems to me safest to adopt the French plan in regard to this; then two pairs of gloves, light grey stitched with black, from Ammann—7½—he knows my number, or rather my size (for the numbers vary); a little bottle of hair-oil, and a small, sharp pair of scissors. That is all for the present.

The safest address for me is that of my journey: c/o Count Myciel-ski, Rawicz, Chocieszewice, near Kröben, viâ Breslau.

Will you be so good as to put in, with the things I have asked for,

---

* A well-known conductor of an out-door orchestra in Dresden.

two packets of Russian paper-cigarettes (Spiglasoff) from Philipp's by the Kreuzkirche; at 12½ silbergroschen the packet.

In all that I have hitherto told you, one thing after another in a mechanical, fragmentary way, there is absolutely nothing to call forth pity in my situation. That, however, is yet to follow, and consists in the want of a grand piano, and, if such a want continues, it will drive me away in a very short space of time. The Count's secretary and manager, who is in possession of the old instrument which the Count promised me I should have for my own use in composition in my room, appears to be unwilling to give it up to me. The Countess, who is of that sweet, condescending amiability which is particularly unpleasant to me, said she had understood I should bring my instrument with me. How the matter will be arranged I do not yet know. I expect I shall have to hire one from the neighbourhood: there must be some to be had.

Dinner yesterday was at 2 o'clock, and tea at 8 o'clock; the hours, and the quality of the food, were both satisfactory to me. The Countess had a visit from some relations . . . an old cousin, with whom I had a good deal of conversation, who had an opportunity of judging of my attainments, and who was very pleasant to me, who had known Chopin intimately, and had seen much in Paris. Also a brother of the Countess, still pretty young, looking awfully bored: and then there was his wife, a young lady, not pretty, but not unamiable-looking, who had such a good memory that she recollected having seen me three or four years ago at a party given by a Polish lady in the Halbegasse.

After dinner I was weak enough to accede to the request to play something, which I did in the cold salon, with frozen fingers. The lady of the house accompanied me with conversation; the men—the old cousin especially—were polite and admired my playing. After tea I repaired, uninvited, to a drawing-room that had been heated, to make conversation, and to be freer and more unconstrained.

I am waiting, for everything that requires alteration, the arrival of the Count: anything I have to say to the Countess I do through the stepdaughters.

How are you? Did you get comfortably home? What a tough hide man has in regard to his troubles! And how much it takes really to destroy the machine!

How did things go on Sunday? Do tell me about the dinner at the Kamieńskis. Or, if you would rather, not a word: or else, just as much as you like.

I am at the moment not disposed to write to anybody else but you. But perhaps later on I shall beg you to pass my letters round now and then.

Have you got a little accustomed to your new house? And how are you off for servants? Has the Cæsar-music been brought back? I do uncommonly wish to hear of a second performance, so that the gentlemen of the orchestra may play something less barbarous.

Please remember me most kindly to Fraulein Dräseke.* How I wish I could have had a chat with her yesterday evening!

Now farewell, dearest mother, and do let me hear from you as soon as possible.

My "colleague" assures me that the postal arrangements are very regular and dependable. Let's hope so. Have the other Polish ladies been to see you?

TO HIS MOTHER.

CHOCIESZEWICE, 19*th October* 1854.

DEAREST MOTHER,

Yesterday afternoon, just as I had given my nineteenth piano lesson, I received your letter. Thank you very much for it, as well as for all the things I wanted. I am answering you by return of post, because, before my letter arrives in Dresden, much time will have elapsed. For in the afternoons a groom rides with the post-bag to Kröben, whence he brings back at night any letters that have arrived for us. The post does not go out from Kröben to Rawicz till the next day, so that a letter cannot reach its destination under three to four days. Of course the delay is far less in letters coming to us here.

You have really sent me too much in sending *three* thalers, for here one has no use for a purse of any kind . . . the only "silver sound" is "Music." This is really a comfort, which you would especially enjoy. For me it has the special charm of novelty.

The only expenditure I have had as yet was buying a Polish grammar, which the Count's secretary, Herr Baranowski, a very pleasant man in his own style and according to the limited circle of his mind, procured for me. I leave the exercise of local benevolence towards the countless calls of a begging nation to the highest bidder, the lord of over 20,000 acres, the proprietor of an estate which is now a bargain at a million, the enviable man who can bear with equanimity the enormous loss of 20,000 to 30,000 reichsthaler (he says 40,000) which the inundation caused him.

I shall also have expenses for tailor's repairs, for shaving, and, eventually, for bootmaker.

The Count has now brought a little order into things, and behaves (until further notice, low be it spoken) very well. I am now well served

---

* Daughter of the bishop, and aunt of the composer Dräseke; a very active-minded and literary lady, who made a metrical translation of Byron.

by a "compatriot," a Vandal brought from Dresden, who does not speak Saxon, and is quite exemplarily methodical. A wardrobe has been made for me by the joiner. As soon as the Count has read the papers he sends them straight to me . . . the *Indépendence* and *Charivari;* of German ones there is unfortunately only the *Schlesische Zeitung*, but on Tuesdays *Kladderadatsch*. He has also begged me to give singing lessons—four hours a week—this of course he will pay for extra . . . but at present, in spite of the most sedulous sleeping and feeding, I have been so done up by my schoolmaster duties that I have not been able to make up my mind to agree to it.

I must briefly give you a sketch of the uniform course of my daily life. As I always go to bed an hour before midnight, and sometimes a couple of hours, I wake and get up, as a rule, not later than 7 o'clock. From 9 to 11 I have to give two "music" lessons, and to instil into my pupils Czerny's Studies, Döhler's Tarantelle and Willmer's 'Schwalben Étude.' That is a tiring "robota" (labour), a torture analogous to the national punishment in Persia, for the wrong notes drip into my ears as constantly as the drops of water on the skull of a Persian criminal. The middle "Countess," I must say, takes much more pains here in Chocieszewice than in Dresden, and shows more intelligence and energy than Fräulein Elisa, whom I have today reproached with her " mollesse slave " (Slavonic indolence). She has, without doubt, the most decided want of talent. Boundless are my troubles with the youngest, thirteen years old, into whom I am drubbing a Quadrille on airs from 'Martha,' for a birthday treat for her Papa. To a certain extent Fräulein Marie is really the most sensible ; she openly avows that she has no vocation for piano-playing, and, indeed, a very great disinclination for it : considering her conviction of her utter want of talent, and in spite of the absurd way her parents insist on her learning, she is comparatively willing, but she has no ear, no sense of rhythm, nor of melody.

C'est vraiment une corvée (it is a real drudgery).

From 11 to 12 I take a walk in the park in fine weather, which hitherto has not failed us, or else I go to my writing-table, and have a rest by reading some book or other—Berlioz' 'Soirées d'Orchestre,' the first volume of Gervinus' 'Literaturgeschichte des deutschen Mittelalters,' and others of that kind. Except to you, I have not yet managed any correspondence. From 12 to 2 I practise pretty vigorously on the new grand piano of Rönisch, which is an excellent one. At 2 o'clock we dine, very well, though sometimes rather limited in quantity—on Fridays "maigre,"—and then have a chat over our coffee in the Count's room, a few useless French phrases about nothing at all. I then go out again till 4 o'clock to warm myself, for we freeze here like barbarians, and the

Count forbids any continuous warming of the rooms as injurious to health (in which he is perhaps right); but it seems to take longer with me to get accustomed to the physical temperature than to the psychical. From 4 to 5 I play again for myself; from 5 to 6 lessons; from 6 to 7 I generally "compose"; at 7 o'clock is supper (hot), and then tea, but this is taken in a most uncomfortable manner at a long table in a cold, and enormously lofty, salon. *After that*, I usually accept an invitation from the Countess to have a little music and conversation in the music-room, because I find it is a good thing to play before puppets when I have not got musical men ("à défaut d'hommes musicaux, mannequins vorzuspielen"), for, after all, the majority of the public consists of the puppets. But about half-past eight, when I have regained my own four walls, I am pretty well "done," and am no good for anything much except reading the papers, which, in the absence of any closer personal interests in my surroundings, I thoroughly devour with the voracious appetite of an old, spectacled subscriber of *Tante Voss.** Up to the present I have not had any indigestion from it.

I have had an old tin-kettle of a piano in my room since Herr Baranowski has been prevented (for a long time, it appears), by a wound in the hand, from slaving at it. It just does for composing, as it has been done up and is in good tune, but for playing it is absolutely unfit.

I have no occasion at this moment to complain of my present situation. It is just a banishment, a punishment for the once "Nihilist," that he has come into the Paradise of a complete negation of all interests. If this negation would extend itself also to my frequent head- and neck-ache it would be a good thing. But I am quite certain that I shall not be able to stand it long without a break. My journey to Berlin, towards the 10th or 15th November, is considered here as a settled thing; it is in every respect necessary to me. I am now working at my instrument with all my powers, with a view to this excursion. I will then give a concert in Posen in December, or—several (during the meeting of the diet); I am sure, then, of doing a *good* business, and Count M[ycielski] has promised me his best assistance.

At the beginning of next year, Breslau. Whether there will be anything to be done with Hamburg is a question. First Berlin: but how? Of this more anon.

When is Johanna Wagner's friend† going to Berlin?

No, I must not let myself be buried, even with the prospect of the most glorious resurrection after a year's grace! My "colleague," a Herr

---

* Familiar name for the *Vossische Zeitung*.
† Helene Kamieńska.

Schneider,* is a very good and, as such, a moderate Saxon. I am going to study English with him, the elements of which he already knows. Next Sunday we are going a mile and a half to a little nest of a place called Kobylin. His post here is altogether of a very inferior nature to mine, because he does not speak French.

Please forward the enclosed note to Isa as soon as you can. On the 25th some strangers (ladies) are expected here ; a Countess Potocka and her daughters, etc.

I sent my serious and absolute (not my relative) best remembrances to Fräulein Dräseke.

Once more, best thanks for your letter, and please write to me very soon and fully. *Your* loneliness is nothing in comparison with *mine*, and the wretched postal connection delays our correspondence so.

P.S.—I strongly recommend to Fräulein Dräseke Bauer's 'Russland und das Germanenthum.' I have enjoyed it very much—it helped me over the first dreadful days. It is so masterly in its power and manliness, so "free," that is, written also with such freedom from party-spirit, and so utterly different from what either of you would imagine, that I am right in recommending it to you.

TO HIS MOTHER.

CHOCIESZEWICE, *5th November* 1854.

DEAREST MOTHER,

     I have just received your letter, and, according to my present custom, I set myself the same evening to answer it.

From Isidore I have twice had news, although very incomplete, for she has sent me two numbers of the *Gazette musicale* by book-post. That is a very practical, cheap kind of correspondence, where it is only a question of giving a sign that one is alive ; but, after my two last letters, which were not unbrotherly, she might have done more than scribble a mere address. In my last letter I had already warmly encouraged her to make the most of her stay in Paris, and to let me know all the many things—even if it concerned merely the masses of houses—that it would interest me to hear. Twice I have also asked whether Mrs. Joy would like me to send her a list of music for playing or singing, and she does not answer me about that either. If I have a spare moment tomorrow to enclose a note to her, and to beg her again to extract some sweets from her stay in Paris, and to tell her explicitly some things that I remember reading, I will be sure to do it; if not tomorrow, then another time, that is, of course very soon.

---

* In a later letter Bülow says : "his name is 'Schreiber,' not 'Schneider.'"

With regard to the music for which I asked her, it is the Romance ' La chaîne anglaise ' for Mlle. Kamieńska, whom I shall very soon surprise with an ' Albumblatt ' of Liszt's. You can tell her about it beforehand; that does not matter. Yesterday I received a letter from my Pest friend, Eugen v. Soupper,* who is now in Weimar, on the last page of which Liszt had written a friendly greeting, and promised to send me very soon what I had begged for.

Why don't you write me a word about the ' Crown Diamonds' ? † I don't know the opera. It is said to be amusing—therefore allowed. I am looking forward to Thursday, for then I shall hear a string twanged once more. There is to be a small ball, for which a band is coming from Kobylin : double-bass, two violins and a flute.

Just fancy how modest we are ! Early this morning I drove in a wretched carriage (an open one, in every way most countrified and primitive) to the Jewish village of Kobylin with Herr Schreiber, who is not a bad fellow at all, and not without a grain of art. In the coupé with us sat the cook's chief kitchen-boy, who understands no German, and with whom I exchanged a few words of Polish jabber. At Kobylin we went to the Catholic and Protestant churches, and stayed a while for the service. Then we bought ourselves some pen-knives at 3 neugroschen, chocolate, blue ink, etc. Finally we went to the confectioner's, where we read the French and German papers, which we had taken with us on purpose, while we ate cakes and tried to imagine we were sitting at Trepp's, and that the mud-bank before the window was the Schlossgasse, and the Polish peasant-women (as a rule brutally ugly) the beautiful Polish ladies one sees coming out of the Catholic church at twelve o'clock, etc., etc. Soon after that, some well-dressed ladies came into the cake-shop, and began an interesting discussion as to whether *pigs* might be fed with *diseased potatoes.* A Protestant thought they *might*, a Catholic thought *not ;* a Jewess, who perhaps, in the words " diseased potatoes," thought they were alluding to her, ran away.

The return ride was interesting. Our carriage was packed choke-full with all sorts of purchases, when, at a farm hard by, they packed in also a dead pig—as a *cushion to lean against and to sit upon.* We were tremendously tickled, and laughed till the tears ran down our cheeks. At dinner I entertained them with a lively description of what had happened : ' Nous avions une société charmante ; d'abord pour compagnon de voyage un garçon cuisinier, avec lequel nous avons parlé polonais—puis le cadavre d'un cochon, avec lequel nous n'avons pas fait la conversation polonaise—

---

* A concert singer, and countryman of Liszt's.

† Opera by Auber.

mais qui nous a servi de sopha,' etc. The Count thought that, in the excessive cold, that must have kept us nice and warm. I began to laugh over again; c'est champêtre! c'est champêtre!

The Count has not yet repaid me the money for my journey, consequently I have not been able to go to ' Lohengrin ' at Breslau. I did not want to ask him for it now; the right moment will come of itself. But, in case of a longer *stay here* (of course including the journey to Berlin), I do require a few more thalers, and should be very grateful if you could send them as soon as *possible*—registered.

The Kamieńskis—the plural is *skie* for ladies—are mad; first they work themselves up, then you, and so forth. First I must try the *metropolis*, then the *provincial towns*. The other way about would be nonsense.

Countess *Mycielska* (! ! !) and the Count *ski* have something else to do than to lend me a helping hand in my concerts. Their guests of the time being cannot and will not by any means do anything for a pianist who is unknown to them, and who, further, neither can nor will ask for their protection. Prince Sułkowski comes on the 9th November— *perhaps* he may chance to interest himself somewhat more for me, though I don't really think he will. What can I *begin*—and that is the principal thing—without funds, without the necessary capital in hand, or at any rate at my disposal, in case of extremity, for a first concert in Berlin? If Madame Schumann takes the concert-public, with Joachim, in Berlin in November, it is all over with a poor, forsaken beggar like me. And I endure it here too. It is a sad, empty life; and yet this supreme indifference, in which irony almost gives place to a certain *bonhommie* (*bon-enfantie*), and which I breathe in all my surroundings here, has its advantages; one learns to moderate and restrain one's self completely, and to value the charm of an ordinary vegetable existence. I am content, in the evening, when I have seen my "hostess" or "principal" once in the day, or even less, for she irritates my nerves in conversation and in her whole being, and thus lends a flavour of virtuousness to my frequent attempts to be amiable: I am content when my pupils have done pretty badly and pretty trivially (in " *expression* ") on the *poor* piano : am content when Mlle. B., " qui est bête comme une oie," as the Count sympathetically agrees with me in thinking, and Herr v. Baranowski have talked *moderate* rubbish at table over the political questions of the day. That I am *happy* when I have eaten well, not been too much frozen, have slept well—that goes without saying. Last night I had the adventurous enjoyment of a mouse-chase. The morning sun showed my *raven* * Hermann the glorious result of the fallen prey.

---

* Refers to Elias, whom the ravens fed.

The Count is niggardly, and talks big, but in the main he is a man of a great deal of *bon sens*, and of proportionate, *very* proportionate humanity; and, as I said, of very sound views; in politics, for instance. In his outer man he has that generous-sentient *pli* (wrinkle) which amused me in Lemaistre, like the head of a confiding cat—I can't put it in any other way: that element of animal-intelligence which, in its natural truth, is so infinitely above a subtle-human stupidity. He venerates *Kladderadatsch* with understanding and enthusiasm, and it warms my heart to hear him hold forth about it. He lets himself be carried away by the spirit of it, and that is a great deal; if I have a joke he is usually my public, and just of the kind I like—not outwardly admiring, but visibly and inwardly consuming it.

Where on earth am I wandering?

Madame Laussot's book, ' Comédies par Alfred de Musset,' is read through and through, and has given me many pleasant moments. My greetings to the donor. Ditto to Fräulein Dräseke; I will write her a Funeral March for Korniloff. How could I go now to Warsaw? What châteaux en Espagne, or rather, Poland! It is all one.

Can you send me ' Richard II. ' in German? We have begun to read it in English, and it is difficult.

Do, for Heaven's sake, read something! at least the *Revues*, the *Deutsches Museum*, the *Grenzboten !* What does the supplement to the *Augsburger* give? Please keep me a little *au fait* of this, dear Mamma! —Lipinski? . . . The Czartoryska* is giving a concert for the sufferers from the inundation very shortly; it is already announced. I will, if possible, pluck up my courage to write letters to Berlin tomorrow.

Farewell, and shorten the time for yourself by writing to me often!

15th November.

Life here is, in the main, horribly uncomfortable and uninteresting. One vegetates. Yet so great is the power of habit that, frankly, I don't feel inclined to go to Berlin, and would much rather keep on staying here, where the days go on unwinding themselves with their accustomed functions, like a ball of thread. On Sunday it is the name-day of

---

* "Madame la Princesse Czartoryska, musicienne parfaite par le savoir et par le goût, distinguée, pianiste en outre . . . Après une quintette de Hummel, qu'elle venait d'exécuter avec une supériorité magistrale, quelqu'un me dit :

' Décidément il n'y a plus d'amateurs !' . . . ' Oh '—répondis-je, ' en cherchant bien—vous en trouverez peut-être—même parmi les artistes. Mais en tout cas la Princesse est une exception.' "—Berlioz " Mémoires " : vol. II. page 198.

Fräulein Elinka ; I shall present her with the dedication of a Mazurka, which, with a still unfinished Notturno, I am going to offer to Schott.

The Count went, the day before yesterday, with a few guests who are still here, to pay a visit to the neighbouring estate of Herr v. Stablewski ; they came back at mid-day today, but were expected yesterday. On that account we dined yesterday at 6, and today at 4 o'clock. This irregular way of living does not suit me at all. If one cannot command according to one's own humour, then there ought at least to be a hard and fast rule as regards the day's arrangements, from which there is no deviation.

Do you still read *Kladderadatsch ?* It has been uninterruptedly capital, especially the last double number.

Write soon, dear mother, and thank you once more for all your care and sympathy. I hope, in my next letter, to be able to tell you more definitely about my journey, etc.

Your grateful son

HANS.

TO HIS SISTER.

CHOCIESZEWICE, 6th November 1854.

ISIDORE ! ISA ! ISIDORE !

It is really unpardonable and unwarrantable of you that you have never deemed me worthy of a line in reply to my repeated requests. What lots of things you could write to me from Paris which would, which must, especially interest me, as a man not knowing Paris, and as Hans von Bülow ! Even if you only told me of the rough impression made upon you by the masses of houses—I should say, of the impression made upon you by the high, rough masses of houses, which of themselves have such manifold historical interest, that would at least be *something,* and I should indeed be more grateful to you for that than for sending me a couple of numbers of one of the most stupid musical papers, such as has not its equal in all Germany. Not merely so awfully stupid, but so insipidly *dull,* so silly were the contents of this paper present, on which the only interesting thing was the address in your handwriting. Just consider what a piece of luck you are having, and how many of your companions—quite apart from me, for instance, would envy you for living in the city which is the centre, not merely of the civilised, but also of the uncivilised, world. And even if you went to no theatre, and saw no museum, what an immense deal there is still left in the way of streets, palaces, gardens, squares, and so forth. From your very window, what an interesting panorama — the faces of the passers by, the *toilettes* of the ladies and gentlemen—I am speaking quite seriously : even *that* would interest me !

I have several times asked you direct, and through Mamma, for an answer to my question, whether Mrs. Joy would like a list of music from me, either for playing or singing, and you have not yet answered me, so that it has been impossible for me to send it ! Is that French Romance, of which I wrote to you, really not to be had at Brandus', Boulevard des Italiens ? Who knows when you will see Paris again ! So open your eyes and ears wide ! Read, look and listen ! It is indeed well worth the trouble. Keep a diary, and write me a *decent* letter for once !

You see today I am very cross and churlish, but for a month past I have been bored out of my life, and it is allowable to want a little relaxation, after having given 70 piano lessons.

Don't take my ill-humour amiss, and let me give you a little advice.

No doubt you have already found your way to Versailles ! to see the museum there : Horace Vernet's pictures of the times of Napoleon (battle of Jena and others) ; the deeds of the French army in Algiers by—I can't remember whom ; the portraits of Robespierre, Mirabeau, also Voltaire : these are all well worth seeing.

Foyatier's statue of Spartacus in the garden of the Tuileries must be very beautiful : have you seen it ? Have you been to the Louvre ? Be sure to see Murillo's Madonna supported by angels ; portrait of Philip II. ; the child drawing water with St. Augustine ; Titian's Christ ; Raphael's Madonna ; Christ seizing St. John by the head ; Caravaggio's fortune-telling gipsy.

Gros : Napoleon in the fever-hospital at Jaffa. ⎫
Géricault : Raft with rescued shipwrecked people. ⎬ Modern.
David : Portraits. ⎭

Have you been to the *Gobelin factory* — the celebrated tapestry pictures ?

The sculpture portion of the Louvre must also contain some magnificent things : the Borghese gladiator ; Melpomene, etc.

Have you been to the Invalides ? Have you seen the Emperor's grave ?

Have you not yet been once to the theatre ? And if so, which ? Do write to me about it. What papers are you reading ? Is the *Figaro* amusing ?

How is Berlioz looking ? Is he contented ?

Have you paid a visit to Jouvin, "*gantier*" (1 rue Rougemont), to Guerlain, "*parfumeur*" (13 rue de la Paix), to Julien, "*patissier*" (Boulevard des Italiens), "*Pâte-Paris, gâteau du soleil*" . . . ? Just look about you and "*dis-moi de leurs nouvelles.*" The best guide to

Paris is "*Les quartiers de Paris, par* St. Fargeau." That you ought to get for yourself, and in a year's time I'll buy it from you.

I believe the following are very amusing, and help one to a knowledge of Parisian life: "*Les petits-Paris*"; and, in separate little brochures, "*Paris viveur; Paris restaurant; Paris bohême; Paris boursier*, etc.; which are to be got at Tarido's, the publisher, Galerie de l'Odéon.

Don't you subscribe to any reading-library? How do you actually spend your days? Describe to me how you live, and let me have a good long letter from you soon; or else I shall soon lose patience also, and shall not send you any more messages. You have neglected me too shamefully. Mind you thoroughly enjoy the beautiful city where the most wretched beggar can get more amusement than a poor devil of a fellow like me here in this desert country of Posen. Adieu meanwhile, dear but most unsisterly sister!

Farewell!

As ever,

Thy faithful brother.

TO HIS MOTHER.

CHOCIESZEWICE [*Middle of November* 1854.]

DEAREST MOTHER,

Many thanks for your dear letters and their accompaniments, the parcel of linen and cigars as well as the 30 thalers, which I have safely received.

Since the day before yesterday we have winter, as winterly as possible; showers of snow, cold and tempest. It will be difficult to get away from here on the journey to Berlin. I don't believe there is such a thing as a close carriage in the Count's coach-house. I shall therefore have to wait for a fine day, even though it only takes about two hours with the Count's horses to drive to the little town of Gostyn, where we take the Post *viâ* Lissa to Glogau, whence the journey by rail to Berlin is of course quite an easy matter.

My fingers are still so frozen that the writing does not get on at all, or rather does not progress towards resigning gloriously the remains of my Saxon nationality. Since yesterday, Sunday, evening I have been re-installed in my former large room, which on Wednesday evening I was obliged to exchange for a little chamber in the adjoining building, as the housing of an unexpectedly large number of birthday guests required all the accommodation of the castle. I was not in a very comfortable frame of mind those four days. The endless confusion in the whole house, the unpunctuality (once we dined at 5, another time at 6, the third day at half-past six), and in addition being obliged to walk 50 paces of the most disgusting road in thin elegant dress at different times of day and night in order to slip into the castle,—all this had so pulled me down, that soon after sitting down to table on Saturday I was attacked by such an excessively severe sick headache and feeling of faintness that there was nothing for it but to go to bed at once. I did not get up till noon yesterday, and felt still better in the afternoon.

I could not find any time to go on with my letter yesterday. It was very uncomfortable in my room last night, what with a smoky lamp, insufficient fire and so forth. I spent the whole day at the piano. I had been obliged to exist without one for four days. So yesterday I began to practise again, and in a furious manner did three hours without stopping. After dinner I went to the billiard-room for the first time, and gave myself up to a game which Herr Schreiber was so kind as to teach me, and found the motion a judicious contrast to pianoforte-playing. Four hours of teaching, three of furious practice, two of billiards, a little drawing-room conversation and strumming in the evening—so the day slips away, without any consciousness at night of anything achieved.

The company which had come hither for " St. Theodore's day " * was, as I said before, very numerous, but it consisted chiefly of relations, some of them being named Mycielski. Prince Sułkowski and his wife, _née_ Mycielska, niece of Count Theodor ; the Prince's brother-in-law Count Wodzicki, who, like his wife (_née_ Sułkowska) has something much more distinguished about him than the Prince ; Count Plater ; Herr von Stablewski, etc. : in short from 40 to 50 people,—men, women, and children too. . . .

Again I have let a day pass without finishing and despatching this letter. But, in the first place postal communication was interrupted today, and then I could not bear to banish myself to the writing-table. Ever since I have known that I should soon be going to Berlin, and that a great and fundamental question would have to be settled for me there, I have not a moment's peace, and find myself dreaming by day of nothing but concert-programmes, and all sorts of trifles appertaining to my concert- and evening-dress, which needs thoroughly renovating. Having been three weeks without a place to keep my things in, and without anyone to mend them for me, my clothes have got into rather a bad state. How all this bothers my head !

For the rest, I must tell you I was pretty well satisfied with myself at the piano today. It is certain that by regular good practice here I

---

* The Count's name-day.

have made decided progress. My probable first (Chamber)-concert-pro-
gramme, which I played to myself today, went smoothly all through.
1. Prelude (C minor) for the organ, by Bach (transcribed for the piano
by Liszt); and Beethoven's 32 Variations, C minor. — 2. Liszt's
Patineurs.—3. Chopin's Berceuse, Étude, and Barcarole.—4. The big
Lucrezia-Fantasia by Liszt. For the second concert I should have again
an interesting series of pieces : 1. Bach's Organ Prelude and Fugue,
A minor (transcribed for piano by Liszt).—2. Beethoven's Sonata in F
minor or A major. — 3. Ballade or Scherzo of Chopin. — 4. The
Rossignol-Paganini Étude; a Waltz of Liszt's.—5. Sonnambula; the
second Lucrezia or Lucia or the Midsummer Night's Dream by Liszt.—
For the third I should have no difficulty in finding novelties.

For the theatre, where I should certainly have to play first of all, I
should have the Beethoven Concerto and the three approved pieces for
pianoforte and orchestra of Liszt to bring forward as show-pieces.

I do not think Redern's acquaintance will avail me much. It seems
to me very uncertain whether it will help me to let my light shine
before His Majesty, to whom—if it came to that—I should have to play
the Russian National Anthem.

I will, likewise, not play for nothing at the opera-house, because at
the worst one must be prepared for further concerts. First of all I am
now going to write and ask Schlesinger when Frau Schumann intends to
fix her soirées in conjunction with Joachim, so that she may not clash
with me, and that I may not be at a loose end on leaving here, spending
unnecessary money.

Do not be vexed with me that I say all these things out to you in
my letter *sans façon*, just as I used to do vivâ voce. But as I can't
consent to keeping a regular diary, and as there is not the least opportunity to be communicative to anybody in this confounded castle, you
must be motherly, and kindly allow my tongue, which is incapable of
carrying much, to send part of its luggage by the pen.

Where shall I stop in Berlin ? I forget the name of that *Hôtel garni*
where the Tiecks' Friederike can take me in.

Liszt wrote to me the day before yesterday, a letter of a few words,
almost as good as nothing, but containing a very elegant, charming little
manuscript for Helene Kamieńska. There was however one pretty thing
in the letter, which is that Liszt wants to do the Cæsar Overture at one
of the Stadthaus concerts. So you would have to be so good as to send
the score and orchestral parts to Weimar. You have probably seen Lipinski ere now, and heard from him that my work is not thought worthy of
a second and more satisfactory performance. And the Cæsar is also probably no longer in the *répertoire*. But when the opportunity occurs I will

just let the Dresden orchestra know that we are quits. Please tell
Lipinski so.

After all I must tell you what my pen has resisted till now, that on
the 9th and 10th I played before the grand-ducal Poledom, and that my
audience treated me very well. They listened attentively and as quiet as
mice, and gave me a little pleasure in return by the manner of their
applause. The most marked instance of it was that they said openly, and
with *piena voce*, that my talent was greater than that of their countrymen Wieniawski and that special favourite of the Poles—Kontski (who
is great as a charlatan and—also in *technique*). They all showed the
utmost politeness to me, which I had, sure enough, set myself systematically to draw forth, by having, on the previous days, when guests had
already arrived, absented myself immediately after meals, and on Wednesday had even distinguished myself by not appearing at all! and an
extremely conciliatory visit of the Count, who came as their emissary, I
had met with an indefinite, unexpressed dissatisfaction. And in the
mornings also, when the guests were having music amongst themselves,
I kept away, so that then, when I *did* appear, they had double *égards*
for me.

TO HIS SISTER.

CHOCIESZEWICE, 19*th November* 1854.

DEAR SISTER.

To set you an example I heap coals of fire on your head,
and answer your long letter received yesterday without further delay.
The quickness of my reply must atone for the shortcomings of my letter
as compared with yours. I have already told you, and you will believe
from my hasty sketch of the bare framework of Polish country seclusion,
that here in Chocieszewice there is no news to *give*, but only to
receive.

I have already given my 103rd music-lesson, and smoked the 103rd
paper cigarette ;—I have fallen so low that to kill time I keep count of
things like this. But a week ago I found a resource of which I had
never even thought, and which I now employ with ardour several hours
a day, namely billiards, into the mysteries of which Herr Schreiber, the
drawing-master and my fellow-sufferer, has initiated me. It is an extremely delightful game of skill, and with the winter fully upon us since
the 10th of November, and the incessant snowstorms, it is a healthy
exercise for us without having to leave the room.

It will be settled in the course of this week whether and when I go
to Berlin. I am daily expecting letters from there to tell me whether I

should have any chance there and should not encounter too great competition. I shall not set out, in any case, for a fortnight; and it certainly
would not do to bounce in in the Christmas-time. I should much like to
get a favourable answer, as I am just now in good practice, and have got
Bach, Beethoven, Chopin and Liszt well at my finger-ends.   Be sure
answer me here in any case till you hear further from me about Berlin.
I have unfortunately not received the *Journal des Débats*, which interests
me far more than the musical paper. As you are so good as to bestow
such things as these on me, I beg you will send me *every* article of *Berlioz*
as quickly as possible. As for musical papers, please look at the *sommaire*
(contents) first, and then decide whether you think they will interest me.
Send me also, when there is an opportunity, a few numbers of the comic
papers *Corsaire* and *Figaro*. They take *Charivari* here, but it has gone
down very much and become monotonous.

When will the performance of Berlioz' 'Trilogie Sacrée' take place?
What is the name of the concert in which it is to be heard?

You are mistaken in thinking that the Princess's letter to Liszt's
daughters is not so good an introduction as a letter from their father.
Quite the contrary, and for this reason. The children's governess (a
Madame Patersi, I believe) was the governess of the Princess Wittgenstein herself, and possesses her entire confidence; has indeed been
put into this very situation by her.

Have you called on Liszt's mother? Do pay a little attention to the
old lady, with whom you can talk German because she would very much
like to be settled in Austria.   Let Liszt's daughters (Erlking's
daughters?), whom I beg you to describe most accurately to me, take
you to see her.

Your little lecture which was called forth by my wish for the
'*Corde sensible*,' has amused me immensely. Here is the explanation
of the riddle. The old Frau von Kamieńska wished to let her daughter
sing this Romance, which she knows, and which could not be got in
Dresden, and she begged me to procure this *horreur* for her. This is
why I want you to send the wretched thing to Mamma in Dresden.

And even though the music of this Romance is really so uncommonly
common and trivial, still I must beg you to send another copy of it to
me immediately. I then get by heart this little affair of one of my
pupils, whom I also occasionally "Schurigle"* in singing,—and that
will then give much pleasure to her Papa who cares *only* for that sort of
music. So there!

Here is a list of music for Mrs. Joy, with my most respectful regards.

---

* An allusion to Isidore's early singing-master, named Sehurig.

What you write of her interests me, and although you have often been enthusiastic about many women, this liking, I know not why, seems to me more reasonable and likely to last.

If Paris suits your health so well, why do you write to Mamma about returning? You should try to acquire a little more of the French ease in society (how often have I insisted on this!), and to find out the peculiarities, I mean the *good* side of the people, and bring out that side. Madame Berlioz must have her good side too.

Will you go tomorrow straight into the second room of the Louvre and send me every bit of print that you think worth sending.—Say all that is nice to Berlioz; ask him whether I shall arrange the Overture to the ' Roman Carnival' for four hands once more—it has been badly done by Pixis; and say I shall be glad if he will employ me for the Overture to the 'Corsair,' as such a piece of work, especially here, would be an amusement to me.

Ask him also how much my first concerts in Paris would be likely to cost me, where I ought to play first, etc., and tell me everything exactly as he has said it to you. By this you will be doing me a great service! I will not forget the commission to the Arnims.

Farewell for today, beloved sister; be very sensible, give up that hankering after impossibilities which don't exist: then your life will be easier and more joyous.

TO FRANZ LISZT.

CHOCIESZEWICE, 20*th November* 1854.

My very dear and illustrious Master,

How good you are! A thousand thanks for this little *chef-d'œuvre* of a manuscript which you have granted in response to my indiscreet request. Frankly, I would just as soon, or rather, I would prefer to, keep it for myself . . . this autograph, which is the most really autograph, since every note bears the characteristic imprint of the style of your last period. It has such an exquisite delicacy, such a subtle grace! But . . . as I asked for it for Mlle. de Kamieńska, who is not without deserving such a favour as an encouragement to her good intentions, I shall have the honesty to send it to her, with the delightful tidings that you will go and see her during your next stay at Dresden. She, however, already enjoys the pleasure of knowing you; for she, with her mother, was one of those at the supper at the ' Hôtel de Bavière,' which followed the first performance of the sublime horror, of the poor *chef-d'œuvre*, which is almost—unknown—under the name of the opera 'Genovefa.'

Excuse me if I refer to the allusion you make, in your very kind letter, to a second autograph which you thought of sending by the same opportunity; without wishing to be importunate I confess that I tremble at the idea that it may have been lost; for the envelope (addressed, as it seemed to me, by Hoplit's hand) only contained one, "l'appassionato," in F sharp major.

The prospect of a performance of my two orchestral pieces under your conducting has given me, and still gives me, many happy moments. I have written to Dresden to tell them to send you the new score of the Overture to 'Cæsar,' together with the orchestral parts, which are fairly correct, with the exception of a few slight errors in the parts for the first horn and the second clarinet. You did receive the orchestral parts of the Fantasia some time ago, did you not?

How glad I should be to hear that this last piece, after its re-petition, seems to you capable of producing some effect on the hearer! Would it interest you to cast your eye over a few lines that Wagner has written to me about this last score? If so, I will send them to you. In spite of much indulgence and kindness, his last word is not as favourable as yours. The chief thing with which he reproaches me—of making cacophonous harmony—brought forth, however, a humble protest from me against his accusation that I had departed from the serious side of art with a frivolous indifference, by striking home at "Pelištim"* to the verge of eccentricity (*Ohrfeigen für feige Ohren*—a box on the ears for the ears of cowards). I do think, nevertheless, that he is right in finding much fault with the last but one chord of the seventh (or rather, the triad with the diminished fifth: f♯—a—c, for the d♯ is an anticipation), on which the *crescendo* works up to its climax on the final harmony of the tonic. Are you also of opinion that it would be better to change this harmony into that which I employ at the beginning of the intro-duction?†

Have you glanced at the manuscript of the duet from 'Tannhäuser'? Will you be so kind as to give me your opinion sometime, without restriction?

---

* "Pelištim," an Old Testament expression for "Philistine." Raff, with the intention of composing, as he afterwards did, an opera 'Samson,' to which he himself wrote the text, was at that time studying the Hebrew language; and some expressions from that language were employed in joke by the young artists.

† Probably the Symphonic Poem, which was afterwards worked up and published under the title of 'Nirwana,' is here meant. In the present form of the work the passage above referred to does not exist.

P

It is possible that I may yet succumb to the temptation to give some concerts in Berlin this winter. In that case I shall go there not later than in a week or a fortnight from now. Johanna Wagner has several times offered to make an exception in favour of my concerts, by singing at them. Would you allow me to play in Berlin your ' Caprice Turc,' supposing that I have the advantage of an orchestra to accompany it; and, in that case, might I ask you *to be so good as to send the orchestral parts to Schlesinger ?* I myself have the score, as well as that of the Hungarian Rhapsody. I venture to submit to you herewith the *répertoire* from which I shall draw. I have only chosen pieces that I know perfectly well by heart.

The six weeks that I have just been spending in an exile which would be intolerable in the long run, have at least been of advantage to my playing of piano and—billiards. The business of schoolmaster reacts so strongly on my nerves, that it renders me incapable of any serious work. When I am a little more inured to it by habit I hope it will be different. I have just given my 104th lesson, and I assure you that, with my nature of a great pedant (great *only* as a pedant), it is a perfectly servile task to make the same individuals study, for four weeks without interruption, pieces suited to their respective capacities — such as the ' Hirondelles' of Willmers, the ' Tarantelle' of Döhler, and Strauss' Quadrille from ' Martha,' the favourite piece of " Papa."

" *Il faut que j'empêche mon cerveau de moisir,*" as Macchiavelli says; and it is just with this object that I shall make excursions, whether for pleasure or business, from time to time : it goes without saying, that I reckon my concert-tours among the latter. Country life in winter offers few charms, especially in that part of the Grand-Duchy of Posen which is as little favoured by nature as it is possible to imagine; a land uniformly flat, without a suspicion of a hill as far as the eye can reach. Although the castle is not yet emptied of its more or less passing guests, yet I have not met one person with whom I should have been tempted to form a closer acquaintance. It is not, however, that I have not met there some very *comme il faut* people, such, for instance, as Mr. de Stablewski, Count Potworowski and his family, and Count de Wodzicki, whose wife is the sister of Prince Sułkowski. As to X., he is a toady, something between a butcher-boy and a hairdresser's assistant.

I am encroaching on your precious moments by gossiping in a way that will perhaps prove to you that my brain has already begun to "*moisir.*"

Thank you for the letter which introduced my sister to your daughters. My sister writes me word that Berlioz' ' Trilogie Sacrée' will be given at a coming concert, and also that, at the opening of the Exhibition, an Overture which he has composed expressly for it will be played.

Will you let me have news of you again very soon, dearest Master, either direct, or else through Hoplit, who does not condescend to correspond with me any more : I am so anxious to hear something about ' Faust,' and a thousand other objects of lesser importance.

TO HIS MOTHER.

CHOCIESZEWICE, *25th November* 1854.

BELOVED MOTHER,

I have received your letters; but, as is usually the case with the wretched postal arrangements, sometimes 4 and indeed 6 days after they have reached Kröben.

I have now decided to set out this, Saturday, afternoon viâ Posen, where Tyszkiewicz is stopping, on whom I shall call early tomorrow morning, as he could perhaps be helpful to me for a concert to be given there later on.

I wrote to Johanna Wagner ten days ago, also to Rellstab, begging them to announce my coming.

Schlesinger and Kisting, whose grand piano I shall use, also already know of my coming.

There were indeed other reasons for my irresolution and delay as regards the journey to Berlin than that of my innate procrastination, which I have conquered. I am always in extremes—at one time tremendously courageous, at another endlessly apathetic and dejected. And now for the chief thing—money !

The Count, who was recently elected for the first Chamber, but still awaits the King's ratification of it, will likewise come to Berlin towards the 1st of December. He was at the ball the day before yesterday, and bought two horses from Sułkowski for 1000 reichsthaler. The same night a daughter was born, and now we cannot either play the piano or play at billiards for some time to come, and it is extremely horrid in this Polish desert.

On Tuesday I had to pay the quarterly tax of 1 reichsthaler 20 silbergroschen ! In order to get my passport I had to send an express messenger at my own expense to Rawicz, 3 miles distant. These are not the only pleasures I have had of that kind. For the last week I have been execrating the laundress, who always keeps me waiting, and has now given me the slip. Contemptible rural life ! Vile country ! Worthless existence !

Excuse the shocking writing ; I did not want to write till I was quite certain about setting off. For the first and second days I shall have to put up at a great hotel (Meinhardt's Hotel). I assure you from experience this expense is unavoidable ; I *have* to do it. After as short a stay as possible I shall try, if the plan of giving a concert seems not too risky, to find a cheap lodging, and shall first inquire of [Tieck's] Friederike.

If I can neither play at Court nor in the theatre (where I can command acoustic arrangements suitable for pianoforte-playing) I shall go back again to Chocieszewice after a few days, so as not to waste money unnecessarily. I hope that it will not be so bad as Schlesinger most discouragingly describes. Should that be the case—then I shall come to Dresden at Christmas for a few days, to recover my spirits.

I *must* once again hear some music, something else than my own everlasting practising !

I will write to you about Berlin as soon as I have anything to tell you.

I am curious how it will fare with me this time ! Please forgive the wretched hasty scrawl, in writing which it just occurs to me to say that Isidore wrote me a long letter a week ago, to which I replied at once.

Farewell meanwhile, dear good mother.

Many thanks for the credit note to Ernst, of which, alas, I shall soon have to make use.

Liszt has long heard from me !

Long in both senses.

TO HIS MOTHER.

BERLIN, 30*th November* 1854. Evening.

BELOVED MOTHER,

I ought, as the proverb says, to have "sought an honest living" *in the country*, instead of going out into the world, where I shall have to go through the old experiences again.

What an abominable journey have I had, and spent two nights and a day and a half over it !

And, if I had not given the postillions and guard enormous tips on the way from Lissa to Glogau, I should have had the pleasant prospect of spending another night in Glogau, as I had already been obliged to do in that little Polish hole Gostyn.

The consequence is that the very first time I went out, by the help of the raw stormy snowy air of the Berlin weather, I caught a shocking influenza cold, which has been getting worse ever since the day before yesterday. I think it has come to a climax today, and I hope that by tomorrow I may venture out again on foot to make some of my countless calls.

It is impossible that, among pianists, there can be a man more worried than I am.

Frau Schumann—at present unaccompanied by Joachim—arrives on the same day as I. She gives her first concert on the 4th of December. There are no others here at present with whom I could clash.

Hülsen, to whom I sent my card at once, requesting to know when I might call on him, showed me very scant courtesy. He is strikingly like the picture of him in the Tannhäuser-caricature in *Kladderadatsch*, which I must reproach myself with not having, after all, told him.

Countess Dönhoff has not yet sent a word, although I begged her to let me know when I could call upon her. Count Redern has received my card and has not yet answered it. That is more excusable, because the Court wedding-festivities occupy him very much.

Friederike Schwabhäuser (Wilhelmstrasse 43 B) was very pleasantly surprised by news of you, but had not, alas, a single room at liberty.

I have looked round but found nothing. I am stopping for the present in Meinhardt's Hotel, unter den Linden No. 68, 3rd étage, where it does not seem to be so immoderately dear. Especially with my present indisposition it would be risky to move.

Johanna Wagner, who had replied, giving me every encouragement to come at once, was recently very friendly, repeated all her amiable promises to me, and said she had spoken with Meyerbeer and Count Redern about my collaboration in the Court concert, but had only received evasive replies. Moreover the Court was largely represented at yesterday's Court concert (in the white hall), and the performers had the pleasant prospect of accompanying the card-playing and conversation with music. Countess Kamieńska was equally polite, and—naturally— grateful for Liszt's interesting manuscript.

Among my acquaintances here, Kroll and others, none have as yet found it worth the trouble to come and return my call. Herr v. Kolb alone visits me frequently, accompanies me on my walks, and takes me a little out of my very depressing loneliness.

I have found a grand piano today (by Eck in Cologne—a rich-toned instrument) ; Kisting had nothing in stock. I have already called on Rellstab, Truhn, Marx, and Frau Zimmermann. The former had yesterday announced my arrival by a mere line. In his own personal opinions he is moreover a—bull-dog. I never yet heard anyone speak with such contempt of people like Spontini and Berlioz (especially the former) as he did today. I must get a forbearing drum to my ear. After I had racked my brains for several days as to whether I should do better and be wiser to go back again to Chocieszewice, I have resolved to give no heed to these suicidal emotions, and have nerved myself for a concert next Wednesday.

Bote and Bock will manage the affair.

I engage Liebig's orchestra (which Madame Schumann also engages—and which, as Rellstab and all the others tell me, gives almost as good Symphony-soirées as the permanent orchestra) and the hall of the Academy of Singing. I am obliged to pay both beforehand—75 and 50 thaler, *i.e.* 125 thaler. I shall have two Overtures played, and shall myself play the Beethoven Concerto, and a manuscript of Liszt's with accompaniment. Johanna Wagner has faithfully promised me to sing twice. The total expenses will amount to about 150 thalers.

In no other way can I give a concert in Berlin, that is, if I am to make my *début* here in a proper manner, not unworthy of myself. May I now borrow the 100 thalers from Ernst, as you kindly told me to do? Does he know about it?

If I do not get through, I shall not make another attempt. To-morrow I am writing to Marpurg (Conductor of the theatre-orchestra in Königsberg) and to Tyszkiewicz in Posen, to ask whether I could give a concert there, with the arrangements for which they would help me.

If the worst comes to the worst I shall at any rate have enough to get back to Chocieszewice. My head is in a whirl, as if driven by a wind-mill. What racing about, and what expenditure of time and money, are before me!

But, in fine, it has become a fixed idea with me to risk an orchestral concert in Berlin,—to let myself be properly heard in the city where, above all others, I should have to seek my public.

If I could only first get rid of this terrible cough and cold, which are really dreadfully bad this time.

You must help me this once more! It shall be the last time, and then I will patiently do my self-worryings round about in Posen or *ailleurs.* I am, then, so unscrupulous as to ask for the 100 thalers which you promised me. Either, or! But to go away from here again, intimidated, would be too inglorious. At least one must make the attempt! Concerts in aid of the sufferers from the floods, which seemed the only way to get anything out of Berlin, and which have abounded up to the present time, now seem to be falling off.

Please send to me here the Cæsar and all the parts belonging to it, etc., as soon as possible. As I have to pay the orchestra I shall allow myself *that* amusement.

Stahr is here, but ill, and could not see me when I called lately.

Frau Schumann plays this week in Breslau. I have not yet seen her; Bargiel will go with me to her. He seems to like me very much, and also to be touched by my real interest in him.

Write to me at once, beloved mother; forgive my bad writing and disorderly style.

I have been to see the Circus, and the 'Bummler von Berlin,' for a little amusement, as no one has yet invited me.

The royal theatre and opera-house do not at the present time offer any temptation.

I hope I shall be able to give you somewhat better news next time.

TO HIS MOTHER.

BERLIN, *8th December* 1854.

DEAREST MOTHER,

It is all over 36 hours ago. But I did not write to you yesterday because I wanted to wait for the criticisms, and because the Kamieńska (my good angel) is starting for Dresden at mid-day today, and will give you verbally her own views and outpourings about my concert, together with mine. Hers may and will appear, in part, rosier than mine.

Comfort yourself, however, before you read this letter, by my assurance that I am in a good humour and full of satisfaction with myself, which is the principal thing.

D'abord . . . the financial side; don't be alarmed! The expenses amount to 160 reichsthalers: 38 tickets at 1 reichsthaler were sold; I have therefore 122 to pay.

Vieuxtemps has had to pay altogether 300 reichsthalers out of his own pocket for his three concerts here. *Cela revient au même.*

You have made a great sacrifice for me; but I must tell you that I accept it without remorse.

I played very well, with immense steadiness, and to the satisfaction of all the more talented connoisseurs.

The first criticism appeared yesterday evening in the *Kreuzzeitung*. It was an excellent one, and as the King reads that paper he must read the whole column (which is a pretty ample one for the "*feuilleton*" of this paper), and thus must observe, and possibly become curious about, my name and talent. *One* result.

I have just this moment got the *Tante Voss*, which I had sent for. Rellstab has eaten his own words. He inveighs against my performance of the E flat major Concerto, which I played in a masterly manner, and cuts me up, with *égards*. He does not allow that I had any delicacy or expression in the Adagio, whereas it was just these two attributes that moved my friends to tears, as they assured me with heartfelt emotion after the concert.

Truhn predicted this transformation beforehand. He assured me that Rellstab has gone mad, and that in all his recent criticisms he rides to death the idea of "aberrations." This *prophétie* was so true that Truhn won two bottles of champagne from someone with whom he had a bet about it after the concert. I am delighted at that! Johanna Wagner also comes in for her share of "aberrations."

Kossak, the most dreaded of all the critics, the most able, the wittiest of them all, who reports for Königsberg, Breslau, Cologne, etc., was, on the other hand, delighted, and, in spite of his being most tremendously busy, he has begged me to play to him *privatim* next Sunday. I am very much pleased at this.

Madame Schumann was so un-colleague-like as to advertise her big soirée with Joachim, which is to take place on the 11th, on the very day of my concert.

Of course I cannot give a second concert now, just at Christmas-time, and indeed no second one at all, unless Joachim were to be so amiable as to play with me, which is possible, if he has not too completely allied himself with Clara Schumann. Perhaps also Vivier * will play for me. The expenses of a concert *sans orchestre* would be 50 to 75 reichsthalers, according to the room.

Stahr will write about me, first in the *Weimar'sche Zeitung*, and then somewhere else. Bruno Bauer was quite delighted with my playing of Bach. Emil Naumann paid me some enthusiastic compliments, of course not genuine, but still he could not help making them.

At the rehearsal I played, in fact, almost better. The Liebig orchestra, who supported me very well, put down their instruments after every piece, and applauded me with great warmth. People said things to me which it warmed my heart to hear.

Kullak, and others also, have strongly advised me to go to Posen: I shall therefore take the necessary steps to bring this about.

Johanna is an angel! You would have kissed and hugged her, if you had seen her with me—I mean, if you had seen how she was with me.

---

* A horn player.

Both your letters I have received. A thousand thanks for all your love.

Half an hour before the concert I got a dear, dear letter from Liszt, by which I felt myself raised and strengthened to an uncommon degree.

I cannot tell you how much good it does me to have the hearty sympathy of all the young artists here whom I respect, and for whose opinion I care. It makes quite a different man of me. I have here so many friendly relations with people who live in the same element as myself, and who, by their greater repose and intelligent self-command, act in a most beneficial and not exciting manner on me.

Marx invited me lately to dine with him ; he then made me, half and half, the most remarkable proposals : Kullak is leaving the Conservatoire, and I am to think it over whether I will take his post as Piano Professor.

It is not a Government, but a semi-official musical, appointment, pecuniarily fluctuating. Nevertheless it is worth considering.

It would be more likely to lead to something, than playing the schoolmaster in the country in Poland. Today or early tomorrow I shall go to him. I will write to you more definitely within 24 hours.

Now I must make haste to finish my letter. Spener's paper, and the ministerial papers, give me, on the one side, high praise, and on the other a slap in the face, only not *à la* Vienna press.

The *Nationalzeitung* will have its long article in tomorrow, written by the blind Gumprecht, an enormously clever and kindly musical critic.

The concert has come to 132 reichsthalers, and not 122, as I have just learnt from Bock.

Two letters have just this moment reached me from University friends of mine, one of whom is referendary in Dantzig, and the other in Posen. Possibly these two old friends may be able to help me in what I eventually undertake.

I have caught a little cold, and have a cough.

Tomorrow morning I will write to you again, so please be satisfied with these hasty lines for today. If you only knew how wearied to death I have been all this time—on Tuesday I had to drive about the town for 3 hours—you would not take it amiss that I have not been able to look about any further for private rooms.

Farewell, beloved mother !

More anon, and, it is to be hoped, more definite news.

When does Giacomo come back here ?

TO HIS MOTHER.

BERLIN, 14th December 1854.

BELOVED MOTHER,

I shall very likely have to leave here soon and go back to Posen, because I am spending such an enormous amount of money here. But at any rate the result of it has been that I have enjoyed eight very pleasant, almost unclouded, days.

Every hour I expect news from Königsberg telling me whether I can play in the theatre there, which is more desirable even than in Breslau, where Clara Schumann also gave her two concerts in the theatre.

Do not expect me to write to you in an orderly manner—I am so excessively preoccupied by all sorts of things, and have so very little time. In the early morning hours I have calls from young artists and friends, who are so good as to bring me the latest-published favourable articles about me. Truhn wrote lately really enthusiastically about me, and turned the comparison provoked by Frau Schumann to my advantage. A very witty critic, who himself edits his paper, *Phönix*, has today noted down a lot of little particulars about me, partly absurd and partly interesting. As Dr. Klein is a friend of Johanna Wagner's, she will probably send this paper to the Kamieńska, and you are sure to hear it read there.

I have left a card for Meyerbeer, begging him to fix a time when I can see him.

Joachim was very pleasant to me at yesterday's concert, and came constantly to my seat where I was applauding the Schumann, and talked to me during the intervals. She played the Kreutzer sonata roughly, but, on the other hand, played a great pianoforte piece by Schumann with such understanding, so much tone and energy, that I was really quite lost in admiration. I believe I must not think of a second concert just now. Joachim will *have* to play with Frau Schumann once more, and by that time Christmas will be upon us. 'Tis a pity, a pity, a pity! *We* two should have done more with the Beethoven sonata here also; it went far better that time in Erfurt.

The answers from Königsberg, and about the Court concert here, are the two matters which, on the ground of expediency, still detain me.

Next Thursday I am to be proposed at the "Liedertafel" and— accepted, as an honorary member. This society in particular gives me now already an incitement to composition. But in provincial towns, Dresden and the like, and in Chocieszewice—whence can one get encouragement for *practical work*?

I had a few words lately with Marx. He seemed to avoid mentioning the subject of my last letter, which rather confirms the report, which has reached me from various quarters, that Frau Schumann will occupy the third place at the Conservatoire, between Stern and Marx, in place of Kullak.

Yesterday morning I played at Dr. Fürst's—where they were, moreover, very polite to me. Dr. Kossak had begged me to play Liszt's later compositions to him at his room.

Now for the most interesting thing I have to tell you, which comes late because, with my confused brain, the pen mechanically outruns the thoughts.

On Friday evening I found an invitation to Count Redern, to go at 9 o'clock next morning to hear the band of 80 men play the military music composed by him for the torch-dancing in his entrance hall.   I go in a plain coat "*sans façon.*" Who should be sitting in the breakfast-room but the Prince of Prussia—Prince Friedrich, his son Prince George, and a Prince of Mecklenburg! I was introduced to them all, and talked with them for some time.   At the conclusion of the military spectacle I was requested to play something to them in the drawing-room.   The Prince of Prussia had, alas, already taken his leave.   At the instigation of Prince George, who is a very cultivated musician and moreover delightfully amiable in conversation, I played the 'Patineurs,' and made a great effect with it.   Their Highnesses stood round the grand piano, where I was obliged to repeat some of the most "incredible" passages, to their astonishment.

I received your letter yesterday, Tuesday, morning, but, alas, not much good news in it.   The way you write to me about Joachim and Clara Schumann has hurt me.   I had unfortunately behaved rather haughtily to the latter—quite without intention, and she had felt so injured by it that Joachim made friendly remonstrances to me, and I determined to do all I possibly could to make up for my involuntary error.

I think I may assume that on the receipt of my letter you will think differently about these things from what you did when writing to me.

"*Die ignobelsten Feinde des Menschen: Neid und Furcht*" (the most ignoble enemies of mankind; Envy and Fear); these often attack me also; but I have always victoriously subdued them by my best inner forces.   And, though quite determined to make my way without looking back, still I shall never make use of any means for which I should have to blush before my old friends, and I assure you I have kept none but the *most honourable* people as my friends.*

---

* What kind of remarks are here referred to is shown in a letter of his mother's to Isidore at that time.

"Joachim is playing with Frau Schumann in Berlin! Hans is, nevertheless,

Yesterday I went to see Meyerbeer, who had fixed the morning at 12 o'clock for my call. We talked freely and pleasantly for three quarters of an hour. He also promised, in the event of his own absence, to ensure my being invited to the *great* Court concert of the Carnival, probably in January. It was moreover very possible that a Court concert would be arranged for in the course of a few days. (That would certainly be more immediately pleasant to me.) But he said that these matters are usually ordered so " *à l'improviste* " (on the spur of the moment), that very often he was only told about it himself the evening before. He is just now rheumatic and cannot leave his room.

I went to see Count Redern in the morning. He said he had spoken of me to their Majesties on Sunday, and that they are quite disposed to hear me. Patience then; but I cannot delay my journey after Tuesday. On Monday I will, if possible, hear Roger, whose talent as yet I only know from report.

You may as well read the *Vossische.* * Someone told me yesterday that Rellstab, in spite of many criticisms in it, speaks of me as "standing alone among the modern virtuosi."

Today I dine with Ernst, and play beforehand with Charlotte von Bülow. At 4 o'clock I must go to a Symphony concert of Liebig (the Hünerfürst of Berlin—only more so—whose orchestra lately accompanied me), to hear the Prize-Symphony by Ulrich † (Dehn's pupil, a friend of Cornelius). Joachim goes with me. (Tickets, 5 silbergroschen, no smoking.) This evening I shall go to the play, where Calderon's ' Medico de su honra ' will be done; and then to a party at the house of Geheimräthin Storch, who gave away the complimentary tickets I sent her, and paid for her seats, which I think was decidedly nice of her.

Why have not you sent me the music to ' Cæsar '? It is true I should not have performed it, but I should have played the score to my friends. Can you still do so ?

Also, *Johanna* has promised Prince George Wagner's ' Nibelungen,' which I lent to Helene. Has Helene given you the book back ? If so, be so good as to send it to me *by return.* If Helene still has it, Johanna's order to return it directly will soon reach her.

I received lately from Isidore a letter 20 pages long. I am glad I complied with your wish and have written to her frequently. It has at

---

splendid ; so noble, so great in character and spirit, that I am the more hurt about it."

* The *Vossische Zeitung.*
† Professor of Composition at Stern's Conservatoire.

any rate had a good influence upon her; it has stimulated and animated her.

I am learning by degrees, in Macchiavellian fashion, to make the reverses which I meet useful to me. But it would be impossible, with the best intentions, to tell you more fully the details of my life here.

I shall go today to see Stern, who expressed his esteem for me in a letter of "Alberti"-an * courtesy the day before yesterday, with apologies for not having yet thanked me personally for the tickets, as he is confined to his bed.

Joachim is still a splendid fellow. I suspect that he no longer takes a fee from Frau Schumann, any more than Johanna does from me for her assistance. The latter really grows more beautiful, more ideal-looking every day. In her morning negligé yesterday, her hair imprisoned in curl-papers, she looked so charming that I could hardly help falling on my knees. Clara Schumann is also, in her way, a really beautiful and very remarkable woman.

Enough for today, so that you may not be kept waiting. How hard it is to me to go back to Posen! As hard as for a vestal virgin into the open grave!

Without black coffee, without any excitement, shall I be able to play the piano thus as I *ought* to play it? Impossible. The critic of the *Nationalzeitung*, who calls me Percy Hotspur, has likewise a different opinion from yours.—Lately I took coffee with Dr. Dohm, editor of *Kladderadatsch*. He is a remarkable, assiduously good-natured person.

You ought surely to feel satisfied with my present style of letter. I cannot now write differently. Fare thee well and without headache, dear mother.

TO HIS MOTHER.

BERLIN, 17th *December* 1854.

DEAREST MOTHER,

Best thanks for your letter! I have some news for you.

Professor Marx has this morning now definitively offered me a post of first pianoforte teacher in the Conservatoire conducted here by himsel and music-director Stern.

The contract, which I shall probably sign, is to be laid before me in a few days.

---

* Presumably a running-stream of courteous expressions.

"Alberti-Bass," so named after Alberti (born in Venice 18th century), who introduced a bass, consisting of broken chords, into compositions for the *cembalo*.

The material advantages are very trifling, but that does not signify ; for the private teaching which I shall be able to give in Berlin will, I hope, amount to much more.

I have to begin on the 1st April, but ought to be here a week or a fortnight earlier, so as to look into my work. I shall get 300 thalers for the first year, and have to give 1½ hours daily, making 9 hours a week. That is in itself more worth having than Mycielski's compensation for my tortures.

Kullak could not get on with either of them.

Marx is an authority to me ; I will willingly defer to him wherever necessary ; we are moreover quite agreed on the chief points of musical education.

If the thing comes to pass—for one can neither know nor predict what may happen—then I shall at last have one foot in the stirrup, and the beginning is made.

I think that, with self-restraint, and a Buonaparte-like tenacity and energy of will, I am capable of getting on. It is true that you will have to help me again at first, self-sacrificingly ; later on a rise of salary, and indeed a considerable one, is guaranteed to me.

But now please have the kindness to send, after all, to the restaurant of the Dresden theatre-orchestra, to get out the score and parts of my Cæsar Overture, and to address the packet to Liszt in Weimar, as he is going to have it performed at a Stadthaus concert.

Tomorrow I shall at length get the answer from Beerenmayer as to whether I can play at Court now, or not till January at the great Carnival concert.

I must now stay here a few days longer, to arrange my immediate future. It costs me money, but that can't be helped. Mycielski must advance me the money for the return journey, or else—but he will do it.

In January, moreover, I come here again for the great Court concert, then to Dantzig and Königsberg, where I can earn money to spend again in giving concerts in Berlin.

Joachim gives up his position in Hanover because an intriguer there has disgusted him with it. Disgraceful lot of fellow-beings !

To make your mind easy, let me tell you that I have only seen Bruno Bauer for about five minutes in all, in his very remote dwelling, whither I went to take him two concert-tickets, because he is such an admirer of Bach and Beethoven.

I shall go this evening to the Wilhelmstadt theatre, in order to calm myself a little, and see ' die Bummler von Berlin.'

Frank was at my concert with his son. I have spoken with him a couple of times in the street. Was very friendly.

Tomorrow I shall give a manuscript to a publisher, and hope I may receive a considerable sum for it : ' Impromptu à la Mazurka,' dédié à Mlle. la Comtesse Elisa Mycielska.

Make many excuses for me to Madame Laussot for having as yet sent her no other answer than my concert-programme, which I was obliged to settle definitely just when I got her letter. I owe her my thanks, for I had almost the greatest success with the Bach, which I had really intended to give at the second concert.

Farewell, dear mother ; my arm aches. Yesterday evening I sent Clara Schumann a beautiful bouquet before her concert. Was not that gallant ?

Send me the Nibelungen directly, and ditto the Cæsar to Liszt ! Please, please !

The Arnims are certainly not in Berlin ! ! !

Remember me to Fräulein Dräseke !

TO ALEXANDER RITTER.

CHOCIESZEWICE BEI KRÖBEN, 25th December '54.

DEAR SASCHA,

You have indeed long been my comfort, but if you were ambitious enough to become still more so, I can now give you an excellent opportunity.

Thus—if there is anything in the fate of one, transplanted from the life-stream of Berlin to this herring's-pond of Polish solitude, Willibald Alexis, calculated to move you without the need of Anglo-frenchifying my Ukase with my snuffing eloquence,—then tie on the clogs of friendship and put on the comforter of obligingness, and betake yourself first and foremost to Cronstadt, not in order to breakfast there (as Napier forgot to do from want of appetite), but (I mean) to Meinhardt's Hotel, and ask the slow-coach at the door if any letters, etc., are awaiting me there. If by this time the bad weather has not obliged you to change your clothes, be so kind as to exchange the enclosed note at a neighbouring stationer's (in case the post-office cannot) for 12 sheets of long-shape music-paper for piano, five staves with a moderate space between ; also a quire of letter-paper like this pattern, with somewhat larger white or blue envelopes. Should you then have about 12 silbergroschen over, it would be uncommonly friendly of you to get me a packet of Spiglasoffs, the only kind of cigars which I can allow myself here.

If you can grant my request, I want you simply to tie the paper, cigars, and any letters from Meinhardt's Hotel together, and to send them as quickly as possible by post to me in my Steppe, like an oasis in my desert.

In this case be assured of my apostolic blessing, my hearty New Year's wishes, my unbounded esteem, devotion, readiness to serve, and musical well-wishing. The music-paper is the most important thing, as in my spare time (which I hope will only last a fortnight) I wish and am obliged to make some four-hand arrangements from Tannhäuser for Meser.

If you are writing to Carl—do do so—give my greetings and say I will soon answer him. But beg him to send me as quickly as possible 2 or 3 copies—at any rate 1, of the 'Alcibiades.' I shall be able to make it known.

My warmest regards to your wife. Give a suitable message from me to your gifted sister-in-law. Ask her if I may compose the sea of waving corn for her, if I don't let the breakers roll too high.

My greetings to Berlin, and enjoy yourself there enough for both of us. Is there any news from Weimar?

Be sure not to prepay the parcel. It is a disgusting business with the postal communication here. Write to me moreover about all sorts of things. Get up a quarter of an hour earlier, for you will have plenty of time before 10 o'clock to do and to leave undone everything possible. Adieu.

Send me the *Kladderadatsch* Calendar too, if you have read it. I will make some fun with it for an unhappy comrade here.

TO MADAME LAUSSOT.

CHOCIESZEWICE, 28*th December* 1854.

MY DEAR MADAM,

You have already shown me many kindnesses, for which I, faithful to the natural disposition of a born egotistical recipient, have not yet once thanked you. But the benefactor certainly does not stick at that. And—as my mother wrote, to my great joy— you have no doubt understood my indirect answer, which I *printed* in the Berlin papers, to your kind letter.* Nothing could have happened more "*a tempo*," for your excellent advice played into my hands like a "host ex machinâ," just at the very moment when I was brooding over

---

* The public announcement of the concert-programme suggested by Madame Laussot.

the arranging of my programme; and, though I had had tea for my breakfast, in opposition to Moleschott, not a single drop of practical spirit from the tea would pour from the sieve of my pen.

Possibly some of the Berlin criticisms about me may have come under your notice, through my mother. In that case you will have seen that it was my Bach, principally, that swelled the measure of commendation given to me by the papers, and that the contrast with the Chopin Ballade also answered a good purpose to me; consequently you will certainly have congratulated me for having followed your counsel. But whether you will now finally allow me to give myself over to a devout superstition, and to beg for your kind advice and good wishes on another occasion—this is a question which, indeed, it is not for me to answer in the affirmative.

How much I am indebted to you that you have brightened up so many hours for my dear mother by your delightful society. Not on my mother's account alone, but on my own, am I indebted to you for this. It seemed to me, in my correspondence with her latterly, that there were many traces where, through the delicate insinuations of your eloquence, some modifications had already crept into certain of her views of art and of society, which had been so diametrically opposed to mine. Now no one can have less talent and vocation for softening down contrasts or opposition than I; and how often I have wished, just in living with my mother, that I had this faculty which is wanting in me. Now as I am to enter into my new position in Berlin on the 1st April of the coming year, and as my mother will also very probably settle in Berlin next Easter, which would be a great satisfaction to me personally, I like to think that you, dear Madam, have somewhat paved the way for me in these matters; for it is, of your own free choice, your special mission to destroy prejudices, and in the home circle—that final and most snug resort of all sorts of unreasonable opinions—to do this most radically and effectually. When I saw you again the first time in Dresden, you spoke to me about this very subject. I was struck by your words at that time; for I thought you only meant that you would make an attempt you had not yet made, and I did not know that you possessed the power of accomplishing it, and that it was the conscious-ness of being *able* to do a thing that had led you to *wish* to do it.

I do not, however, altogether agree with your view about the "public," although I acknowledge that yours is more normal, healthier, and more objectively reasonable than my subjective feeling and opinion.

I have gradually learnt, not through the channel of the understanding, but rather through my feelings, to renounce my reverent worship of the "Spirit of Universality," of the god "Humanité" of certain pantheistic

Q

French Socialists and of Feuerbach who preceded them. Yes, I confess it openly; I hate that ideal police-god just as—without drawing a parallel —Voltaire persecuted the Nazarene God.

At present I am by belief an " Individualist," and, if I do not always manifest it in action, I am all the more absolute and zealous in my theoretical impulses. In general I think we may give much more consideration to our ideal aspirations in practice than in theory. A methodical Idealism becomes coarse, heavy and measurable, and annihilates itself where it does not become simply absurd. So I, for my part, confess in theory to a feeling of respect only for that fraction of the " Spirit of Universality " to which I myself belong. Now as regards the little I may have accomplished in my Art, the value of which consists in undeniable perfectibility alone; and as regards my claims to a recognition of it by the public, that is, by a handful of the " Spirit of Universality ;" I am only susceptible to the influence of applause in moments of nervous physical excitement. In cooler moments the judgment of a mass of people never exercises any attraction or influence upon me, however much I feel the value of winning the sympathy of some of its individual members. Every one of its manifestations has some sort of bribe to action. But true Art never bribes, directly or indirectly. Were I not restrained, by my individual subjectivity, from reducing my theory to practice, and had I the means to do it, I would not hesitate a moment (supposing they were able to do me the same service) to win over my audience in the same way as Louis Napoleon won his French army. In acquiring those advantages which admit of the individual's ceasing for a moment to ignore the "Spirit of Universality," it is success alone which determines the excellence of the means. You see I am a Jesuit also ; and you were afraid your advice would seem Jesuitical to me ! But what says the Italian proverb ?

" Vincasi per fortuna o per inganno—
Il vincer fu sempre laudabil' cosa."

I have a peculiar predilection for Louis Napoleon ; that is to say, not so much for his person as for the indigenous compendium of the 19th century which he represents to me. As such he is a child, a result, of the latest German philosophy, that is to say, of that which has become rational through emancipation of itself. Buonapartism is a philosophical system reduced to practice and to policy—i.e. the Buonapartism of 1850 par excellence. But I have also, personally, a certain kindred leaning towards "Napoléon le Petit." It seems to me that I, in my proportions to Franz Liszt, my uncle by election, stand in a very similar relation to that which Napoleon III. bore to the great Emperor ; and it pleases me to think that the mentally-adopted nephew might perhaps have as much luck, as he has little real genius, vis-à-vis of the uncle.

For a first letter to you, it seems to me that I ought to make a post-script of excuses for a heap of stupidities I have written. For the rest, I imagined to myself what I have written above, solely with the view of thereby evading, in a "good" manner, your friendly invitation to me to tell you about my concert and all my other experiences in Berlin. Spare me the description of miseries—of the disagreeable, as well as of the agreeable side, for that, in short, is the substance of all that I should have to tell.

I have renewed, in Berlin, an interesting personal acquaintance with Karl Lührss, the composer, a pupil of Mendelssohn, who composes *western* music.

Allow me to recommend to you the following of his compositions : 'Märchen,' kleine Tonstücke; 3 books. Op. 25, Trautwein (Guttentag), Berlin. 'Barcarole' (G flat major) ; and 'Trois Danses brillantes.' Senff, Leipzig. I take this opportunity of mentioning to you also two very important piano-pieces, by the composer Julius Schaeffer : 'Fantasiestücke' Op. 1 ; and Fantasia—'Variationen' (E minor) Op. 2, Breitkopf & Härtel, Leipzig.

From Wagner I have heard nothing for a whole month. The last time he wrote to me he said he had begun the third Act of the 'Walküre,' and he appeared to be freed from his most pressing difficulties. From Liszt you have no doubt had news direct. *A propos*, Wagner has lately become tremendously enthusiastic for Arthur Schopenhauer, the philo-sopher so long ignored by his fraternity. Do you know any of his works ?

For the present of Alfred de Musset I thank you once more "*en connaissance de cause.*" But, just in those selections you have marked, it would be interesting to me to hear your opinion of them in detail. In several of them the essential, main idea seemed to me to be so very slightly connected with the otherwise charming form.

May I beg you to remember me most warmly to the Ritters? Karl wrote to me not long ago, but not a word about himself, and I had a couple of delightful days with Sascha in Berlin. I am longing for the time of my removal thither ; life in the country puts one dreadfully out of tune, and a schoolmaster's functions in the country would hurry one into one's dotage, or back into puerility, a thing from which a great city preserves one.

Thank you once more, my dear lady, for the interest and kindness you have shown me, and allow me to reciprocate your good wishes to

Yours most respectfully,

HANS V. BÜLOW.

BRESLAU—POSEN—BERLIN

CHAPTER XI.

BRESLAU—POSEN—BERLIN.

WINTER—SPRING 1855.

BÜLOW was now on the eve of leaving Chocieszewice again. In a letter to his mother, from that place, dated 2nd January 1855, he says :—

Next Saturday, 6th January, I go to Breslau, and shall play for the first time in Truhn's concert. If they like me very much, then I shall arrange matters with the theatre in the same way that Clara Schumann did.

The ensuing months seem to have been anxious ones for Bülow's mother, owing to the irregularity and scarcity of letters from her son. The following extracts from the mother's letters to her daughter, who was still in Paris, show how difficult it was for the young virtuoso to get so far in his profession as to attain pecuniary independence. In spite of the great interest and pleasure he awakened, in the long concert-tours in Germany which now ensued, yet expenses were so great, and receipts as yet so insufficient, as to necessitate a continuance of help from his self-sacrificing mother.

FRANZISKA VON BÜLOW TO HER DAUGHTER.

" At last comes a letter from Hans ! He still sticks at Breslau, but contentedly lets himself be admired and dragged hither and thither to such a degree that he never gets so far as to write a word to me. He still decides to go to Königsberg. Tonight he is playing to the students at Breslau. On Sunday there is to be a monster-concert, at which he plays, and where he hopes to make some money. God grant it, if one may trouble God about such a thing."

In the middle of February the mother complains that the latest news of her son has come to her only through the papers : tidings of a farewell-matinée in Breslau, and of a concert on the same day for the sufferers at Keuth.

" This, however, is all I know about him. What has happened next ; and has he money, or has he none ? I fear it is the latter. To have such a child, rushing about the world in all sorts of adventures, is truly no sinecure. As our shoemaker lately said : ' The Herr Sohn has become a genius.' "

On the 19th February she writes :—

" At last a letter from Hans. He has given nine concerts in Breslau, and has at least earned enough to pay his five weeks in the hotel. He has been quite taken up there by the army, the cuirassiers, hussars, &c., and has been constantly amongst them. Now he is in Posen, where he finds it terribly cold. . . . If he only becomes reasonable at last! He won't take any advice from me. It is a great misfortune for him that he has lost his father, for *he* did understand how to influence him. . . . He has only sent newspapers : they give him great praise, but regret that the concerts were so *empty*."

TO HIS MOTHER.

Posen, *February* 28, 1855.

Dear Mamma,

Thanks for your letters. I wanted to wait over the third concert, yesterday, before writing to you. It was such a pity that we did not get so far as the question of expenses. I despise the whole Polish race to the nth power ! For the rest, it is a curious city, Posen ! Such a separation as there is between the German and Polish elements I never met before. The second concert, in which my singer became hoarse, and so I had to play the piano for two whole hours, was hardly attended by any but Poles—the result being 69 thalers, which was enough to cover the expenses of the two first concerts together. Yesterday's audience was exclusively German (with the exception of Mycielski's brother, who came over from his estate to hear me again, and is a pleasant, well-bred, and musical man), headed by chief president von Puttkammer, who conversed with me most amiably, and sent his card today to invite me for Friday evening. Of course the concerts are continuing ; we have to give 5 or 6 of them.

The Germans mostly pay nothing for concert tickets, but are very lavish with invitations. Herr von Hindenburg, the chief of the police ; Herr Buttendorf, the chief of the post office ; Justice Dönniges, amongst others, have delightful houses.

I once dined at Count Dzialyński's. Now I give daily lessons to the youngest Countess, who is not a pretty girl, but very charming and full of talent. I shall either take no fee or present her when I leave with an extremely valuable album, because I like her so much. There is something really poetical about her. I shall dedicate a *Rêverie* to her. The Kamieńska is to have a Waltz.

Explanation of enclosure No. 1. *

The Pole who signed the enclosed had heard that I was to teach the Countess Dzialyńska. Immediately, from a love of rivalry—peculiar to the Pole,—he wishes his daughter to learn from me also. After his call I send him a card on which is written "*est disposé à donner des leçons pendant son séjour à Posen—à* 1 *ducat la leçon.*" Thereupon he answered thus—I of course took no notice of it:—On a tour—in hotels—as a virtuoso I could not—according to Truhn—possibly take less than one ducat an hour.

I have now considerably enlarged my Chopin-*répertoire* :

Ballade, two Scherzos, four Nocturnes, two Impromptus, two Polonaises, four Mazurkas, Barcarole, Berceuse, and various Études.

Truhn has just written to Bromberg, which is in every respect more favourable than Posen, as he knows from experience. Only we must get away from here first. Finally there would also be the theatre to play in, to which the well-known conductor Wallner has invited us with increasingly favourable conditions, but which we have, notwithstanding, always refused. We must now leave this arrangement to Justice Dönniges. He is a very good sort of man—takes concert-tickets even when he is unable to use them.

Have you no indirect news from Weimar? I should so like to know whether Liszt has already set off for Vienna.

The Countess Dzialyńska has just written to me that it will not be possible for her to take a lesson before Saturday, as she has too much else to do. I have refused the invitation for this evening, and shall moreover go to no more Poles.

I am writing today to Professor Marx about the Conservatoire, and will let you know his answer.

If I am going to be condemned to waste my life for a year in Berlin I shall of course yield to my fate without complaining, only I shall then be obliged to beg you to remove thither quickly. You must make this sacrifice for me. My theoretical wits are not equal to undertaking household matters. Moreover I must be very careful of myself—all my strength belongs to my art, and nothing else matters to me.

Our life here is uncommonly respectable. I have quite given up going to the "*Kneipe,*" even at the risk of being thought wanting in good fellowship. And Truhn is also too much of a gentleman and too particular for it.

Think lovingly of your son,

HANS VON BÜLOW,

"*le plus enguignonné* (unlucky) *des pianistes.*"

---

* The enclosed letter, here referred to, which Bülow sent to his mother, is no longer extant.

TO FRANZ LISZT.

POSEN, *14th March* 1855. Bazar.*

MY VERY DEAR AND ILLUSTRIOUS MASTER,

You have several times given me the precious permission to write to you about myself. I have always tried not to abuse this kindness, by not writing to you at times when I could only have told you of the thousand and one miseries in the career of a Lilliputian pianist, which would have sometimes appeared to you incomprehensible. Nevertheless I have not been without a few agreeable weeks at Breslau, where I gave about eight concerts in company with Mr. Truhn, to whom I joined myself at the beginning of the New Year, and for whom I feel a friendship which has been strengthened between us by his own amiable qualities of a true artist and a practical and useful man, as well as by our mutual sympathies in art. Breslau is a town which might well have a certain musical future in the future. I do not say this *because* I have found a publisher there, but *in spite of* this fact.

We did a very bad business at Posen, where we gave four concerts, the latter ones of which did not even suffice to pay the expenses of this unlucky undertaking. In spite of letters of introduction, by means of which I thought I should have some success, the Poles were much less kind to me than Mr. de Puttkammer and the few Germans who live at Posen. I felt the Poles to be rather freezing; but these impressions led me nevertheless to respond to them in a manner quite in harmony with anti-Mortier † principles, which I have continued to profess in my career, and which I cannot reproach myself with ever having violated up to now. After having given a passably good first concert at Bromberg on Monday, the 12th March, I have returned to Posen, to play tonight in the theatre, in a performance that the Poles have arranged for the benefit of the poor.

I shall return to Bromberg in a few days, to give a second concert there, which will be a much more brilliant one than the first. Then we go again to Dantzig, and finally to Königsberg. I should be very grate-ful to you if you would have the kindness to give me an introduction to Mr. Louis Köhler.

On the 1st April I shall have to enter on my duties as professor at the Conservatoire. I would give everything in the world to be able to

---

* The name of a hotel.

† Mortier de Fontaine (1816-1883), a *soi-disant* Beethoven-player, who attained a passing celebrity by his great *technique* and also tremendous puffing. We are unable to state what principles of Mortier's are here referred to.

set myself free from this engagement, which promises me but little satisfaction. I have however a mission to fulfil in Berlin, and I shall use every means to attain my object. A war of extermination against "Mendelssohnianism";* that is what ought now to be the most pressing business of the "coterie Brendel." In regard to this I have a very urgent request to submit to you. I read the other day Robert Schumann's article in the *Neue Zeitschrift* for the year 1837, in which he draws an ignominious parallel between the 'Huguenots' and 'St. Paul.' I have been for some time past preparing an article in which I am delighting to avenge somewhat the occasionally mud-stained poetry of Meyerbeer, of the unjust respect which has been too long accorded to the impertinently-*bourgeoise* prose of Mendelssohn. Not even the fear that Hoplit, that most corruptible man, might in his *amour-propre* proclaim me as his colleague, will be an obstacle in carrying out this project : it, however, cannot be realised unless you were to be so very kind as imperatively to authorise my article in embryo to "Tante Brendel." †

For a long time I have been erroneously thinking that you had left Weimar, about the middle of January, to go to Vienna or I know not where. I think I remember Ritter having spoken to me of this intention on your part, but with a certain amount of mystery. I cannot tell you how I feel almost tortured by the longing to see you again and to kiss your hand. I hope my holidays in the months of July and August will enable me to come to wherever you may then be, if you will allow it.

I shall venture to submit to you shortly some *bagatelles* for piano, which are going to be published at Breslau, and in which your indulgent eye will perhaps note a little progress, if you bear in mind the individual difficulties I have to conquer in writing for your instrument. The piano at those times seems to evade me, and becomes intractable when I endeavour to express my ideas on it. It is true that it often has to complain of the bad treatment it receives at my hands. But it is also true that the thought of you, when it is vividly and persistently before anyone,

---

* It should be clearly understood that Bülow's antipathy, which is here so strongly expressed, is directed, not so much against Mendelssohn himself, as against the immense *over-rating* of his works which was at that time so much in fashion, and which especially provoked all the adherents of the new school to strong antagonism. It is well known how, in later years, when a reaction set in, and the *over*-estimation had changed into *under*-estimation of Mendelssohn, Bülow was constantly to the fore in defence of the Master he had so highly honoured in his early youth.

† Refers, no doubt, to Brendel's paper.

as is the case with me, tends more to discourage than to encourage those
who believe themselves sufficiently advanced in their art to have the
right to admire you.

Might the great politico-physical event which has just taken place at
St. Petersburg make it possible to suppose that those matters which you
have most deeply at heart will now take a turn more favourable to your
views? Has death rendered you a service?

I hope Raff will not be long in publishing an 'Ouverture solennelle'
in honour of the accession of the Emperor Alexander, and I shall be
delighted to see the admirable counterpoint with which he will adorn the
Russian Hymn.

Excuse what I have now to tell you. There is a certain Mr. Greulich,
to whom we especially owe it that we have done such bad business, and
I am obliged to enlighten you a little about him, because you have seen
him at Weimar, and he boasts everywhere that he corresponds with you,
and declares that he possesses brilliant certificates from your hand about
his miserable compositions. He has been trying for a long time to set
himself up in opposition to his elder brother Mr. Oswald Greulich, who
is not an especially talented man, but a good piano teacher, and a person
whom one can take seriously. The fellow has not yet succeeded in
doing this, and he did me the honour to select me as the victim or
stepping-stone of his intrigues.

He took the initiative in a correspondence when we were at Breslau,
by begging me to entrust to him the arrangements of our concerts,
promising us the most brilliant success, and speaking of his influence
and relations with the Polish aristocracy, but which his brother in
reality possessed. As Mr. Truhn was detained at Breslau by illness, I
set out alone for Posen, Mr. Greulich having mentioned to me the *least*
propitious day in the week as the most favourable for a first concert. I
had to put up with a heap of disagreeables, thanks to the swaggering and
lies of this gentleman, who, without exaggeration, ruined our chances at
Posen, as I have been assured by the most competent judges, and as I
found by my own experience. Just imagine what a trick he played me
at my first concert, which took place the day after my arrival: he took
the programme I had dictated to him, to let the printer have it; and,
without letting me know a word about it, he added to it some of his own
compositions. He had brought me a parcel of them the evening before,
and I had had the weakness to correct some of them in playing them to
him. As a pendant to what I have told you, I enclose some bits of the
German paper in which Mr. Greulich endeavoured to throw on to me the
mantle of ridicule which has covered his own shoulders since he has been
at Posen.

Do you still think that you could make one trial, at a rehearsal, of my Fantasia for orchestra? I am so curious to see whether this trial would make any effect whatever, whether disagreeable or flattering; this latter supposition would, however, be over-modest.*

Sometimes in my concerts I join the 12th Rhapsody with the Frischka of the 2nd Rhapsody. Truhn compliments me every time on the *crescendo* I bring out, which often carries away the majority of the public. The Bach Fugues, which you transcribed so splendidly, have been most useful to me everywhere; and the Schubert Waltzes, the Patineurs and the Sonnambula equally so. I also play all the Chopin Nocturnes which have not been too much drummed into our ears by Mesdames Clauss and Schumann. There remain, thank Heaven, enough "show-pieces" of this kind.

Please do not forget me on *your* side; I am so sensitive to the reproach of being forgetful that I am trying to rid myself of it in the greatest haste.

À propos, I have come across a little prodigy here, such as I could never have imagined to exist. It is the son of a precentor at the synagogue, a Mr. Ketten from Hungary, a child of scarcely seven years of age, who has completely stupified me by his remarkable musical talent. The little lad reads at sight anything that is placed before him, and plays with the utmost care and correctness all the "middle parts" in the most complicated compositions. He even transposes into other keys pieces which he is reading for the first time. This little fellow is really interesting, both by the astonishing agility of his fingers, which seem *made* for the piano, and by his marvellously acute ear. He can tell you the most out of the way chords without ever making a mistake in a single note, even when one plays them rapidly one after another. He can even classify, and give the technical names to, the harmonies he hears. I played him the first bars of 'Prometheus,' and it nearly made my hair stand on end to hear the exactness of his replies. The father, to whom I am constantly preaching not to "*exploiter*" his son, wants very much to bring him to you at Weimar, and to beg you to allow his musical education to be taken in hand by one of your pupils. Of course it would be impossible to place such an exceptional child in the Leipzig or Berlin Conservatoire. Mr. Ketten wants very much to know how much longer you expect to be in Weimar, as he intends first to go to Berlin, and to try to interest Mr. Paul Mendelssohn, or possibly even the Government, in his child, in order to obtain pecuniary assistance for him.†

---

* As the composition is of a very severe character.

† Henri Ketten, born 1848 at Baja in Hungary, studied at the Paris Conservatoire, and afterwards made a brilliant, if passing, success as a virtuoso. Died in 1883. Wrote many effective pieces for his own instrument, besides songs, etc.

TO LOUIS KÖHLER.

BERLIN, *3rd May* 1855,
BEHRENSTRASSE, 4. *2nd étage.*

HONOURED SIR,

Whilst in Dantzig and still in hopes (which, as you know, I had to relinquish) of visiting Königsberg, and of making the acquaintance of one whose writings had proved him to me so worthy a companion-in-arms, I received the enclosed letter from Dr. Liszt, which introduces his pupil, but also very likely contains special information for his friend. I have long reproached myself with keeping these lines from you, and will not put off sending them any longer.

As you may perhaps have heard, I am now officiating as Pianoforte teacher at the old Conservatoire of Messrs. Marx & Stern, as successor to Kullak.

A large number of fresh notifications of pupils has insured the continuance of the institution. In spite of being tied here, I hope nevertheless to come next winter in any case to visit the birthplace of the composer of " The last days of Pompeii ";* and if possible to open the concert-season there.

If your time permitted, I should very much like to enter into correspondence with you. Perhaps there may be a hope of welcoming you in Berlin for the performance of 'Tannhäuser,' which is to take place, at last, in November.

FRANZ LISZT TO LOUIS KÖHLER.†

MY VERY DEAR FRIEND,

Hans von Bülow will bring you these lines. You must enjoy yourself in *the* artist who, above all other active or dying out *virtuosi*, is the dearest to me, and who has, so to speak, grown out of my musical heart.—When Hummel heard me in Paris more than twenty-five years ago, he said, " Der Bursch ist ein Eisenfresser (the fellow is a *bravo*)." To this title, which was very flattering to me, Hans von Bülow can with perfect justice lay claim, and I confess that such an extra-ordinarily gifted, thorough-bred musical organism as his has never come before me.

---

* An opera by Pabst.

† Liszt's Letters, edited by La Mara, translated by Constance Bache. Vol. I. page 233. (Grevel, London.)

Receive him as an approved and active friend, and do all you can to make his stay in Königsberg a pleasant one.

Yours in friendship,

F. LISZT.

WEYMAR, *March* 16, 1855.

The following extracts from letters written by Franziska to her daughter about this time (Spring, 1855) give us a slight sketch of the kind of life Hans was leading in Berlin, in company with his mother.

"Hans has just received 4 louis d'or for his latest composition, the 'Rêverie fantastique,' dedicated to the Princess of Hohenzollern. This has put him into a somewhat better mood. . . . I wish he might get to feel at home here ! I have the feeling that Berlin might become a home to us ; I like it so much, and a great city is what Hans requires.

. . . God grant me good news from you, and grant Hans contentment and plenty of lessons."

"On Thursday evening there was a party at Bülow's. Hans, Madame Decker (once a celebrated singer) and Karl Bronikowski played and sang duets from Fidelio and Figaro ; Hans accompanied, and also played alone, to people's admiration. . . . On Saturday Hans intended to work hard, but in the evening came Herman Grimm, who was very pleasant. In the daytime too come numbers of callers, mostly young people ; artists, referendaries, and people who are just passing through, as Hans has so many acquaintances."

"Today with Countess Bohlen to the Exhibition, where there is a beautiful show of pictures for the benefit of the sufferers from the inundation. Just listen in whose company I found myself there : the Prince of Prussia, the Savignys, Herr van Olfers, old Wrangel, &c. ; *je vous fais grâce des autres!* Olfers explained everything to us so nicely ; but I tore myself away, from a sense of duty, from the lovely pictures and good company, and jumped into a carriage, as Hans and lunch were waiting ; then came Ernst, Fräulein Genast from Weimar, &c. At the present moment I am at my writing-table ; this evening I go to a concert given by a couple of Frenchmen, singers, and at which Hans plays. That is how one lives in Berlin. Hans gets into pickles again after his own fashion."

BERLIN, 25*th May* 1855.

"Meanwhile things have gone quite well here also. I don't know if I have already told you that Hans had an invitation from the Duchess of Sagan, to pay her a visit of 3 days on the 29th, during the stay of the Princess of Prussia at Sagan. He accepted : meanwhile he receives, on Sunday, a letter from Amalie Sternberg, the governess to the Princess of Prussia's daughter who has just been confirmed here. This letter was to ask Hans to give her a lesson every day during her short stay here. So he now goes daily from 11 to 12, and he much likes going among the very highest families. Not that it specially impresses him, but it puts him in a good humour. In other respects he is working hard with composing and arranging, and has but little spare time. He is now received everywhere with distinction, and begins to be regarded as a star of the first magnitude. With all this he can be charming when he will, and seems to have grown much more reasonable."

TO HIS SISTER.

SAGAN, 30th May 1855.

MY DEAR SISTER,

I wrote to you lately to Paris, and you have also doubtless received my letter. It is quite my turn to write to you again before I can receive an answer, for you have often done just the same to me. And I have today moreover something new—low be it spoken—something good to tell you.

Since yesterday I have been here with the Duchess of Sagan, who had sent me an invitation to visit her that I might have the opportunity of being presented to the Prince and Princess of Prussia, and might play to them. This introduction had in the meantime already taken place in Berlin. At the beginning of last week I suddenly received a communication from Fräulein Amélie v. Sternberg, asking me, at the wish of the Princess, to give a few music-lessons to the young Princess Louise, to whom she is governess. So this came to pass. My royal pupil, who had come to Berlin for her confirmation, is now, alas, returning to Coblence, and the pleasure—for such it was, because the young Princess has really beautiful musical talent, and is a very amiable charming creature—this pleasure, I say, was of very short duration. Still there is a prospect of the Princess coming to Berlin next winter for a longer time, and then I alone shall be chosen for her piano-teacher again. The Princess-mother—whose appearance, by the way, reminds me very much of Frau von Lüttichau—has overwhelmed me with kindness. Only last Saturday she arranged a matinée in my honour, because she thought "I was still too little known in Berlin, and that it would make me better known." To this matinée she invited a great number of Royalties and their suites, also artistic magnates such as Meyerbeer, the Court-painter Hensel, &c. So I played the piano a great deal, and played altogether an important and pleasant part.

I came hither yesterday morning from Berlin by the same train as the Prince of Prussia, etc., and shall probably return there tomorrow by a special train (part way). For the past eight days I have been living as if at Court, attending, of course, all their breakfasts and dinners, &c. The Duchess is extremely agreeable; the sojourn splendid. A castle of rare beauty and grandeur, a wonderful and immense park, charming visitor's apartments for me, where everything is arranged for the greatest comfort. Drives in Court carriages; this evening a theatrical performance at the Castle; illuminations; these are the exceptional diversions which one likes sometimes as a change. I do not speak of the *menus;* they could only be mentioned with reverential awe. I should like to live like that all my life! In the evenings, alas, I have to endure great torture—in trying to bring out from a villainous old grand-piano (which is unfortunately considered very valuable by its possessor) strains which shall sound as little as possible like caterwauling. If I could only have more assurance, and were not deceived by the idea that the audience is as musical as myself, and as unpleasantly moved by sticking and discordant notes as I am! But after the experience of yesterday I intend, if I am asked to play again to-day, to pound the old tin-kettle quite boldly and pitilessly as regards myself, and with such self-possession that at the *fortissimi* no one can hear his own voice, and at the *piani* no one can hear any sound at all!

The theatre begins in half-an-hour; the Duchess has been obliged to engage a dramatic company from Glogau. I am afraid it will be very bad, and yet not bad enough to be amusing.

I have had such numerous and repeated calls in Berlin from people— chiefly, of course, musicians by profession, whom I got to know while travelling—that I have been very idle, and have accomplished but little of all the work I had planned. But that shall be changed on my return, even should the weather continue as fine as now.

These late occurrences delight Mamma in truth more than they do me. Till now they have cost me more than I can hope to gain by them! I only wish there may be a reaction and an after-effect of them in Berlin, so that I may rise in the estimation of the better portion of the public, and that some people may wish to learn from me in consequence.

The sketch of Hans von Bülow's youth, which these pages are designed to give, cannot be better concluded than by his mother's own words. None of the young artist's earlier victories had been so hard, none so important, alike to his inner peace of mind and to the further development of his powers and his character, as the complete conquest of the prejudice which she had always maintained, up to the present time, against his chosen career as an artist; a prejudice which had its origin in her deep parental solicitude. Whereas Frau von Bülow had written to her daughter only a year ago from Dresden, "I comprehend less and less how this artist's life can and does satisfy him"— she now sums up her impressions in the following words:

"Hans has played perfectly, his tones float ethereally upwards, and his

R

conceptions and their realisation form a drama. He knows how, both by look and tone, to keep the public in rapt attention, hardly daring to breathe, till at the conclusion they break out into a storm of applause. In this power, which he exercises over his audience, he finds the charm of playing in public. The faintest dying breath in Chopin's Nocturne was at once audible in the most distant corner of the crowded hall. With quiet, distinguished deportment he bows slowly with complete unconcern, then carelessly places first one hand and then the other on the keys and begins. Whether the tones now roll forth in the wildest storm, so that one would imagine an orchestra playing, whether they are now heard in the most pearling runs, or die away like the most beautiful human voices in the purest azure, there is always the same composure, the most finished beauty, the complete mastery of thought shown : there one learns to comprehend what *Tone-colour* means. It is indeed a transcendent talent ! Something supernatural ! May he at last win recognition and a position worthy of him.   FRANZISKA V. BÜLOW."

THE END.

INDEX

INDEX.

264 INDEX.

Kühmstedt, 111.
Kullak, 29, 42, 57, 232, 233, 235, 238, 254.
Kummer, 176.

Lachner, 83, 189.
Lacombe, 191.
La Mara, 254.
Langer, 119.
Laub, 181.
Laube, 96, 145.
Laussot, *see* Hillebrand.
Lehr, 21.
Leiningen, Count, 172.
Lemaistre, 216.
Lenhard, von, 147.
Levy, 203.
Lewald, 82, 83, 133.
Liebig, 230, 232, 236.
Linanges, Count de, 175.
Lind, 108, 176, 185.
Lindpaintner, 18, 20.
Lipinski, 10, 72, 154, 198, 199, 204, 216, 221, 222.
Liszt, Franz, 5, 13, 19, 32, 33, 34, 35, 42, 48, 51, 52, 56, 57, 62, 63, 66, 67, 70, 72, 75, 76, 77, 81, 82, 84, 85, 86, 87, 88, 89, 91, 92, 93, 94, 95, 96, 97, 98, 99, 100, 101, 102, 103, 104, 105, 106, 107, 108, 109, 110, 111, 112, 113, 114, 115, 116, 117, 118, 119, 120, 121, 122, 123, 125, 126, 127, 128, 129, 130, 131, 132, 133, 134, 135, 139, 140, 141, 142, 143, 144, 147, 148, 149, 151, 152, 153, 154, 155, 156, 157, 158, 160, 165, 166, 167, 168, 170, 171, 172, 173, 174, 181, 182, 183, 184, 185, 186, 188, 197, 201, 202, 203, 205, 206, 207, 214, 221, 223, 224, 228, 229, 230, 233, 235, 238, 239, 242, 243, 249, 250, 254, 255.
Liszt, Eduard, 140, 143, 144.
Litolff, 12, 13, 19, 36, 40, 41, 87, 94, 121, 147, 183, 200.
Lobe, 110.
Lortzing, 63.
Löwy, 140, 144.
Lührss, 243.
Lully, 19.
Lüttichau, von, 3, 101, 133, 141, 145, 154, 174, 175, 184, 198, 199, 256.

Macchiavelli, 226, 237.
Mangold, 113.
Mangolt, von, 104.
Marastoni, 159.
Marpurg, 230.
Marschner, 104, 185.
Marx, 229, 233, 234, 235, 237, 238, 249, 254.
Marxen, 189.
Mayer, 10, 19, 48, 176.
Mayer-Wordmüller, 60.
Mecklenburg, Prince of, 235.
Méhul, 20, 58.
Mendelssohn, 6, 11, 19, 20, 30, 66, 83, 101, 112, 146, 166, 190, 191, 243, 251.
,, Paul, 253.
Meser, 173, 240.
Meyerbeer, 66, 74, 120, 229, 234, 236, 251, 256.
Milanollo, 145, 148, 152.
Milde, von, 105, 109, 120, 187.
Mirabeau, 218.
Moleschott, 241.
Molière, 10, 205.
Molique, 17, 18, 19, 20, 21.
Montenuovo, Count, 147.
Moritz, 83.
Moscheles, 11, 29, 30, 101.
Mosewius, 207.
Mozart, 18, 31, 36, 59, 66, 99, 176.
Müller, 12, 121.
Münch-Bellinghausen, Freiherr von, 148.
Murillo, 218.
Musset, de, 216, 243.
Mycielski, Count, 202, 203, 207, 208, 212, 215, 220, 238, 248.
,, Daughters, 211, 217, 239.

Napier, 239.
Napoleon, 12, 140, 218, 242.
Naumann, 232.
Nehse, 120.
Nero, 205.
Noëls, 133.

Olfers, 255.
Orleans, Duchess of, 112.

Pabst, 254.